LATINO CIVIL RIGHTS IN EDUCATION

Latino Civil Rights in Education: La Lucha Sigue documents the experiences of historical and contemporary advocates in the movement for civil rights in the education of Latinos in the United States. These critical narratives and counter-narratives discuss identity, inequality, desegregation, policy, public school, bilingual education, higher education, family engagement, and more, comprising an ongoing effort to improve the conditions of schooling for Latino children. Featuring the perspectives and research of Latino educators, sociologists, historians, attorneys, and academics whose lives were guided by this movement, the book holds broad applications in the study and continuation of social justice and activism today.

Anaida Colón-Muñiz is Associate Professor in the College of Educational Studies at Chapman University, USA. She teaches in the Multiple Subject, Master of Arts and Doctoral programs and is the Director of Community Education for the college's community-based bookstore.

Magaly Lavadenz is Professor in the Department of Educational Leadership and Founding Director of the Center for Equity for English Learners at Loyola Marymount University, USA.

Series in Critical Narrative
Donaldo Macedo, Series Editor
University of Massachusetts Boston

The Hegemony of English
by Donaldo Macedo, Bessie Dendrinos, and Panayota Gounari (2003)

Letters from Lexington: Reflections on Propaganda
New Updated Edition
by Noam Chomsky (2004)

Pedagogy of Indignation
by Paulo Freire (2004)

Howard Zinn on Democratic Education
by Howard Zinn, with Donaldo Macedo (2005)

How Children Learn: Getting Beyond the Deficit Myth
by Terese Fayden (2005)

The Globalization of Racism
edited by Donaldo Macedo and Panayota Gounari (2006)

Daring to Dream: Toward a Pedagogy of the Unfinished
by Paulo Freire (2007)

Class in Culture
by Teresa L. Ebert and Mas'ud Zavarzadeh (2008)

Dear Paulo: Letters from Those Who Dare Teach
by Sonia Nieto (2008)

Uncommon Sense from the Writings of Howard Zinn (2008) Paulo Freire and the Curriculum
by Georgios Grollios (2009)

Freedom at Work: Language, Professional, and Intellectual Development in Schools
by Maria E. Torres-Guzman with Ruth Swinney (2009)

The Latinization of U.S. Schools: Successful Teaching and Learning in Shifting Cultural Contexts
by Jason G. Irizarry (2011)

Culture and Power in the Classroom: Educational Foundations for the Schooling of Bicultural Students
by Antonia Darder (2011)

Changing Lives: Working with Literature in an Alternative Sentencing Program
by Taylor Stoehr (2013)

Seeds of Freedom: Liberating Education in Guatemala
by Clark Taylor (2013)

Pedagogy of Commitment
by Paulo Freire (2014)

Latino Civil Rights in Education: La Lucha Sigue
edited by Anaida Colón-Muñiz and Magaly Lavadenz (2016)

LATINO CIVIL RIGHTS IN EDUCATION

La Lucha Sigue

Edited by Anaida Colón-Muñiz and Magaly Lavadenz

NEW YORK AND LONDON

First published 2016
by Routledge
711 Third Avenue, New York, NY 10017

and by Routledge
2 Park Square, Milton Park, Abingdon, Oxon OX14 4RN

Routledge is an imprint of the Taylor & Francis Group, an informa business

© 2016 Taylor & Francis

The right of Anaida Colón-Muñiz and Magaly Lavadenz to be identified as authors of the editorial material, and of the authors for their individual chapters, has been asserted by them in accordance with sections 77 and 78 of the Copyright, Designs and Patents Act 1988.

All rights reserved. No part of this book may be reprinted or reproduced or utilised in any form or by any electronic, mechanical, or other means, now known or hereafter invented, including photocopying and recording, or in any information storage or retrieval system, without permission in writing from the publishers.

Trademark notice: Product or corporate names may be trademarks or registered trademarks, and are used only for identification and explanation without intent to infringe.

Library of Congress Cataloging-in-Publication Data
Latino civil rights in education : la lucha sigue / edited by Anaida Colón-Muñiz and Magaly Lavadenz.
   pages cm — (Series in critical narrative)
   Includes bibliographical references and index.
   In English.
   1. Hispanic Americans—Education. 2. Hispanic Americans—Civil rights. 3. Discrimination in education—United States.
4. Educational equalization—United States. I. Colón-Muñiz, Anaida, 1951– II. Lavadenz, Magaly C.
   LC2669.L34 2016
   371.829′68073—dc23
   2015017432

ISBN: 978-1-138-94332-2 (hbk)
ISBN: 978-1-138-94333-9 (pbk)
ISBN: 978-1-315-67252-6 (ebk)

Typeset in Bembo
by Apex CoVantage, LLC

Printed and bound in the United States of America by Publishers Graphics, LLC on sustainably sourced paper.

We dedicate this book to all Latino civil rights advocates, such as the families in the Mendez et al. v. Westminster et al. desegregation case of the 1940s, who helped to inspire this book, especially Sylvia and Gonzalo Méndez, who continue to advocate for students throughout the country. It is also dedicated to the tireless work of Dolores Huerta and her heroic fight on behalf of Latino families. She is a beacon to Latino and Latina civil rights activists and scholars who carry on the struggle for social justice.

The book is also loyal to the memory of Evangelina "Gigi" Brignoni and Luis Fuentes, both contributors to the book who succumbed to illness prior to its publication. They served us well throughout their lives in their commitment to educational justice and courage in pursuing a better society. Their stories help us to record the history of struggle for civil rights in education along with all of the memories of resistance, labor and love that accompanied each of the other authors in the book.

We thank our mentor and guide, Donaldo Macedo, who encouraged us to record these critical histories and challenged us to strive for powerful storytelling so that we could make an indelible mark in the readers about the importance of civil rights in Latino education. And we thank Sonia Nieto, Latina scholar and dearest friend who was first to submit her civil rights account to inspire us.

While the narratives are written by Latinos, we want to ensure that this is a valuable text for all people concerned with social justice and critical education. Graciously, Suzanne SooHoo and Peter McLaren took the time to read our book and write our afterword, and we sincerely appreciate their critical lens and endorsement because we view our struggle as part of a universal struggle for justice.

Gracias to our colleagues, friends, and especially to our families who allowed us the space in our lives and gave us the support we needed to be able to complete this manuscript. This is a labor of love, hope and continued resistance because we know that the struggle continues . . . LA LUCHA SIGUE.

CONTENTS

Foreword—Latina(o) Civil Rights Movement: A Deferred Revolution   xiii
Donaldo Macedo

   Introduction   1
   Anaida Colón-Muñiz and Magaly Lavadenz

1   Latino Educational Civil Rights: A Critical Sociohistorical
    Narrative Analysis   15
    Anaida Colón-Muñiz and Magaly Lavadenz

2   Recognizing Inequality and the Pursuit of Equity:
    A Legal and Social Equity Framework   24
    Alberto M. Ochoa

3   The Lemon Grove Desegregation Case: A Matter of
    Neglected History   47
    Mike Madrid

4   The Meaning of Méndez   58
    Sandra Robbie

5   My Recollection of a Failed Attempt to Return
    the Schools to the Public   65
    Luis Fuentes (narrated by Anaida Colón-Muñiz)

6 The BC 44, Ethnic Studies, and Transformative Education   72
   Sonia Nieto

7 Memoirs of El Centro: The Impact of the Civil Rights
   Movement in Higher Education   88
   Pedro Pedraza

8 The 1968 Los Angeles Chicano Walkout   100
   Herman Sillas

9 *La Lucha Sigue*: An Interview with Dolores Huerta   109
   Magaly Lavadenz and Anaida Colón-Muñiz

10 I Am a Chicana, I Am Union, I Am an Activist: The Struggle
   for Cultural, Educational, and Linguistic Justice   121
   Theresa Montaño

11 Operation Chicano/a Teacher: A School-Based Teacher
   Equity Recruitment and Retention Program   133
   Marta E. Sanchez

12 I Don't Speak My Mother's Tongue   143
   Evangelina "Gigi" Brignoni

13 Becoming Me in the World   147
   Anaida Colón-Muñiz

14 Proposition 227 and the Loss of Educational Rights: A Personal
   Perspective and Quest for Equitable Educational Programs for
   English Learners   158
   María S. Quezada

15 Latinos and Social Capitalization: Taking Back Our Schools   170
   Magaly Lavadenz

16 Latino Parent Engagement: Struggle, Hope, and Resistance   177
   Pablo C. Ramírez

17 A Concise History of the National Latino/a Education
   Research and Policy Project: Origins, Identity,
   Accomplishments, and Initiatives   188
   Angela Valenzuela and Patricia D. López

Afterword *Peter McLaren and Suzanne SooHoo*	194
Appendix: A Chronology of Educational Experiences of Latinos in Latin America and the United States 1500s–2012	*201*
About the Authors	*214*
National Latino/a Education Research and Policy Project: National Advisory Board Members	*218*
Index	*220*

"Students I have had the privilege to meet many of you, and I am thrilled to find out that you are working so hard to show the world you are our future leaders. You must continue to persevere and never give up. I remain so proud of all of you, especially the ones that have made it, and are now giving back to the community."

Sylvia Méndez, of the 1946 Mendez et al. v. Westminster et al. desegregation case. January 1, 2015

FOREWORD

Latina(o) Civil Rights Movement: A Deferred Revolution

by Donaldo Macedo
UNIVERSITY OF MASSACHUSETTS BOSTON

For some time I have been encouraging my colleagues and friends, Anaida Colón-Muñiz and Magaly Lavadenz, to edit a book that would bring together Latina(o) voices of the courageous Latina(o) students and community activists who either participated in the Civil Rights Movement or continued the important work of those who put their careers, and sometimes their lives, on the line to denounce the oppressive conditions under which Latina(o) students were and continue to be mis-educated in segregated schools. Even after the promulgation of the Civil Rights Act and the subsequent Supreme Court victory in *Lau v. Nichols* in 1974 "which held that offering language-minority children only instruction in a language they could not understand violated the Civil Rights Act,"[1] a very large proportion of schools in the United States adopted a posture that would project an image of concern for the astutely mis-labelled Latina(o) educational failure problem while remaining largely in connivance with institutional racism—an entrenched racism that was never eradicated even in the heyday of the Civil Rights Movement. The subsequent Court orders designed to ameliorate apartheid conditions that generated, guided, and shaped the mis-education of an unacceptable high percentage of Latina(o) student population in schools where most teachers who were also mostly White did not stop the continued mis-education of Latina(o) students. The mostly White teachers would begin their school day by engaging their Latina(o) students and themselves in a pedagogy of lies through the recitation of the Pledge of Allegiance without the slightest idea of the inherent contradiction in the Pledge given the rampant discriminatory practices leveled against Latina(o) students. I say a "pedagogy of lies" because this "expression of fealty" can only be embraced by teachers who have been ideologically blinded by the doctrinal system from which they reap benefits and rewards for engaging in a social construction of not seeing—a process whereby they willfully develop an inability to separate myth from reality. This inability to live "within truth" pushes these indoctrinated teachers to a perpetual flirtation with historical hypocrisy—a hypocrisy that was not undetected by David Spritzler, a 12-year-old boy who could see readily the Pledge of Allegiance as "a hypocritical exhortation to patriotism" in that there is not "liberty and justice for all."[2] Hence, for David, the Pledge is an attempt to unite, as he explained, the "oppressed and the oppressors. You have people who drive nice cars, live in nice houses and don't have to worry about money. Then you have the poor people, living in bad neighborhoods and going to bad schools. Somehow the Pledge makes it seem that everybody's equal when that's not happening. There's no justice for everybody."[3]

The Pledge plays also the role of a magical transformation where the recitation of the Pledge becomes a kind of Disney Magic Kingdom with no fun, particularly for lower-class non-White racial and ethnic students, "no mermaids or princesses to be seen,"[4] but a mere attempt to reconcile the obscene fact that in California, for instance, in "high schools in the top two deciles in the state . . . one fourth of White [attend compared to] 1 in 30 Latinos."[5] The not-so-magical reality is that the promise of the Civil Rights Act as a tool to desegregate schools and racial and ethnic communities has been defanged by the very Courts appointed by Republican Presidents since Ronald Reagan while the ongoing Civil Rights Act backlash has forced many schools in the nation to re-segregate to the point that Latina(o) students populate some schools in California by over 90 percent as exemplified by many urban school districts which, according to Gary Orfield, "[have] been transformed in the half century since the civil rights era by immigration and huge changes in demography and that face profound inequality by race and class, inequality directly linked to schooling opportunities and educational outcomes."[6]

Against a landscape of re-segregation of communities and, consequently, of schools, which has led to the extreme *barriofication* of Latinas(o) communities, I strongly urged both Anaida and Magaly to ask Latina(o) educators and civic and community leaders what happened to the Civil Rights Latina(o) Movement that struggled so courageously to demand an end to segregation, inequality, and mis-education—a movement filled with rightful indignation and ire as young Latina(o) students in the 1960s paralyzed the entire Los Angeles School System and defiantly proclaiming "no más" (no more) inferior education and no more school segregation. What happened to the Latina(o) leadership as courageously embodied by César Chávez and other Chicana(o) activists? Today the Latina(o) voice of protest has somewhat re-submerged in a silenced culture—a silenced culture where there is no outrage even when Barack Obama, the first Black President, gave in to deporting the 57 thousand Latina(o) children who were stuck at the U.S./Mexico border back to their countries of origin where they face unimaginable violence, hunger, and dire poverty.

The quasi-national indifference regarding the eagerness to quickly deport 57 thousand Latina(o) children was articulately denounced by Joanne Springer, a graduate student in a seminar I taught last summer at Boise State, Idaho. She urged the class to reflect on the level of dehumanization experienced by those individuals who remain indifferent to the cries of Latina(o) children who were victims of rape, physical abuse, psychological violence, and inhumane poverty. Filled with indignation, she asked us to reconcile the nation's ideals inscribed in the Pledge of "one Nation under God, indivisible, with liberty and justice for all." She somberly ended her challenge to the class by asking: "what would these same individuals who were aggressively proposing immediate deportation of the 57 thousand Latina(o) children stuck at our borders do if it were announced that there were 57 thousand dogs stranded at our borders with Mexico?" She ventured to guess that the abandonment of this massive number of dogs would cause a national outcry ironically led precisely by individuals who support the deportation of 57 thousand Latina(o) children but who would rally the country to find safe homes and loving families to adopt these stranded dogs. This student's critical reflection on the biases with which we selectively demonstrate empathy and how the ingrained White supremacy ideology dehumanizes us to the point of remaining indifferent to the suffering of human beings who have been *othered*. Paraphrasing the famous Mexican author, Carlos Fuentes, who so poignantly explained the dehumanization of the oppressors in the process of dehumanizing the oppressed, stating that if we cannot see our humanity in others, we cannot see it in ourselves. Hence, the lack of a national outrage regarding our inability to see our shared humanity with these 57,000 Latina(o) children stuck at our borders with Mexico points to "a kind of intellectual disease . . . [as the English historian Paul Johnson suggests] . . . fundamentally irrational and highly infectious. It exerts great self-destructive force, severely harming countries and societies that engage in it."[7] One of the major challenges for the U.S. society is to eradicate its imperialistic desires that are inherently racist—desires whose foundation lies with the American exceptionalism, which, in turn, fuels White supremacy and fosters a form of derangement that "condemns [the society] to decline and weakness."[8]

These Latina(o) children were fleeing violence, dire poverty, and human misery largely because our foreign policies have generated, shaped, and maintained, for decades, support for brutal right-wing dictatorships in these children's respective countries. Thus, there is a direct link with the expansion of undocumented refugees from Latin America and our disastrous interventions in Latin America. Consequently, the continued extreme *barriofication* of Latina(o) communities very much mirror a form of third-worldization of the U.S. society that is now marked by the shrinkage of the middle class which, in turn, has led to the normalization of a huge expansion of the lower class characterized by poverty, alienation, and hopelessness. The hope etched in *"Sí se puede"* so brilliantly engendered by Dolores Huerta was emptied out by President Obama with his false promises contained in the usurped "Yes, we can" slogan. I say false promises to the extent that President Obama easily acquiesced to the right-wing Republicans and many center-right Democrats as evidenced by his lukewarm actions and his inaction with respect to most progressive causes that were part of his presidential campaign platform. As the first Black President, he has remained ominously silent regarding race relations as unarmed and innocent Black men, including a 12-year-old boy, are killed by police with impunity. President Obama's troubling silence is, however, welcome news to most White Americans who falsely convince themselves that racism is over and, as Chris Matthews, a liberal MSNBC host, put it, "[President Obama] is post-racial . . . I forgot he was black tonight for an hour. You know, he's gone a long way to become a leader of this country, and past so much history, in just a year or two. I mean, it's something we don't even think about."9

What White Americans fail to realize, as exemplified by Matthews' remarks, is that we can never become post-racial without first de-racing and to de-race implies cultural identity transmogrification of the White supremacist ideology that views leadership and the denouncement of racism as being mutually exclusive. That is why many racial and ethnic individuals embrace a social construction of not seeing racism as they move to leadership positions. Afraid of being accused of taking sides or favoring people from their racial group, they tend to adopt a posture of inaction with respect to affirmative action and race relations issues. In their inaction, they willingly support institutional racism that requires assimilation to the White ideology—a process that expects non-Whites to stop being in order to be. In other words, one is tolerated as Black so long one does not act too Black. That is, one must first be colonized by the White ideology before one is allowed entrance as a colonized subordinate into the dominant power structure. Thus, the post-racial proposition is a euphemism for forced and subordinating assimilation that is not too dissimilar from "the imperialist colonial domination [that] tried to create theories which, in fact, are only gross formulations of racism, and which, in practice, are translated into a permanent state of siege on the indigenous populations."10

In other words, the post-racial theory embraced by most White Americans, including White liberals, is yet another attempt to deny non-Whites their cultures with the false promise that race and ethnicity no longer matter just because the Civil Rights Act made it possible for Blacks and Whites to use the same public bathrooms and to share the same lunch counters. However, we cannot have too many individuals from non-White racial and ethnic minority groups occupying positions of leadership and power. I am reminded of a search for the deanship of which I was a member of the search committee. When the committee was leaning toward the selection of a Latina, the Chancellor reminded the headhunter that "we had one of them already." That is, while it is natural to have all White leadership, it is unnatural to have more than a token non-White representation in leadership positions. Hence, the lie within a post-racial theory that is astutely reproduced by White ideology through the individualization of racism—a process that disarticulates personal acts of racism from the insidiousness of institutional racism. The defanging of the Civil Rights Act and the re-interpretation of affirmative action mandates that were designed to shield members of protected groups are readily seen when institutions remain largely immune from racial harassment cases leveled against them. For example, as a Latina(o) professor or teacher, you can be harassed *ad infinitum*, and unless the author or authors of the harassment utter a term comparable to the "N" word that applies also to the Latina(o) ethnicity, the institution's reaction is always "it is not racism. They just don't like you. It has nothing to do with your ethnicity." In essence, institutional racist structures will protect those who racially harass so long as the authors of the harassment do not revert to name calling or similar acts of personal racism.

While race remains a central challenge in the U.S. society, our first Black president opted to "transcend race,"[11] a figment of White Americans' imagination to the extent that no matter how much the Supreme Court judge Clarence Thomas and other assimilated Blacks or Latinas(os) try to transcend race, they remain locked in the collective imagination as "people of color"—a category that functions to make Whiteness invisible and deprives non-White racial and ethnic groups of a language to identify themselves. The insidiousness of making White ideology invisible through the erasure of language is yet again another assimilatory mechanism that attempts to impose White ideology "without damage to the culture of the dominated people—that is, harmonizes economic and political domination of these people with their cultural personality."[12] Thus, even critical Latinas(os), Blacks, and members of other non-White racial and ethnic groups in the U.S. refer to themselves always as "people of color" without realizing that the very acceptance of this false linguistic category reinforces White supremacy through the invisibility of White ideology. That is, by not questioning the identifier, "people of color," it is assumed that only non-White racial and ethnic groups have color and Whites are colorless—a proposition that is semantically unviable to the degree that you cannot have "colorless White." Through this ideological manipulation, the invisible White becomes the norm against which all other subordinated racial and ethnic groups are measured as Anaida Colón-Muñiz and Magaly Lavadenz, the authors of this edited volume, explain that "in the United States Latinos have fallen into the same labeling and overarching hyphenated categories as have European-Americans, African-Americans." However, there is a marked difference: due to the Europeans' socially perceived White skin color, they were able to eventually and fully assimilate and now enjoy *full* citizenship since they have become part of the economic system that benefits Whites while groups perceived as non-Whites continue to be excluded from full participation and citizenship as evidenced as the need to hyphenate African-American, Asian-American, Mexican-American, among others. It is no longer necessary to hyphenate German-Americans, Dutch-Americans, or Irish-Americans. Members of these groups identify themselves simply as Americans. If there is a need for ancestry identification, they typically identify simply as German, Dutch, and Irish. Thus, the hyphenation process points to the not-yet-full citizenship status of the hyphenated people as promised by the colonizing assimilatory process while the same process maintains the necessary linguistic mechanism to signal distinction as separate from the full citizenship status enjoyed by Whites only. In reality, the distinction marked by hyphenation, more often than not, functions to devalue, to discriminate, and to dehumanize those that have become "*othered*" in the colonizing assimilation process.

What is important to highlight is that assimilation theory falsely promises to create "a brand-new national identity, carried forward by individuals who, in forsaking old loyalties and joining to make new lives, melted away ethnic differences."[13] This assimilation false promise shows its cancerous underbelly whenever the hyphenated "*other*" begins to take the assimilation myth seriously and acts as a full member of society and attempts to enjoy full citizenship as in the case of Louis Gates, an African-American professor at Harvard University who was arrested by a White policeman as he struggled to open the door to his multimillion dollar house in Harvard Yard and who wondered aloud if this obscene form of racial profiling happens to most young Black men in America. While within the academic context of Harvard and other universities Professor Gates enjoys full citizenship, he remains fundamentally a Black man in the vast majority of societal contexts where his Harvard pedigree is unknown. Thus, to the White Cambridge policeman, Professor Gates is just another Black man who fits the profile of the racial "*other*" who does not belong in an upper-class White neighborhood and who must be subjected to the same indignities that most African-American men suffer.

The arrest of Professor Louis Gates became international news and President Obama, as the first Black President, failed to use the presidential pulpit to launch a national dialogue on race-relations, particularly when racial profiling, re-segregation, and racist exclusion have now become routine after the 9/11 attack on the Twin Towers in New York. Instead, President Obama summoned Professor Louis Gates and the White Cambridge policeman who had wrongly arrested Gates to the White House for a beer conversation, which trivialized and vulgarized the complexity of race relations in the United States. The White House beer conversation also futilely attempted to reconcile the proposition of post-racial society with the ever-growing economic gaps between Whites and other racial and ethnic groups, the incessant assault on Black and Latina(o) people by the legal system, and the *Civil Rights Act* backlash that increasingly target Latinas(os) and Blacks as they are routinely funneled through an expanded prison-pipeline which has become the 21st-century new form of lynching.

Had Professor Gates traveled a few miles from his Harvard Yard to have a meaningful dialogue with thousands of young Latina(o) and Black man in Dorchester and Roxbury, he would have quickly learned that these young men are always suspect, frisked, and sometimes killed with impunity by virtue of their ethnicity and race and the subsequent stereotypes generated by White supremacy in America—an America that remains fundamentally racist and classist while denying the persistent role that both race and class play in the reproduction of the White supremacy ideology.

What this important edited volume, *Latino Civil Right in Education: La Lucha Sigue,* succinctly demonstrates is that the United States of America is far from developing a post-racial society due to its inability to de-race institutional structures so that race no longer matters—a de-raced society where "Latino scholars who have been inspired by their predecessors to continue social justice work in education . . . [without having to engage] . . . in a silenced discourse due to restrictions put upon them by academia," which remains largely White, classist, and discriminatory. A de-raced society would create democratic structures so that Latina(o) submerged voices can emerge free from the shackles of what Colón-Muñiz and Lavadenz describe as "Latino history interpreted by non-Latinos . . . [who] have brought a colonizing perspective and perpetuated a dominant narrative that continues to misconstrue our [Latina(o)] experience." While Colón-Muñiz and Lavadenz report locating "a number of significant works written by Chicano/Boricua/Latino scholars over the past 20 years who pose theoretical, analytical, historical and critical perspectives on our [Latina(o)] history," we should also use this critical perspective for self-critique and point out that we should be aware that race and ethnicity are no guarantee in the struggle for social justice. We all can name countless Latina(o) educators who benefitted tremendously from the tools of the Civil Rights Act and yet remained colonized and indifferent from the discriminatory practices that shape and guide the U.S. Latina(o) educational experience. These colonized Latina(o) educators and scholars are often used by the dominant system as functionaries whose connivance with the dominant ideology serve to exclude Latinas(os) and prevent their submerged voices from emerging. Hence, what is important is to avoid falling into any form of essentialism that romanticizes *Latinoness* while suffocating the struggle for social justice that working-class Latinas(os) yearn and deserve. Thus, what is important is not so much the color of one's skin. What is important is the color of one's ideology to ensure that the principles of democracy, social justice, and freedom are never sacrificed at the altar of careerism through which the accommodated Latina(o) professional's main task is to represent the oppressed Latina(o) left behind. By their role as representatives of the oppressed Latina(o), these accommodated careerists generally become apologists who are eager to protect their new middle-class status newly gained through the Civil Rights Act, as they are beholden to the very system that sustains that status. It is for this reason that merely having a Latina(o) last name is not sufficient to move forward a revolutionary pedagogy that would have, on the one hand, embraced a societal transformation where the 57 thousand Latina(o) children stranded at our borders with Mexico would be welcome instead of deporting them back to countries in Latin America where "a hundred children die of hunger or curable disease every hour, but doesn't stem their number in the streets and fields of a region that manufactures poor people and outlaws poverty . . . [countries that] squeeze them dry, watches them constantly, punishes them, sometimes kills them; almost never are they listened to, never are they understood."[14]

Against the backdrop of the human misery suffered by an unacceptable number of Latin American children in their respective countries, the task of Latina(o) educators in the United States is to never allow the imperfect tools of the Civil

Rights Act to be used to hire and promote middle- and upper-class individuals from Latin American countries who benefit tremendously from the oppression of children. Many of these middle- and upper-class international Latinas(os) who may have come to the United States to pursue graduate studies are hired to occupy leadership positions as representative of Latina(o) communities and, as a result, have a second chance to oppress the U.S. Latina(o) children they were hired to represent. Too often, educational institutions in the United States gravitate toward class solidarity and favor middle- and upper-class foreigners over domestic community individuals who are generally consigned a lower-class status and experience systematic and continued subordination. Often these foreign middle- and upper-class individuals identify more with White dominant values than they do with U.S. Latina(o) community members' ways of being even though they share the same ethnicity. In some cases, they even disdain American lower-class members of their own ethnicity.

While the dominant institutions feel more comfortable with foreign middle- and upper-class Latin American individuals than they do with American lower-class community people, given their shared dominant class values, it is important to point out that the imperfection of the Civil Rights Act tools that are based on ethnicity, race, and last names must be rectified so that the submerged voices of Latinas(os) left behind, locked in *barrios,* do not continue to be muffled by educators and functionaries who are hired as representative of American lower-class Latinas(os) simply because they share a last name. In essence, many of these representatives fail to see that the reformist agenda of the Latina(o) civil rights movement could only produce a deferred emancipation of Latinas(os)—an emancipation that is fast becoming fossilized as we witness a retrenchment from progressive causes and democratic ideals espoused by Dolores Huerta, César Chávez, Boricua leaders, among others, which are so eloquently and poignantly described, analyzed, and critiqued in this important edited volume.

Against a legacy of pragmatic careerism where many Latina(o) educators and leaders often sacrifice their principles in order to serve the dominant power structure through a form of colonized accommodation instead of serving the very community of people they represent, the authors of this important volume embrace a form of educational activism that guarantees not only a spirit of critique but also a necessary independence of thinking. In other words, they embrace what Edward Said and Paulo Freire believed: that an educator (who is also an intellectual) must always have the courage, the ethical posture, to denounce so as to be able to announce a world informed by a language of critique as well as a language of possibility—a language of critique that can justly denounce the lack of coherence revealed in President Obama's inability to walk his talk as he sloganized "Yes, we can" so as to re-infuse "*Sí, se puede*" with the necessary courage and activist hope of Dolores Huerta when she passionately crafted "*Sí, se puede*" as a means to speak truth to power. Dolores Huerta's embrace of a language of possibility also means activism and militancy in order to overthrow all forms of oppression leveled against Latinas(os) by any means necessary, as Malcolm X so courageously put it. And her engendering of *"Sí, se puede"* also means to not accommodate and align oneself with the interests of the powerful ruling class and to not submit to a system that constantly rewards individuals for obedience, complicity, and their contributions to the reproduction of an ever-expanding and inherently discriminatory and undemocratic assault on Latinas(os). In addition, the Latina(o) civil rights movement embodied in Dolores Huerta's *"Sí, se puede"* is an expression of an activist hope that goes beyond President Obama's flowery but empty embellishment of hope that promises but never delivers. The Latina(o) civil rights movement was infused with a kind of radical hope that is best characterized by Henry Giroux as a force that "can energize and mobilize groups, neighborhoods, communities, campuses and networks of people to articulate and advance insurgent discourses . . . Hope matters only when it turns outward, confronts the obstacles in its paths and provides points of identification that people find meaningful in order to become critical agents capable of engaging in transformative collective action."[15] Given the current incessant attacks on Latinas(os) in the United States, it is high time that we re-engage the radicality of *"Sí, se puede"* as a means to move Latinas(os) from the present object position of cheap labor or potential electoral votes to a subject position where they become agents of history who can think beyond the manufacturing of Latina(o) leaders as representatives or celebrities who eagerly don the "stardom" badge and act as spokespeople to represent all Latinas(os), while the vast majority of Latinas(os) are abandoned in the human misery of *barrio* life and never allowed to be present in history.

Notes

1. Gary Orfield, "Tenth Annual Brown Lecture in Education Research: A New Civil Rights Agenda for American Education." *Education Researcher*, August/September 2014, Vol. 43 No. 6, p. 276.
2. Donaldo Macedo, *Literacies of Power: What Americans Are Not Allowed to Know* (Boulder, Colorado: Westview Press, 2006), p. 10.
3. Ibid., p. 10.
4. John Goreman, "Superintendent says student doesn't have to recite pledge." *The Boston Globe*, March 11, 2015, p. J1.
5. Gary Orfield, "Tenth Annual Brown Lecture in Education Research: A New Civil Rights Agenda for American Education." *Education Researcher*, August/September 2014, Vol. 43 No. 6, p. 273.
6. Ibid., p. 273.
7. Jeff Jacoby, "The anti-Semitic derangement." *The Boston Globe*, January 14, 2015, p. A11.
8. Ibid., p. A11.
9. Jesse Washington, "Matthews' remark exposes complexity of 'transcending race.'" *Yahoo News*, January 28, 2015.
10. Donaldo Macedo, *Literacies of Power: What Americans Are Not Allowed to Know* (Boulder, Colorado: Westview Press, 2006), p. 43.
11. Jesse Washington, "Matthews' remark exposes complexity of 'transcending race.'" *Yahoo News*, January 28, 2015.

12. Donaldo Macedo, *Literacies of Power: What Americans Are Not Allowed to Know* (Boulder, Colorado: Westview Press, 2006), p. 43.
13. Arthur M. Schlesinger, Jr., *The Disuniting of America: Reflections on a Multicultural Society* (New York: Norton: 1992), p.40.
14. Eduardo Galeano, *Upside Down: A Primer for the Looking-Glass World* (New York: Picador, 2000), pp. 13–14.
15. Henry A. Giroux, "Authoritarianism, class warfare and the advance of neoliberal austerity policies," *Truthout*, January 5, 2015, p. 7.

INTRODUCTION

Anaida Colón-Muñiz and Magaly Lavadenz

"I stole your slogan," President Obama sheepishly admitted to Dolores Huerta when they met. In her inimitable acerbic style, she replied, "Yes, you did!" *Sí se puede* has been the fervent cry of the farmworkers since Dolores Huerta coined the phrase at the heart of the Farmworkers Union Movement working alongside César Chávez. Even today, rooms filled with thousands enthusiastically shout the phrase: *"¡Sí se puede, sí se puede, sí se puede!,"* clapping into a roar. As educators we have chanted ardently along with Dolores Huerta each time that she attends our education conventions to motivate us in addressing issues of educational inequity. When President Obama usurped the slogan, *Yes We Can*, for his 2008 presidential campaign, those of us who know Dolores Huerta and her work noticed right away that no credit had been given of its origin. "Hey, that's our slogan," we thought. It caught on as a popular cry and supported the election of our first African-American president. But, in our hearts we kept waiting for the recognition that this slogan came from Latinos and our fight for equity.

It is said that the famous slogan came to be in El Campito, in Arizona, as César Chávez fasted for farmworker rights and Dolores Huerta got the crowd energized to fight the good fight in what is now Santa Rita Hall in Phoenix.[1,2] This catchphrase came from the cries of the poor demanding a better world for themselves and their children. It wasn't until Ms. Huerta confronted the President that he finally made it public and acknowledged that *Yes We Can* is indeed *¡Sí Se Puede!* On May 29th, 2012,[3] Dolores Huerta received the Presidential Medal of Freedom, but it wasn't simply because of a slogan; it was for the many years that she struggled for the rights of farmworkers and for her continued work through the Dolores Huerta Foundation.[4]

Latinos honor and revere Huerta's work, and especially her fearlessness and passion for fighting for civil rights. As Latinas, we look up to her even more, because of the dearth of acknowledgment of women leaders, especially Latinas. We don't yet have a day to recognize Dolores Huerta as we have for other great Americans, but that will surely come, because she is as deserving as anyone for the inroads that she has made in the area of civil rights. For her voice and action Huerta was arrested 22 times for participating in non-violent civil disobedience activities and strikes. She has traveled all over the country and internationally to lecture and address human rights and continues to advocate on behalf of farmworkers, the working poor, Latina women and children. She is a Board Member of the Feminist Majority Foundation; Secretary-Treasurer Emeritus of the United Farm Workers of America; and President of the Dolores Huerta Foundation, which she founded in 2002.[5] Progressive causes are her calling, so she has served on the boards of People for the American Way, and the Consumer Federation of California. Even today as an octogenarian, Dolores Huerta has not completed her work, as she so aptly states, "la lucha sigue," the struggle continues.

About the Text

This edited anthology of *his* and *her/stories* captures some of the civil rights struggles in the education of Latinos in the United States. It was inspired by the 1946/47 Mendez et al. v. Westminster et al. case, which was barely known until recently in our history. In learning of this case, the authors saw the need to publish the stories of other Latino histories in education. Thus, this anthology includes narratives and counter-narratives written by Latinos/as involved in civil rights activities aimed at improving the condition of schooling for Latino children. It includes the perspectives and research of Latino educators, sociologists, historians, attorneys, and academics whose lives were guided and influenced in one way or another by this movement.

Latinos in the United States have had a long and arduous trajectory with regard to educational and other civil rights (Donato, 1997; Bell, 1998), despite the myth that we are not part of the tightly knit fabric of this country. Historical documents, records, articles and books that do chronicle this history seldom share it from the perspective of the very people who either participated directly in civil rights events or from those who followed their footsteps in that quest (MacDonald, 2004). Moreover, Latino scholars who have been inspired by their predecessors to continue social justice work in education are often engaged in a *silenced discourse* due to restrictions put upon them by academia (Reyes & Rios, 2005; Padilla & Chavez Chavez, 1995), or redirected by publishing houses driven by a market economy. As editors and authors represented in this book, we recognize that it was barely a generation ago when most of Latino history had been interpreted and written by non-Latinos (Hess & Petrilli, 2009); while more recently, many are great allies who have empathized with us and tried to describe our Latino history (McLaren, 2006; Miksch, 2008; Wainer, 2006), Logan and Turner (2013) and others have brought a colonializing perspective and perpetuated a dominating narrative that continues to misconstrue our experience (Gonzalez, J., 2011). However, we found a number of significant works written by Chicano/Boricua/Latino scholars over the last 20 years who pose theoretical, analytical, historical and critical perspectives on our history that have helped to frame and address the issues impacting Latinos in education (Darder, 1991/2012; Donato, 1997; Gonzales, 2011; Gonzalez, G., 2013; Gonzalez, J., 2011; Guerra, 2004; MacDonald, 2004; Murillo, Villenas, Galván, Sánchez Munoz, Martínez, & Machado-Casas, 2010; Melendez, 2003; Ogbar, 2006; Ruiz, 2006; Ruiz, 2008; San Miguel, 2013; Sanchez, 1993; Vargas, 2010). While not all of these directly address educational issues as we intend with the narratives included in this volume, these contributions represent Latina/o history, political and sociological analyses *by* Latinas/os.

To this body of important literature we wanted to add documentation on the Latino education experience giving light to personal trajectories—oral histories that need to be heard. We aimed at providing a social and historical accounting that could narrate for the larger society the personal impact of and response to ongoing abuses and neglect in schools and communities stemming from policies that have traditionally denied Latino students their basic educational and civil rights (Aoki & Johnson, 2009; Nieto, 2004; Rodriguez, 1999; Rodriguez, 2004; Vasquez, 2007). Traditional history textbooks used in schools typically fail to reflect the richness and complexity of the life, work and struggles for equality of Latinos in the United States. These omissions not only offend our existence as citizens, but nullify the validity of the numerous contributions made by Latinos for the betterment of society in America. According to historian Vicki Ruiz (2006), "histories of pre–United States settlements, if acknowledged at all, became reduced to romanticized images of quaint New Mexican villages or crumbling California missions" (p. 656).

Narrating the struggle for Latino civil rights in education comes not only from the past; these firsthand accounts also bridge with the future and the ongoing struggle of the fastest growing minority in the United States, now at approximately 60 million in 2014. According to the last census (U.S. Census, 2012), projections went from 53.3 million in 2012 to 128.8 million projected for 2060. Latino U.S. residents and our cultural traditions, stereotypically known for salsa dancing, tacos, cigars, and barrio life, actually represent the diversity of over 21 nations south of the border, totaling over 423 million people internationally. In fact, the United States has representation from every country in Latin America, although the majority are from Mexico, Puerto Rico and Cuba.

Rationale

That in the United States Latinos have fallen into the same labeling and overarching hyphenated categories as have European-American, African-Americans and

Asian-Americans, is of course not surprising, although we are mostly abbreviated into *Hispanic* or *Latino*. It has been convenient to put us under mega-categories to satisfy the needs of the market place, but we are as diverse within these "unifying" categories as we are between them.

According to the United States Census Bureau, "in the 2010 Census 'Hispanic or Latino' refers to a person of Cuban, Mexican, Puerto Rican, South or Central American, or other Spanish culture or origin regardless of race" (NCES, 2012). The socioeconomic, cultural, racial and linguistic differences we embody include North and South American, Meso-American and Caribbean people of mixed racial backgrounds that are belied in homogenous terms such as Latino or Hispanic. Regardless of the labeling, many of us have felt the inequity that has been bestowed upon us in the United States. We have adopted these titles to name our social, cultural and political condition. But, even with these generic terms, we sometimes struggle with what to name ourselves in different contexts. Guerra (2004) explains this best:

> In Chicago, most of the time but not always, soy hispano o latino. In Texas, soy tejano. In Mexico, soy mexicano americano. In Washington [S]tate, soy chicano. When I am out of my element, I refer to myself as Mexican or mexicano. And when I am around Anglos who are not quite sure what all of these words ending in "o" mean, I tell them—and yes, I admit that I still grit my teeth and bite my tongue before I speak this phrase—that I am Hispanic. At this point in my life, I want to believe that whatever singular label I may prefer to use to define myself in theory is no longer as important as the multiple labels I must choose to identify myself in practice.
>
> (p. 7)

While it is true that similarities in language and culture have been factors that unite us, there are also sociocultural factors that create different sociohistorical experiences. For example, while given little regard, the realities of indigenous people from Latin America, also labeled as Hispanic-American or Latino in the United States, are quite distinct. Many have a home language that is not Spanish, but rather one of many indigenous Amerindian languages (some in danger of extinction). In another example, racial and economic classification systems of Latin America predate the Latino existence in the United States that stemmed from European colonial racial and class stratification. While most of the immigrants come to the United States for economic reasons, others may represent elite social classes that come to get a higher education, or for political, cultural or social reasons. It becomes clear that we are complex and multifaceted. Given the limitations of a book such as this, it would be presumptuous of us, to say the least, to assume that we could capture the vast number of civil rights stories, efforts and events encompassing the experiences of U.S. Latinos. Nevertheless, the greatest numbers of Latinos who have sought their luck on American soil, even begrudgingly, are those whose civil rights have been violated primarily for reasons of color, language, ethnicity and poverty issues, and are the focus of this book. American history is replete with stories, many untold, where discrimination showed its ugly face and subjected Latinos as others to the menace of racism, bigotry, cynicism, hypocrisy, inequity and poverty. Then again, there are those wonderful accounts[6] and recounts of Latinos who have responded to these assaults with bravery, challenging the oppressive conditions that limited them and others to change these very conditions. These are some of the stories we have attempted to collect and share in this volume.

Like our African-American counterparts and countless others who have suffered discrimination because of race, religion, gender or socioeconomic status, we have people to thank for the inroads that have been made. Those who came before us and struggled towards civil rights left an indelible record of known individuals and groups, but the record is incomplete. In the United States we tend to "individualize" movements under one person, at the expense of ignoring the masses, as if by eliminating the deemed leader, entire groups could be controlled (Carson, 2000). But, we know this is not the case. There are little-known and unknown individuals and groups of people who contributed to the progress we have made and continue to do so because of their willingness to speak up and do something to improve the conditions of K–12 schooling and access to higher education. So, we also stand on the shoulders of those who took to the streets (and continue to do so) to protest an injustice, stepping forward to speak up for the community and whose names we may never know.

Inspired by our predecessors and the continued need to work towards social justice in education, these 16 narratives provide an historical foundation and social context from their perspectives. We believe this volume will serve to further the knowledge base of community members, agents of change and activists, educators and students. We also hope that it will further the research interests of future scholars. These chapters include personal narratives that reveal the thoughts, opinions and experiences of the authors as both scholars and community activists. We present the book in this narrated way to demystify agency or taking action, with the hope that others will be inspired to become agents of change for civil rights in education, speak up against injustice and take an active role in their schools and communities no matter what their role or rank in society—parent, student, community member, worker, professional or scholar.

How the Book Is Organized

This book documents the lives and efforts of a group of Latinos in American history struggling to attain equity in education through their involvement in civil rights. It begins with an analysis of the narratives by the editors, followed

It includes a brief historical overview of the case, and an examination of the social, political, and economic forces and conditions that fostered segregated schools for children of Mexican descent in California and the southwest.

Chapter 4: The Meaning of Méndez

Sandra Robbie

The author recounts how the 1946 Mendez et al. v. Westminster et al. case exploded into her awareness and changed the direction of her life. She describes the Méndez case, led by Mexican-American Gonzalo Méndez and his Puerto Rican wife Felicitas, and details the parallel prejudice experienced by people of many colors in California at the time of the case. This chapter reveals the electric human connection between the American civil rights struggles of Latinos, Blacks, Asians, Native Americans and Jews in creating the freedoms we have today.

Chapter 5: My Recollection of a Failed Attempt to Return the Schools to the Public

Luis Fuentes (narrated by Anaida Colón-Muñiz)

This narrative is based on the experiences of the first Puerto Rican principal in New York City Schools and his attempt to respond to the needs of parents and children. Even prior to the ASPIRA consent decree of 1974, the city launched an experimental (reform) project that introduced local control and autonomy. It was a milestone in civil rights for Blacks and Latinos as the first coalition effort of minorities of similar economic levels to improve schools that were failing their children. The author describes the racialized power struggle that surfaced in a district in which there were great demographic disparities between the growing diverse student population and homogeneity of the unionized teaching force. He recounts the personal and professional impact of these struggles.

Chapter 6: The BC 44, Ethnic Studies, and Transformative Education

Sonia Nieto

Known for her expertise in multicultural education and her advocacy for teachers, Sonia Nieto outlines the process that she underwent as a young Latina educator in becoming an activist during the ethnic studies movement in New York's CUNY system. As part of the first group of student and faculty activists who protested for a more appropriate representation and selection process for the director of the recently founded Puerto Rican Studies program at Brooklyn College, she narrates her experiences of resistance, the struggle for change and the outcome of the efforts of the BC 44.

Chapter 7: Memoirs of El Centro: The Impact of the Civil Rights Movement in Higher Education

Pedro Pedraza

In his chapter, Pedraza gives an account of the steps that were taken to establish El Centro de Estudios Puertorriqueños at Hunter College in New York in the 1960s. The Center for Puerto Rican Studies has become a highly valued pivotal space for researching the history of Puerto Ricans in the United States as well as for archiving documents to illustrate that experience. From one of earliest staff members and research directors, we learn that it took an arduous struggle to get the Center off the ground and to sustain it amidst the politics and power of American higher education.

Chapter 8: The 1968 Los Angeles Chicano Walkout

Herman Sillas

Following the Watts Riots, the National Guard was called to restore order in Los Angeles. There was worry about the Black Berets as well as about another militant front—the Brown Berets. In the community people were perturbed with the 50 percent high school drop-out rate of Mexican-Americans. Chicano students took action with a presentation of demands, but there was a lack of response from the administration. This is the story of the walkout that took place in four L.A. schools and how within three days, and involving thousands of students, it resulted in violence. The legal case that took place is part of how Herman Sillas got involved in this history: Castro v. Superior Court (1970) 9 Cal. App. 3rd 675.

Chapter 9: La Lucha Sigue: An Interview with Dolores Huerta

Magaly Lavadenz and Anaida Colón-Muñiz

Prefaced with an historical backdrop of her life, the voice of the legendary civil rights activist Dolores Huerta is shared through an interview about her perceptions on the condition of education for immigrant children, the injustices that persist in schools, and her advice to parents about how to help their children succeed.

Chapter 10: I Am a Chicana, I Am Union, I Am an Activist: The Struggle for Cultural, Educational, and Linguistic Justice

Theresa Montaño

In this account Montaño provides a history of the union movement in education as she experienced it, and how it gave her the impetus to become a vital agent of change. It describes the importance of the unionization movement in education and the personal connections between the activism of the author in education and her cultural and linguistic identity.

Chapter 11: Operation Chicano/a Teacher: A School-Based Teacher Equity Recruitment and Retention Program

Marta E. Sanchez

The historical development of a specialized, federally funded teacher training project to respond to the shortage of bilingual teachers is the focus of this chapter. The author details all of the challenges that she faced in getting the program off the ground, its successes and struggles, and the slow demise of the program due to cutbacks in funding.

Chapter 12: I Don't Speak My Mother's Tongue

Evangelina "Gigi" Brignoni

Why would a non-native Spanish speaker work so hard to recuperate her parents' heritage language? It started when she was 5 years old when she realized that her parents' code was not hers. What resulted was years of struggle to attempt native-like fluency, a bilingual teaching credential, and starting a Bilingual Education endorsement at the University of Omaha, Nebraska. This chapter focuses on Brignoni's personal narrative including her social justice advocacy work as a bilingual educator.

Chapter 13: Becoming Me in the World

Anaida Colón-Muñiz

This chapter contests the well-meaning processes inherent in American schooling that wear down at the core of the native language and culture of linguistically diverse children, affecting their self-development. The author describes her personal trajectory as an English learner and how she fought back, gaining critical consciousness and finding hope as a critical bilingual and multicultural educator.

Introduction **11**

Chapter 14: Proposition 227 and the Loss of Educational Rights: A Personal Perspective and Quest for Equitable Educational Programs for English Learners

María S. Quezada

In this narrative, the author shares her personal involvement in trying to defeat Proposition 227, the initiative aimed at doing away with bilingual education in California. As president of one of the largest bilingual education organizations in the country, she discusses the tensions and frustrations she experienced and provides a rationale for the passing of the ballot proposition that resulted in the loss of language and education rights for English learners.

Chapter 15: Latinos and Social Capitalization: Taking Back Our Schools

Magaly Lavadenz

This chapter describes a five-year-long process in the mobilization of a working class Latino community to counter the violation of the rights of parents to choose legally available educational options for their children. The author documents an intensive and collaborative community movement, led by a team of parents and teachers that resulted in two campaigns to elect new representatives to the school board. Collaboration, action and vigilance were central aspects to ensure that politics of schooling along with sound practices are necessary to ensure a positive future for Latino children in the United States.

Chapter 16: Latino Parent Engagement: Struggle, Hope, and Resistance

Pablo C. Ramírez

In this chronicle Ramírez narrates how his lived experiences as a Latino parent advocate and scholar informed action research undertaken in Latino school communities. Critical action research is used to document, expose and challenge inequalities faced by Latino parents. The author affirms that hope and resiliency play a significant role in Latino parent engagement.

Chapter 17: A Concise History of the National Latino/a Education Research and Policy Project: Origins, Identity, Accomplishments, and Initiatives

Angela Valenzuela and Patricia D. López

This chapter provides a concise history of the National Latino/a Education Research and Policy (NLERAP) project, originally formed by a national board of educators, community activists, and university faculty whose research is focused on the education of Latina and Latino youth. This synopsis lays out the historical context, evolution and activities of this national organization and concludes with mention of curriculum development for pre-service teachers, signaling the kinds of systemic changes that are sought for higher education and teacher preparation as a national collective.

Appendix: A Chronology of Educational Experiences of Latinos in Latin America and the United States 1500s–2012

Magaly Lavadenz and Anaida Colón-Muñiz

The editors include this appendix in order to provide a singular timeline of Latino education history from the Spanish colonial period in the Americas and the United States. The chronology is based primarily on the work of MacDonald (2004) and others focused on the education of Latinos. It serves to demonstrate the depth and breadth of the Latino educational experience and the struggle in seeking a fair and equitable education.

Notes

1. Chicanos Por La Causa bought the building with plans to restore it. Now in the fight for federal recognition, Santa Rita Hall is one of the five "nationally significant sites connected to César Chávez and the United Farm Workers movement." Retrieved February 23, 2014 from http://peoplesguidetomaricopa2.blogspot.com/2012/12/santa-rita-hall.html.
2. Dolores Huerta entrevista—"Sí se puede" | AARP. Retrieved February 23, 2014 from http://www.youtube.com/watch?v=qF_OoZJNRCo.
3. Cook, Rachel (26 April 2012). "Dolores Huerta will be given Medal of Freedom, White House announces." *Bakersfield Californian*. Retrieved February 23, 2014 from https://farmworkersforum.wordpress.com/2012/04/28/dolores-huerta-will-be-given-medal-of-freedom-white-house-announces/.
4. "About the Dolores Huerta Foundation." Dolores Huerta Foundation. Retrieved February 23, 2014 from http://doloreshuerta.org.
5. "Dolores Huerta Biography." Dolores Huerta Foundation. Retrieved February 23, 2014 from http://doloreshuerta.org/dolores-huerta/.
6. We use the terms accounts, narratives and oral histories interchangeably in our introduction. While oral history is widely recognized as the collection and recording of personal memoirs as historical documentation, we define narratives and counter-narratives in this volume as the often untold oral histories from the viewpoints of those whose histories/herstories have not been voiced in dominant historical accounts.

References

Aoki, K., & Johnson, K. R. (2009). Latinos and the law: Case and materials. *Harvard Latino Law Review, 12*, 73–101.

Bell, G. (1998). *Telling stories out of school: Remembering the Carlisle Indian Industrial School, 1879–1918.* Doctoral dissertation. Stanford University.
Carson, C. (2000). "Civil Rights reform and the Black freedom struggle." In *The Civil Rights Movement in America*, edited by Charles W. Eagles, 19–32. Jackson: University Press of Mississippi, 1986. Reprinted in *Interpretations of American history: Patterns & perspectives*, edited by Francis G. Couvares et al., New York: Free Press.
Darder, A. (1991). *Culture and power in the classroom: A critical foundation for bicultural education.* New York: Bergin and Garvey Publishers.
Darder, A. (2012). *Culture and power in the classroom: A critical foundation for the education of bicultural students.* Boulder, CO: Paradigm Press.
Donato, R. (1997). *The other struggle for equal schools: Mexican-Americans during the civil rights era.* Albany: State University of New York Press.
Gonzales, R. G. (2011). Learning to be illegal: Undocumented youth and shifting legal contexts in the transition to adulthood. *American Sociological Review, 76*(4), 602–619.
Gonzalez, G. (2013). *Chicano education in the era of segregation.* Denton: University of North Texas Press.
Gonzalez, J., (2011). *Harvest of empire: A history of Latinos in America.* New York: Penguin Putnam Books.
Guerra, J. C. (2004). "Emerging representations, situated literacies, and the practice of transcultural repositioning." In *Latino/a discourses on language, identity, and literacy education*, edited by M. Halls Kells, V. M. Balester, with V. Villanueva. Portsmouth, NH: Boyton/Cook Publishers.
Hess, F. M., & Petrilli, M. (2009). Wrong turn on school reform. *Policy Review, 153,* 55–68.
Logan, J. R., & Turner, R. (2013). *Hispanics in the United States: Not only Mexicans.* Brown University: US2010. March 2013. Retrieved June 16, 2015 from http://www.s4.brown.edu/us2010/Data/Report/report03202013
MacDonald, V. M. (2004). *Latino education in the United States.* New York: Palgrave Macmillan.
McLaren, P. (2006). 5th ed. *Life in schools: An introduction to critical pedagogy in the foundations of education.* New York: Allyn & Bacon.
Melendez, Miguel "Mickey." (2003). *We took the streets: Fighting for Latino rights with the Young Lords.* New York: St. Martin's Press.
Mendez v. Westminster, 64 F. Supp. 544 (S.D. Cal. 1946).
Miksch, K. (2008). Widening the river: Challenging unequal schools. *UCLA Chicana/o Latina/o Law Review, 27,* 111–147.
Murillo, E. G., Villenas, S. A., Galván, R. T., Sánchez Munoz, J., Martínez, C., & Machado-Casas, M. Eds. (2010). *Handbook of Latinos and education: Theory, research, and practice.* New York: Routledge.
Nieto, S. (2004). Black, White, and us: The meaning of Brown v. Board of Education for Latinos. *Multicultural Perspectives, 6*(4), 22–25.
Ogbar, J.O.G. (2006). Puerto Rico in my heart: The Young Lords, Black Power and Puerto Rican Nationalism in the US, 1966–1972. *Centro Journal, 18.1,* 148–169.
Padilla, A., & Chavez Chavez, R. Eds. (1995). *The leaning ivory tower: Latino professors in American universities.* New York: SUNY Press.
Reyes, X. A., & Rios, D. (2005). Dialoguing the Latina experience in higher education. *Journal of Hispanic Higher Education, 4*(4), 377–391 (October 2005).
Rodriguez, A. (1999). Latino education, Latino movement. *Educational Theory, 49*(3), 381–400.

Rodriguez, R. (2004). The state of Latino education: A war against ignorance. *Black Issues in Higher Education, 21*(9), 84–86.

Ruiz, V. L. (2006). Nuestra América: Latino history as United States history. *Journal of American History, 93* (Dec. 2006), 655–672.

Ruiz, V. L. (2008). *From out of the shadows: Mexican women in twentieth-century America* (Tenth Anniversary Edition). New York: Oxford University Press.

Sanchez, G. J. (1993). *Becoming Mexican-American: Ethnicity, culture and identity in Chicano Los Angeles, 1900–1945*. New York: Oxford University Press.

San Miguel, G. (2013). *Those who dared: Ethnic Mexican struggles for education in the Southwest since the 1960s.* College Station, TX: Texas A&M University Press.

Stavans, I. (2001). *The Hispanic condition: Reflections on culture and identity.* New York: HarperCollins.

U.S. Census Bureau. 2012. *U.S. Census bureau projections show a slower growing, older, more diverse nation a half century from now.* Washington, DC. Retrieved February 23, 2015 from https://www.census.gov/newsroom./releases/archives/population/cb12–243.html

U.S. Department of Education, National Center for Education Statistics (NCES). (2012). *The Condition of Education* 2011 (NCES 2011–04).

Vargas, Z. (2010). *Crucible of struggle: A history of Mexican America from colonial times to the present.* New York: Oxford University Press.

Vasquez, O. A. (2007). Latinos in the global context. *Journal of Latinos and Education, 6*(2), 119–137.

Wainer, A. (2006). The new Latino south and the challenge to American public education. *International Migration, 44*(5), 129–165.

1
LATINO EDUCATIONAL CIVIL RIGHTS

A Critical Sociohistorical Narrative Analysis

Anaida Colón-Muñiz and Magaly Lavadenz

Schooling Context for Latinos in the U.S.

Historically in the United States, diverse civil rights groups have been seeking a fair and equitable education for more than 100 years; this quest has not yet ended. The longstanding achievement gap, along with increasing drop-out/push-out rates (Chapman, Laird, & Kewal Ramani, 2010), increased suspension rates, and overrepresentation in special education (Artiles, Harry, Reschy, & Chinn, 2002) attest to this. Table 1.1, for instance, reflects the disparities in reading between White students and students of color (Black and Latino) in 8th grade reading scores, revealing 24–26 point differences. Numerous scholars (Banks & Banks, 1995; Delpit, 1995; Delpit & Dowdy, 2010; Haberman, 1995; Howard, 2006; Huerta, 2011; Ladson-Billings, 1995; Nieto, 2004) have identified contributing factors for persistent underachievement as linked to the lack of culturally and linguistically appropriate instruction for these populations.

English Learners (ELs), comprising approximately 20% of our nation's student population, frequently do not have access to a comprehensive curriculum of high-quality science, social science, and the arts, and have experienced the consequences of "subtractive schooling" as push-outs, drop-outs, and long-term ELs (Olsen, 2010; Gandara & Rumberger, 2004; Valenzuela, 1999).

These statistics are not acceptable and wear away at the conceptual core of a free and democratic public education system in the United States. While issues related to Black youth and the civil rights movement in education have been keenly defined and publicly denounced, issues related to the civil rights efforts of Latinos remain somewhat in the shadows of American politics and policy. There has been mere "lip service" paid to the need for a national focus to address issues of language, ethnicity, poverty, and the academic achievement of Latino students, particularly those underachieving. On the other hand, while there are plenty of

TABLE 1.1 National Association of Educational Progress 2009 and 2011 Comparison 8th Grade Reading Scale Scores by Ethnicity

Jurisdiction	Year	All Students	White	Black	Hispanic	Hispanic-Black (Difference)
National Public Schools	2009	262.29	271.36	245.45	247.83	2.38
	2011	263.59	272.29	247.61	251.30	3.6

media blasts on the failures of Latino students to learn adequate English or meet the cutoffs on standardized English tests, we rarely hear about the students who are beating the odds and excelling in school, which would not only serve to redefine public opinion, but would also help identify and support what works well in alleviating what is considered a Latino education crisis.

The truth is that neither Black nor Latino groups have been fully satisfied with the outcome of one wave or another of so-called educational reforms for integration and academic achievement (Abramson, 1971). Promising educational practices are short-lived or underfunded in some cases, or replaced with yet another wave of compensatory programs that fail to help the students with the greatest needs. The ongoing struggle for underserved and underperforming populations in schools continues and its advocates tirelessly continue to dream of and call for the day when Black and Latino children can be seen as equals in their human potential to become who they are capable of being—not drop-outs, push-outs, underachievers, far below basic or at-risk students. These are labels we know all too well.

Theoretical Framework: Critical Sociohistorical Narrative

Imagining a better world is what brought us to preparing this work. In order to imagine a more just and humane world, according to Freire (1978), it must come from the authentic struggle of people who engage front and center in battling oppressive conditions. Through gaining a greater critical conscientiousness, naming inhumane conditions and denouncing them, problem-posing and defining possibilities through reflection and action or praxis, as U.S. Latinos/as we embrace the hope that comes from standing up for what are inalienable rights as well as changing the conditions that create inequities. We also embrace the hope that exists in the creation of knowledge and a better history.

Using Freire's work as a lens, we selected five historical themes (Freire, 2005) that coincided with many of the stories that we collected for this book and the recurring ideas that surfaced from the various struggles throughout history: 1) concientización, 2) naming and denunciating, 3) problem-posing, 4) reflection and action, and 5) hope. This final theme—hope—comes from the labor of love that inspired the varied civil rights efforts narrated in the book chapters. Analyzing the narratives using this lens we found the generative themes that surfaced from the authors relating their experiences in the struggle for civil and educational rights. Freire describes how people respond to generative themes:

> As they separate themselves from the world, which they objectify, as they separate themselves from their own activity, as they locate the seat of their decisions in themselves and in their relations with the world and others, people overcome the situations which limit them: the "limit-situations."
>
> *(2005, p. 99)*

Some narratives we collected are personal stories of the authors while others recount neglected Latino histories. More importantly, the stories accentuate Freire's capacity to capture that essential need of humans to struggle when they are bound by inequities that restrict their ability to be free and to realize their own potential.

Freire explains critical consciousness as a sociopolitical educative tool that engages learners in questioning the nature of their historical and social situation, which he addressed as "reading the world" (2005). Thus, we used a critical sociohistorical approach as a central conceptual organizing model to examine the narratives of the 17 Latino/a authors, following Solórzano and Yosso's (2000; 2001; 2002a; 2002b) approach to using narratives and counter-narratives as inquiry modes. These are posed to contest and counter dominant forms of documenting history from the standpoint of the people who are central to the struggle. Using a critical sociohistorical approach based on Freire's theory of emancipation, the authors engaged in a critical analysis of the history of civil rights in the education of U.S. Latinos.

Concientización

The goal of critical consciousness, according to Freire, should be acting as subjects in the creation of democratic society. Freire implies intergenerational equity between students and teachers in which both learn, both question, both reflect, and both participate in meaning-making (1970; 1973; 2005).

Naming and Denunciating

Freire points to the importance of naming. He says, "To exist, humanly, is to name the world, to change it" (2005, p. 88).

Problem-Posing

Freire shows us how in problem-posing people are able to perceive critically their existence in a dynamic world that is always in the process of transforming and becoming (1970; 2005).

Reflection and Action = Praxis

One of the key principles of Freire's theory of emancipation has to do with the capability that humans have as creative beings to produce tangible as well as intangible goods, ideas, and concepts. He claims that through the process of reflection and action (praxis), humans create history and their social and historical reality (1970; 2005).

Hope and Love

Love and hope provide the courage to take on oppressive conditions and change them. "Because love is an act of courage, not of fear, love is commitment to others. No matter where the oppressed are found, the act of love is commitment to their cause—the cause of liberation" (Freire, 2005, p. 89).

Our Inquiry Approach

A Call to Contribute

A wide appeal was made by the authors to gather and collect these stories from throughout the country and from various historical periods. Following a review of the key historic and contemporary Latino/a civil rights activists, we identified 25 key participants across a variety of Latino national origin groups. We wanted to include narratives from U.S.-based Latino perspectives. Because education is interdisciplinary in nature, we also invited individuals representing various professions who were engaged in the educational civil rights movement. For example, there is an entry by Herman Sillas, the attorney who defended Sal Castro after the walkouts in Los Angeles. Personal contacts were also made to reach individuals from activist organizations, who might be limited in their time to write their own stories, such as Dolores Huerta of the United Farmworkers Union, whom we interviewed. We also appealed to colleagues in education who we knew had engaged in the education of Latino children, prepared teachers, or dedicated their research and writing to the education of Latinos. Contributors were asked to narrate their stories. We compiled and analyzed 16 written narratives and manuscripts that highlight where we have been as a nation on Latino educational civil rights. The authors have shared the humanity and dignity behind the civil rights movement and they remind us that we are all capable of taking action when we are confronted with injustice and decide to take a stand.

Contributors were asked to narrate their stories according to the following guiding questions:

1. What were the conditions just prior to the action you took?
2. What incident/s gave you the impetus to take action?

3. Tell your story as you remember it using as many dates and facts as possible.
4. What were your observations, feelings, and concerns at the time?
5. What changes came about, if any, relative to your area of concern?
6. How is it now? Have things gotten any better?
7. What is your hope for the present and future of civil rights in the U.S. relative to the particular area of civil rights in which you were involved?
8. What do you propose as a way to create change for the better?

Process

We compiled and analyzed 16 written narratives and manuscripts that highlight the voices of those who have been integrally involved in our national policy, practices, and historical development regarding Latino educational civil rights.

Analyzing Narratives: Freire's Critical Sociohistorical Approach

> I have the right to be angry and to express that anger, to hold it as my motivation to fight, just as I have the right to love and to express my love for the world, to hold it as my motivation to fight, because, while a historical being, I live history as a time of possibility, not of predetermination.
>
> *(Freire, 2004, pp. 58–59)*

Using Paulo Freire's critical sociohistorical approach as the conceptual framework, we then sought to engage with a complementary central conceptual analytic organizer to use with the narratives. Critical sociocultural discourse analysis has its central origins found in the works of Russian psychologist Lev Vygotsky (1978); sociocultural perspectives in language, teaching, and learning can be defined as newer understandings jointly constructed via dialogue and interactions between people. From this viewpoint, communication and learning are inextricably linked and also informed by the social, cultural, and historical experiences of the participants. Thus, we used a critical sociocultural discourse analysis as both a theoretical approach and methodological approach to engage with the concepts, events, and participants of Latinos in educational civil rights in the United States. We applied this approach to both the written narratives of the authors as well as the oral texts (such as in the chapter by Dolores Huerta).

The critical sociocultural discourse analysis described here is also influenced by the work of language researchers in several disciplines. It differs from dialogue in the original sense as treated by Freire; rather, narrative forms of intellectual activity are communicated as an intersection of written, social, and cognitive reflections of experiences in the forms and manners that have traditionally been omitted. Other educational researchers have also devised useful approaches to the analysis of talk based on a sociocultural perspective and have used them in the pursuit of their own research questions.

Critical Discourse Analysis

Critical discourse analysis (Fairclough, 1995; Gee, 2004, 1999; Widdowson, 1998) can be defined as a form of data analysis which "studies the way social power abuse, dominance, and inequality are enacted, reproduced, and resisted by text and talk in the social and political context" (van Dijk, 2003, p. 252). In order to generate the themes from the narratives, we applied Gee's recommendations for extracting both meaning and the understanding about how that meaning was situated within the particular perspective, experience, and context of the contributors to this volume:

> Function means meaning or the communicative purpose a form carries out. The other task is what we call the utterance-token meaning (or situated meaning) task. This task involves the study of correlations between form and function in language at the level of utterance-token meanings. Essentially, this task involves discovering the situation-specific or situated meanings of forms used in specific contexts of use.
> *(Gee, 2004, p. 25)*

Thus, we used this process collaboratively in analyzing the narratives across Freire's emancipatory themes that reflected the actions, words, and insights from our contributing authors as noted earlier: 1) concientización, 2) naming and denunciating, 3) problem-posing, 4) reflection and action, and 5) hope. The next section describes our analysis.

Findings: Analysis of the Narratives and Counter-Narratives

Analyzing the content, we found that there was a strong relationship between the Freirean themes and those that surfaced from the narratives. In all of the manuscripts we found evidence of the five Freirean themes, each story containing at least four of the five. This process resulted in the five final themes. Following are representative excerpts from the authors' narratives:

1. *Concientización.* This equals recognizing the sociopolitical conditions creating devaluing and deficit orientations toward Latino community experiences. Alberto Ochoa states, "By my late teens I was clearly aware of discriminatory practices, lack of academic rigor in my schooling, and the lack of K–12 schooling opportunity to maintain my home language with a high level of academic proficiency."
2. *Naming and Denunciating.* In describing his experience as the defense attorney for Sal Castro, the incarcerated teacher accused in the L.A. Walkouts,

Herman Sillas wrote: "He spoke of assimilation and the stripping of their culture by insensitive teachers and administrators. Our children felt unwanted as a result. As he spoke, I realized that he had described my school journey." It is through the identification of the unjust conditions with an enactment of the democratic principle of the right to protest that this account is described.

3. *Problem-Posing.* Through contextualizing institutional racism and the perpetuating of lack of access to equitable schooling, Sandra Robbie describes the experience of participating in the famous Mendez v. Westminster case, ruling the unconstitutionality of separate schools for Latinos and Whites: "While the disparity between the two schools was vast, what really motivated Mr. Méndez to fight the segregation was the fact that he did not want his children to grow up with hate in their hearts for the children who went to the beautiful school. 'I will fight this,' he thought, 'But how?' At the farm, produce truck driver Henry Rivera told Gonzalo, 'I know of a lawyer who might help.' The families of Méndez, Estrada, Guzman, Palomino, and Ramirez held that the school districts of Westminster, Santa Ana, Garden Grove and El Modena were unlawfully discriminating against their children."

4. *Reflection and Action.* Pedro Pedraza's account of the beginning of ethnic studies in New York revealed that through a dialogic process, people of color engaged in the historic practice of struggle and resistance: "To work on these problem areas five task forces were organized: Puerto Rican studies itself—later to become higher education; history of the Puerto Rican migration; the criminal justice system and prisons; culture in popular expression, visual and performing arts, and literature; and language policy."

5. *Hope.* Sonia Nieto's narrative reveals the enduring self-affirmation of culture, identity, and dignity as foundational aspects of the experiences and resistance of people of color. "It was hard to believe that I was one of the 'BC 44,' an identity foreign to my upbringing and inclination. Yet, my early experiences as the child of working-class Puerto Rican [im]migrants, my training as a teacher, and my work with poor working-class, African-American, and immigrant children during years of great social unrest—all of these experiences serve as the backdrop to how I became one of the BC 44. And as unlikely as it might have seemed at first, they also help explain my social activism in the years to come. . . . For my part, this experience brought me a greater political clarity and a renewed commitment to social justice in my chosen field, education, a commitment that I have maintained to this day."

The long-lasting commitment that these individuals have had over the years to engage in change for social and educational justice for Latinos in the United States is evident in these stories. We found that teachers, researchers, and authors who have been inspired by past civil rights participants have also committed their lives and work to improve the conditions of education for Latino students. For some, like Gigi Brignoni and Luis Fuentes, it meant change from within by recapturing their heritage language and culture. For others, like Sonia Nieto, Herman Sillas, María Quezada, and Magaly Lavadenz, it meant confronting the sociopolitical and economic structures in schools, institutions of higher education, communities, and government.

Significance of the Findings

Using Freire's theory as a framework elucidates the dialogical process that oppressed U.S. Latinos have undergone historically in the search for freedom and equity. They engaged in the formation of their own history, reaching a level of critical consciousness that allowed them to have the courage to reflect and act, thereby engaging in praxis. While Freire cautions mere activism as a futile act, the findings from the analysis of these historically motivated narratives of Latinos in search of civil and educational rights were surprisingly well aligned to Freire's theory of emancipation. This evidently resulted from the dialogical process that preceded the reflection and action. The significance of this study comes in the recognition that oppressed humans can merely act in rebellion, or they can undergo a critical process to transform oppressive conditions into those that are more humane and based on hope and love. Without minimizing the importance of activism in some historical events, the narratives suggest that engaging in praxis is a fluid, dynamic, and dialogical process that continues as we reinvent ourselves to respond to new and changing sociohistorical conditions that may arise.

References

Abramson, M. (1971). *Palante: Young Lords Party.* New York: McGraw-Hill.
Artiles, A., Harry, B., Reschy, D. J., & Chinn, P. C. (2002). Overrepresentation of color in special education. *Multicultural Perspectives, 4,* 3–10.
Banks, C.A.M., & Banks, J.A. (1995). Equity pedagogy: An essential component of multicultural education. *Theory into practice, 34*(3), 152–158.
Chapman, C., Laird, J., & Kewal Ramani, A. (2010). *Trends in high school dropout and completion rates in the United States: 1972–2008* (NCES 2011–012). National Center for Education Statistics, Institute of Education Sciences, U.S. Department of Education. Washington, DC. Retrieved March 24, 2015 from http://nces.ed.gov/pubsearch.
Delpit, L. (1995). *Other people's children.* New York: The New Press.
Delpit, L. & Dowdy, J. K. (Eds.) (2010). *The skin we speak: Thoughts on language and culture in the classroom.* New York: New Press.
Fairclough, N. (1995). *Critical discourse analysis.* London: Longman.
Freire, P. (1970). *Pedagogy of the oppressed.* New York: Herder and Herder.
Freire, P. (1973). *Education for critical consciousness.* 1st American ed. A Continuum book. New York: Seabury Press.
Freire, P. (1978). *Pedagogy in process: The letters to Guinea-Bissau.* A Continuum book. New York: Seabury Press.
Freire, P. (2004). *The pedagogy of indignation.* Boulder, CO: Paradigm Publishers.

Freire, P. (2005). *Pedagogy of the oppressed* (Edition 30). New York: Continuum International Publishing Group.

Gandara, P., & Rumberger, R. (2004). Seeking equity in the education of California's English Learners. *Teachers College Record, 106*(10), 2032–2056.

Gee, J. (1999). *An introduction to discourse analysis.* New York: Routledge.

Gee, J. P. (2004). Discourse analysis: What makes it critical? In: R. Rogers (Ed.), *An introduction to critical discourse analysis in education.* Mahweh, NJ: Lawrence Earlbaum.

Haberman, M. (1995). The dimensions of excellence in programs preparing teachers for urban poverty schools. *Peabody Journal of Education, 70*(2), 24–43. doi: 10.1080/01619569509538821

Howard, G. (2006). *We can't teach what we don't know: White teachers, multiracial schools* (2nd ed.). New York: Teachers College Press.

Huerta, T. M. (2011). Humanizing pedagogy: Beliefs and practices on the teaching of Latino children. *Bilingual Research Journal, 34*(1), 38–57.

Ladson-Billings, G. (1995). But that's just good teaching! The case for Culturally Relevant Pedagogy. *Theory into Practice, 34*(3), 159–165.

Nieto, S. (2004). Black, White, and us: The meaning of Brown v. Board of Education for Latinos. *Multicultural Perspectives, 6*(4), 22–25.

Olsen, L. (2010). *Reparable harm: Fulfilling the unkept promise of educational opportunity for California's longterm English learners.* Long Beach, CA: Californians Together Research & Policy Publication.

Solórzano, D., & Yosso, T. (2000). Toward a critical race theory of Chicana and Chicano education. In: C. Tejeda, C. Martinez, Z. Leonardo & P. McLaren (Eds.), *Charting new terrains of Chicana(o)/Latina(o) education.* Cresskill, NJ: Hampton Press, 35–65.

Solórzano, D., & Yosso, T. (2001). Critical race and LatCrit theory and method: counter-storytelling: Chicana and Chicano graduate school experiences. *International Journal of Qualitative Studies in Education, 14*(4), 471–495.

Solórzano, D., & Yosso, T. (2002a). A critical race counterstory of race, racism and affirmative action. *Equity and Excellence in Education, 35*(2), 155–168.

Solórzano, D., & Yosso, T. (2002b). Maintaining social justice hopes within academic realities: a Freirean approach to critical race/LatCrit pedagogy, *Denver Law Review, 78*(4), 595–621.

Valenzuela, A. (1999). *Subtractive schooling: U.S.–Mexican youth and the politics of caring.* Albany: State University of New York Press.

van Dijk, T. (2003). Introduction to critical discourse analysis. In: D. Schiffrin, D. Tannen & H. Hamilton (Eds.), *The handbook of discourse analysis.* Malden: Blackwell Publishers, 352–371.

Vygotsky, L. (1978). Interaction between learning and development. In *Mind and Society* (pp. 7–91). Cambridge, MA: Harvard University Press.

Widdowson, H. (1998). The theory and practice of critical discourse analysis. *Applied Linguistics, 19*, 136–151.

2

RECOGNIZING INEQUALITY AND THE PURSUIT OF EQUITY

A Legal and Social Equity Framework

Alberto M. Ochoa

Introduction

Arriving in the United States in 1954 as a child, my immigrant Mexican parents quickly settled in northeast Los Angeles, on the outskirts of East Los Angeles. My parents strongly inculcated to their seven children the value that we are all equal and had the right to receive equal access to education. In 1955 my parents moved near Ave. 43 close to Highland Park, a community that at that time was predominantly Euro-American, so the Ochoa family integrated a segregated community. Placed in an elementary school that had no interventions for recently arrived immigrant children from other parts of the world, as a third grader, I was given speech pathology for 15 minutes a week. Knowing how to read and write in Spanish enabled me to survive the lack of comprehensible instruction and the well-meaning teachers who constantly kept reminding me to speak English and not to associate with perceived gang members. I entered one of the most integrated middle schools (Nightingale Junior High) in the early 1960s with African-Americans, Asians (multiple heritages), Latinos (first, second, and third generation), and Euro-Americans, placed at one school site and expected to get along. No cross-cultural education was provided, so lunchtime was a living theater of survival and one of my best-lived cross-cultural experiences in my entire education. Upon completing junior high, I enrolled in Lincoln High School, the first school to have the 1968 student walkouts in the Los Angeles Unified School District. In the late 1960s and early 1970s, Mexican-Americans/Chicanos across the state of Texas also made their voices heard in a civil rights movement that would change the state forever. The walkouts were driven by Latino students' concern for the quality of their education, the high death toll of Latinos in the Vietnam War, and the growing voice of the Chicano Movement. I survived high school and received good grades with an emphasis in mathematics, but was never encouraged to apply to college. However, I did so because my older brother, Jose, had enrolled in college and the Vietnam War was in my face. I applied and was accepted while always looking for part-time jobs to pay tuition, books, and transportation. By my late teens I was clearly aware of discriminatory practices, lack of academic rigor in my schooling, and the lack of K–12 schooling opportunity to maintain my home language with a high level of academic proficiency. In the late 1960s, I continued to encounter racism, often harassed by police for being in the wrong communities late at night, and became an active participant of the Chicano Movement. My drive to continue to further develop my skills and find ways to contribute to social policy, civil rights-oriented educational projects, and social initiatives led me to graduate from the university, obtain teaching credentials, receive an MA in special education, and complete my doctoral degree in education with an emphasis on community development and non-formal education. My persistent passion for educational access in the last 35 years has led me to direct national, state, and local projects and research grants that have focused on equity of opportunity, language policy, community development, and development of biliteracy teachers—guided by respect of voice, representation, dignity, and opportunity to reclaim historical, cultural, and academic presence. This will persist until my last breath on earth.

In this chapter, given my journey for educational social justice for more than 40 years, I will examine prominent civil right cases, educational legal cases, and legislation that I have experienced through my journey in education from 1954 to the present and from a Latino perspective. The legal cases and legislation will touch on the struggle for social integration, equal access, biliteracy/multilingualism, and academic rigor. I will conclude with the significant challenges for voice, equal access, and the right of youth to academic rigor for accessing careers in the 21st century. I examine four sociopolitical periods to contextualize the journey of Latino education since 1848 to the present. Emphasis will be given to the period of 1954 to the present as the journey of my direct engagement in the communities of southern California and that many of the contributors to this book have taken.

Sociopolitical Educational Framework

Four sociopolitical periods are presented, each having significant impact on the lives of Latinos and ethnically diverse communities in the Southwest and the United States. The periods cover the following years:

- 1848 to 1910   Period I   Pre and Post Civil War and Reconstruction
- 1910 to 1954   Period II   Separate but Equal and Segregation
- 1954 to 1980   Period III   The Civil Rights Movement and Equal Access
- 1980 to Present   Period IV   The Movement to Undo Civil Rights Gains

Period of Pre and Post Civil War and Reconstruction

The *first period (1848–1910)* of the sociopolitical framework is marked by the shift of ownership of the present day region of the U.S. Southwest from being a Mexican territory to becoming part of the United States, and the development of the separate but equal doctrine. Table 2.1 provides salient events, cases, and legislation for this period.

Driven by the belief of Manifest Destiny of the God-given right to expand the country's borders from sea to sea and the earlier Texas War of Independence from Mexico (1836), the tensions between the two largest independent nations on the North American continent grew as Texas eventually became a U.S. state. These tensions led to the Mexican-American War of 1846–1848 between Mexico and the United States, with the outcome forcing the Mexican Cession of 1848 of its northern territories. Through the Treaty of Guadalupe Hidalgo the United States annexed the northern portions of Mexico and in return, the United States agreed to pay $15 million to Mexico as compensation for the seized territory. This outcome led to the United States gaining about 15% of its present boundaries. In the new land demarcations, Mexican citizens and landowners lost their rights and were treated as foreigners, marking the beginning of the struggle for land rights, equal access, voice, and political representation. This period also marked the beginning of the Chicano movement and the struggle for self-determination (strangers in their own land); anti-Mexican violence and intimidation resulted in Mexicans being displaced from their lands, denied access to natural resources, and becoming politically disenfranchised.

TABLE 2.1 Salient Cases and Legislation 1848 to 1910

Social & Political Period	Historical Events	Equity Emphasis	U.S. Legal Cases and Educational Policy
1848–1910	• Manifest Destiny • U.S. Civil War • Slavery • Reconstruction • Mexican-American War • Displacement of Southwest	• Civil Rights • de Jure Segregation • Property Rights • Citizenship • "Separate but Equal Doctrine"	• Guadalupe Hidalgo Treaty (1848) • U.S. Constitution 14th Amendment (July 9, 1868) • Invalidation of most Civil Rights Laws of 1875 & 1883 • *Ward v. Flood* 48 Cal. 36 (1874) • *Plessy v. Ferguson*, 163 U.S. 537 (1896)

A divided nation on the issue of slavery led to a Civil War (1861–1865) between the states, with the North opposed to slavery and the South in support of slavery. The South required slaves to work in the farms. The closure of the Civil War led to the approval and addition of the 14th Constitutional Amendment (1868) granting equal protection to all:

> All persons born or naturalized in the United States, and subject to the jurisdiction thereof, are citizens of the United States and of the State wherein they reside. No State shall make or enforce any law which shall abridge the privileges or immunities of citizens of the United States; nor shall any State deprive any person of life, liberty, or property, without due process of law; nor deny to any person within its jurisdiction the equal protection of the laws.
>
> *(U.S. Constitution, 14th Amendment, Section 1)*

In the Southwest, resistance to the equal protection clause of the 14th Amendment of the Constitution in 1869–1870 led the California legislature to pass segregation laws calling for the establishment of separate public schools for African-American and Native American children (Sections 1669, 1670, 1671 of the California Political Code). In 1874, in *Ward v. Flood* 48 Cal. 36, the California Supreme Court ordered that colored children may be excluded from schools established for white children provided that a separate school of equal facilities had been established for colored children. If a separate-but-equal school has not been established, then colored children must be admitted to schools established for white children. By 1890 in *Wysinger v. Crookshank* 82 Cal. 588, the California Supreme Court ruled that public school districts in California may not establish separate schools for children of African descent or exclude them from public schools established for white children. However, in other parts of the nation, Louisiana passed a Jim Crow law mandating separate-but-equal accommodations on railroads for blacks and whites (leading ultimately to the Supreme Court decision in *Plessy v. Ferguson*, 163 U.S. 537 [1896]). In this case the Supreme Court upheld the separate-but-equal law of Louisiana. On June 7, 1892, Homer Plessy was arrested for refusing to sit in the "colored" railcar aboard a passenger train of the East Louisiana Railway. The Supreme Court decided that Louisiana's separate-but-equal law did not violate Plessy's rights according to the 14th Amendment. This decision led to the "Separate but Equal Doctrine" in our nation. Mexico during this period developed as a nation where power would be concentrated in the hands of a select few, while the masses would have no power to express their opinions or elect their public officials. These injustices led to the Mexican Revolution of 1910 that forced many to migrate to the United States. By the end of the century segregation was the law of the land under a democratic government. The debate and legal challenges of what constitutes equal access began.

Period of Separate but Equal and Segregation

The *second period (1910–1954)* of the sociopolitical framework is marked by the actualization of social and educational segregation (separate but equal), the struggle for due process, and the right to equal access. Table 2.2 outlines salient events, legal cases, and legislation for this period.

In the case of the Mexican Revolution, the danger of the revolution, the economic catastrophe, and social chaos surrounding the revolution pushed almost a million Mexican citizens to head north between 1910 and 1920, immigrating to the United States. With the further development of the railroad system in the Southwest, thousands of Mexicans were hired for construction and maintenance of the nation's railroad network. For the most part, male Mexican immigrants began to establish *colonias* (communities) in the early 20th century in places such as Chicago and Kansas City as railroad employment took them further within the United States. During World War I, Latino immigrants also moved in large numbers to Denver, the San Francisco Bay area, and in smaller numbers to Detroit, Minneapolis, and Pennsylvania to work in the steel and automobile manufacturing industry. Others, because of the demand for cheap labor, migrated to South Texas and Oklahoma to work in cotton fields and others followed the summer harvests of fruit and vegetables in the fields of California, Oregon, and Washington.

As colonias were formed (1915–1935), families experienced the effects of the "separate-but-equal doctrine" and direct racism. Five court cases illustrate the challenges facing Mexican immigrant communities as they were targeted groups of segregation by school officials. In the 1930s, in the community of Lemon

TABLE 2.2 Salient Cases and Legislation 1910 to 1954

Social & Political Period	Historical Events	Equity Emphasis	U.S. Legal Cases and Educational Policy
1910–1954	• World War I • Mexican Revolution • Colonized labor force • World War II • Zoot Suit Riot • Korean War • Bracero Program	• Regressive Civil Rights • Due process • Segregation of public schools, public places, and public transportation • Second class citizenship • Access to G.I. Bill of Rights	• *Independent School District v. Salvatierra* (1930, 1931) • *Alvarez v. Lemon Grove School District*, Petition for Writ of Mandate No. 66625, February 13, 1931 • *Lopez v. Seccombe*, 71 F. Supp. 769 (S.D. Cal 1944) • *Mendez v. Westminster School District* (1946, 1947) • *Delgado et al. v. Bastrop Independent School District of Bastrop County et al.* (1948)

Grove in California, in the case of *Roberto Alvarez v. the Board of Trustees of the Lemon Grove School District* (1931), Mexican families challenged the segregation of their children. The case was won by Alvarez, making it the first successful school desegregation court decision in the history of the United States. In *Alvarez*, the court established the rights of their children to equal education, despite local, regional, and national sentiment that favored not only segregation, but also actual deportation. In a similar case, *Independent School District v. Salvatierra* (1930), in Del Rio, Texas, parents sued the town's school board on the grounds that Mexican-American students were being deprived of the resources given white students. While the district judge issued a ruling in favor of the plaintiffs, the state's higher courts later overturned it (Orozco, 2010).

These two legal cases marked the Mexican community's rights and voice towards equality in education for all children in the United States. With Latinos returning to their communities after World War II (1939–1945) and the Korean War (1950–1953), having fought for the right to equal opportunity and democratic representation, Latinos continued to question contradictory social and educational segregated practices. In three additional court cases one finds a consistent and forceful voice of Latinos to seek representation and equal access to educational facilities and services. In the case of *Lopez v. Seccombe* (1944) the court ruled that the ban of "Citizens of Mexican and Latin descent" from public schools and park facilities by the City of San Bernardino was a violation of the 14th Amendment. In the case of *Méndez v. Westminister* (1947), a case that gave impetus to *Brown v. Board of Education* (1954) challenging segregation, the Ninth Circuit Court of Appeals ruled that,

> By enforcing the segregation of school children of Mexican descent against their will and contrary to the laws of California, respondents have violated the federal law as provided in the Fourteenth Amendment to the Federal Constitution by depriving them of liberty and property without due process of law and by denying to them the equal protection of the laws.
>
> (p. 4)

The Court noted that California law did not include the segregation of school children because of their Mexican blood. On June 14, 1947, under California Governor Earl Warren, California's school segregation laws were repealed. Furthermore, with regard to interracial marriages, in the case of *Perez v. Lippold* (1948) in California it was ruled that the laws against interracial marriage violated the Equal Protection Clause of the 14th Amendment. Lastly, under this period the court case of *Delgado et al. v. Bastrop Independent School District of Bastrop County et al.* (1948) also challenged the segregation practices of the state of Texas with a favorable decision rendered on behalf of Mexican and Latino children. By the end of this second sociopolitical period, communities of color openly challenged the contradictions of social policy—in a democratic system of government.

Period of the Civil Rights Movement and Equal Access

The *third period (1954–1980)* of the sociopolitical framework marked a new moral and legal national awakening for equality, equal opportunity, equal access, due process, and equal benefits. The 1950s marked the catalyst of a national civil rights movement. Table 2.3 outlines salient events, court cases, and legislation for this period.

By 1954, the "separate-but-equal doctrine" established under *Plessy* was challenged in the nation's Supreme Court. In the case of *Hernandez v. Texas* (1954), the U.S. Supreme Court case also declared that Mexican-Americans and all other racial groups in the United States had the right to equal protection under the 14th Amendment of the U.S. Constitution. In the case of *Brown v. Board of Education of Topeka, Kansas* (1954), the Supreme Court overruled the decision in *Plessy v. Ferguson* of 1896 that permitted "separate-but-equal" education for children of color in general. Thus, in *Brown v. Board of Education*, the Court ruled that "in the field of public education, the doctrine of: 'separate but equal' has no place. Separate educational facilities are inherently unequal." This decision established a new morality for the nation and the principle of equal educational opportunity for all students. With the launch of *Sputnik* into the earth's orbit, scientific activity provoked federal policies to support foreign languages, mathematics, and science, as well as the creation of the National Defense Education Act in 1958. While foreign language instruction was encouraged for English monolinguals, no educational program was supporting children from limited-English-language proficient (LEP) backgrounds. As a result of the civil rights movement, Congress in 1964 passed Title VI of the 1964 Civil Rights Act (CRA of 1964) that led to the creation of the Office for Civil Rights, and changes in immigration laws that terminated the 1924 national origin quota system. Hope was in sight with the new impetus towards the right to equal educational access for all students. The CRA of 1964 declared:

> No person in the United States shall, on the grounds of race, color, or national origin, be excluded from participation in, be denied the benefits of, or be subjected to discrimination under any program or activity receiving Federal financial assistance.
>
> *(Title VI of the Civil Rights Act of 1964, 78 Stat. 252, 42 U.S.C. 2000d et seq.)*

With the Immigration and Nationality Act of 1965 that abolished the national origin formula that had been in place in the United States since the Immigration Act of 1924, an increase of Asians and Latin Americans entered the country. The need for some type of comprehensible instruction (bilingual programs) became paramount for many school districts. In Florida, due to the Cuban Revolution of 1959, many middle- and upper-income exiled Cubans arrived in Florida and

TABLE 2.3 Salient Cases and Legislation 1954 to 1980

Political Period	Historical Events	Equity	U.S. Legal Cases & Legislation
1954–1980	• Civil Rights Movement • Cold War • Cuban Revolution • United Farm Workers • Student Walkouts • Vietnam War • Southwest Voter Registration	• Civil Rights • Due process • Equal opportunity • Equal access • Equal benefits • Recognition of diversity: race, gender, national origin, disability	• *Brown v. Board of Education of Topeka, Kansas,* 347 U.G.S. 483 (1954) • *Hernandez v. Texas,* 347 U.S. 475 (1954) • Civil Rights Act (Pub.L. 88–352, 78 Stat. 241, 1964) • Elementary and Secondary Education Act (ESEA) (Pub.L. 89–10, 79 Stat. 27, 20 U.S.C. ch.70) 1965 • U.S. Department of Health, Education, and Welfare (HEW), May 25, 1970 Memorandum, 35 Fed. Reg. 11595 • *Diana v. State Board of Education,* C. A. N. C-70–37 R. F. P. (N.D. Cal., Filed February 3, 1970) • *Swann v. Charlotte-Mecklenburg Board of Education,* 402 U.S. 1 (1971) • *United States v. State of Texas et al.,* 5 Cir., 447 F.2d 441(1971) • Section 504 of the Rehabilitation Act of 1973 • *Aspira v. Board of Education of New York City,* U.S. Court of Appeals, New York, Consent Decree, 72 Cir. 400, (1974) • Title IX of the Education Amendments, United States Code Section 20, (1972) • Equal Educational Opportunity Act (1974) • *Lau v. Nichols* (1974) • *Pasadena City Bd. of Educ. v. Spangler,* 427 U.S. 424 (1976) • *Cintrón v. Brentwood* 1977, 1978 (U.S. District Court, Eastern District of New York • *Rios v. Read,* 73 F.R.D. 589, 598 (E.D.N.Y. 1977)

wanted their children to retain their language and culture. In 1963, a two-way bilingual education program was started at Coral Way Elementary School in Dade County, Florida. As an outcome of the Bilingual Education Act and the Civil Rights Act of 1964, many elementary and some secondary bilingual and English as a Second Language (ESL) programs were implemented throughout the United States. These programs had the focus to address the academic, linguistic, and sociocultural needs of students from culturally and linguistically diverse backgrounds. Of importance was also the *Department of HEW, May 25, 1970 Memorandum*, 35 Fed. Reg. 11595 that outlined school districts' responsibility to provide equal educational opportunity to national origin minority group children deficient in English language skills:

> Where inability to speak and understand the English language excludes national origin minority group children from effective participation in the educational program offered by a school district, the district must take affirmative steps to rectify the language deficiency in order to open its instructional program to these students.
>
> *(p. 1)*

In addition, the federal legislation under *Equal Educational Opportunity Act of 1974, 20 U.S.C. 1703 (f)* (EEOA 1974) called for states to prevent the denial of equal educational opportunity. Among them was the failure by an educational agency to take appropriate action to overcome language barriers that impeded equal participation by students in an instructional program. The EEOA 1974 ascertained:

> No state shall deny equal educational opportunity to an individual on account of his or her race, color, sex, or national origin, by . . . (f) the failure by an educational agency to overcome language barriers that impede equal participation by its students in its instructional programs.
>
> *(Equal Educational Opportunity Act, 20 U.S.C. Sec. 1703)*

All of the aforementioned court cases and civil rights legislation led ethnically and linguistically diverse communities to advocate for services and educational programs that provided comprehensible, meaningful, and effective pedagogy and learning. Of importance was the Supreme Court ruling under *Lau v. Nichols* (1974). The *Lau* decision was the result of a class action suit representing 1,800 Chinese students who alleged discrimination on the grounds that they could not achieve academically, because they did not understand the instruction of their English-speaking teachers. The U.S. Supreme Court concluded that equal treatment of English-speaking and non-English-speaking students did not constitute equal educational opportunity and, therefore, violated non-English-speaking students' civil rights. Thus, the *Lau* decision gave impetus to the movement for equal educational opportunity for language minority students who do not speak English and raised the nation's consciousness for the need for bilingual education, encouraging federal legislation. The unanimous Supreme Court decision emphasized that the court in *Lau* was not concerned with the intentions or motivations of the school district. Regardless of how much good faith a school district might be exercising in trying to meet the problem, the only relevant factor is whether the child received a "meaningful" and "comprehensible" education and "effective participation in the educational program." Thus, under the *Lau v. Nichols* decision, the highest court of our nation affirmed the authority of the government to require affirmative remedial efforts to give special attention to linguistically diverse immigrant students. From 1975 to the early 1980s, school districts were required to develop educational master plans to comply with the *Lau* decision. In 1975, the Department of Education (HEW) provided guidelines known as the *Lau Remedies*. The Lau Remedies required approved approaches, methods, and procedures for identifying and evaluating national origin minority students' English language skills, determining appropriate instructional treatments, deciding when these children were ready for mainstream classrooms, and determining the professional standards to be met by teachers of language-minority children.

Given the 1954 Brown Supreme Court decision, by the late 1960s and early 1970s school desegregation became a main concern. A challenge to the societal resistance of integrating the nation's schools was the case of *Swann v. Charlotte-Mecklenburg Board of Education* (1971), where the U.S. Supreme Court upheld busing students to achieve integration and provided all students the right to receive equal educational opportunities regardless of their race. One other case impacting Latinos was the *United States of America v. State of Texas et al.* (1971) in which the court ordered the consolidation of two districts to provide equal educational opportunity and eliminate discrimination on the grounds of race, color, or national origin in Texas public and charter schools. Yet by the end of 1976, the force to take deliberate speed to integrate schools took on a more flexible approach, namely in *Pasadena City Bd. Of Education v. Spangler* (1976). In this case, the court ruled that once a school system complies with the demands of equal protection, it does not need to annually readjust school attendance to ensure a proportional racial balance at each school—disregarding ethnically and culturally diverse student growth and the demographics of schools.

Furthermore, during the period of 1974 to 1982, a number of court cases addressed the educational language rights of language minority students with respect to assessment, appropriate and well-implemented programs, staffing, and evaluation of program quality:

- In the 1974 case of *Aspira v. Board of Education of New York City*, the Federal Court ruled against the New York Board of Education, which was sued by Puerto Rican parents and students who believed that schools were not fulfilling their duty to educate non-native English speakers. The court ruling

resulted in a consent decree where the New York City Board of Education drafted an agreement to create and properly assess non-English-speaking students, provide appropriate instruction, and when necessary, provide materials in the student's native language to educate and support the students.
- In the 1974 case *of Serna v. Portales Municipal Schools, U.S. Court of Appeals, Tenth Circuit,* the court ascertained that Spanish surnamed individuals did not reach the same achievement levels as non-Spanish-surnamed peers. The court ordered Portales Municipal Schools in Albuquerque, New Mexico, to implement a bilingual/bicultural curriculum, revise procedures for assessing achievement, and hire bilingual school personnel. This was the first court to specify bilingual education as a remedy for the *Lau* decision. The court stated that a student who does not understand English and is not provided with bilingual education is therefore precluded from any meaningful education.
- In *Otero v. Mesa County Valley School District* (1975), Mexican-American parents and school-age children residing in a Colorado rural town charged that the school district's educational program and hiring practices discriminated against Chicanos/Latinos. The community requested that the court institute comprehensive bilingual/bicultural curriculum, programs, and require affirmative action in the hiring of teachers. In *Otero*, the court entered judgment for the school district on all counts. In spite of the court's decision, the Colorado legislature passed legislation supporting bilingual-bicultural education. A significant aspect to this lawsuit was the realization by Euro-American educators that they had to take into account the academic aspirations of Latino/Hispanic students.
- In addition, with regard to program instructional quality, in the 1977 case of *Rios v. Read*, the federal district court for the Eastern District of New York ruled that quality of instruction is of importance by asserting that:

    > It is not enough simply to provide a program for language disadvantaged children or even to staff the program with bilingual teachers; rather, the critical question is whether the program is designed to assure as much as is reasonably possible the language deficient child's growth in the English language. An inadequate program is as harmful to a child who does not speak English as no program at all.
    >
    > *(75 C. 296 at 15)*

- With regard to quality of teaching personnel, in the 1978 case of *Cintrón, Elis et al. v. Brentwood Union Free School District et al.*, the Federal District Court set the standard for the courts in examining programs for non-English-speaking students. Cintron required that school districts needed to demonstrate the implementation of a pedagogically sound plan for language minority students, sufficient qualified staff to implement the plan, and a system established to evaluate the program. Yet, by 1978, states and school districts began to argue for flexibility in designing programs for compliance under the spirit of the *Lau* decision.

- In contrast to *Cintrón* and *Ríos*, in 1977 and 1978, the Ninth Circuit federal court in *Guadalupe Organization, Inc. v. Tempe Elementary School District* ruled against the adequacy of a bilingual program that was already being implemented and allowed a remedial English language program to meet the requirement of an "appropriate action" to overcome language barriers.

This period is also recognized for its significant contributions in *gender and discrimination based on disabilities*, challenging attitudinal and behavioral biases while seeking social awareness, and the right of students with disabilities to equal opportunity. In terms of gender equity, this period is also recognized for its Title IX of the Education Amendments of 1972, with the law declaring that:

> No person in the United States shall, on the basis of sex, be excluded from participation in, be denied the benefits of, or be subjected to discrimination under any education program or activity receiving Federal financial assistance . . .
>
> *(United States Code Section 20)*

Beyond confronting gender attitudes and behaviors, Title IX specifically challenged the segregation of services received between girls and boys and instituted the right to receive equal educational opportunities. Among the consequences of Title IX has been the increased participation rates in access to educational and athletics programs, funding, opportunities, equitable facilities, scholarships, and employment.

In the arena of *discrimination based on disabilities*, legislation affirmed a disabled person's right to equal protection and equal educational opportunity under the 14th Amendment of the U.S. Constitution, and in a way that it did not violate either procedural due process or equal protection, leading the educational civil rights for students with disabilities. The rights of students with disabilities was established with the passage of the federal law under the Rehabilitation Act of 1973, with Section 504 protecting the rights of individuals with disabilities in programs and activities that receive Federal financial assistance from the U.S. Department of Education. Section 504 states:

> No otherwise qualified individual with a disability in the United States . . . shall, solely by reason of her or his disability, be excluded from the participation in, be denied the benefits of, or be subjected to discrimination under any program or activity receiving Federal financial assistance . . .
>
> *(Section 504, Regulation at 45 CFR Part 84)*

Also in the 1970s, the courts in time turned to assessment procedures and processes for delivering educational services to culturally and linguistically diverse students. Four court cases (*Diana, Guadalupe, Covarrubias, Jose P.*) involving Latino students examined the issue of overrepresentation and indicted the assessment methods used for determining who was and who was not mentally disabled (Figueroa, 1999). In *Diana v. California Board of Education* (1970), the court mandated non-bias assessment procedures to be used with Chinese-American and Mexican-American students. *Diana* influenced the enactment of federal special education laws in three areas: (a) if a student's primary language was not English, the student had to be tested in both English and his or her primary language; (b) culturally unfair items had to be eliminated from all tests used in the assessment process; (c) if intelligence tests were to be used in the assessment process, they had to be developed to reflect Mexican-American culture.

In the case of *Guadalupe v. Tempe Elementary School District* (1971), the court ruled that other assessment procedures must be used in addition to intelligence tests in considering placement in educable mentally retarded classes and that parental permission must be obtained for such placements. In *Covarrubias v. San Diego Unified School District* (1971), the court ruled that monetary damages could be paid due to misclassifying Mexican-Americans as disabled; in *Jose Peter v. Ambach* (1982), the court ruled that school districts must follow timelines for evaluation and placement of students in special education programs and placement teams should include school personnel who are bilingual and bicultural. The outcome of these court cases led to the identification and assessment guideline that when cultural and linguistic factors apply in testing, it is necessary to do more testing (Figueroa, 1999).

In this third sociopolitical period (1954–1980), collectively both state and federal court cases and civil rights legislation established the right to equal access, equal benefits, procedural due process, equal protection, and in particular the focus in the delivery of pedagogical services to culturally and linguistically diverse students. Yet, the force of law and policy is but one necessary but insufficient condition in the process of attaining equity, with human social consciousness the other necessary condition to provide equal educational benefits to all students.

Period on the Movement to Undo Civil Rights Gains

The fourth period (1980–present) marks a period of educational turbulence and the push to undo the gains of the civil rights period of 1954 to 1980. The policies taken by President Reagan (1981–1989), by President George H. Bush (1989–1993), and by the ruling of the federal courts (1980–present) are identified as neoconservative policies that have worked to undo the civil rights gains from 1954 to 1980. Table 2.4 outlines the salient events, cases, and legislation of this period.

The first policy was *decentralization*—shifting federal responsibility to the 50 states or creating 50 different social and educational policies. The second policy was *deregulation*; rather than having national guidelines to shape social and educational policy, the new direction was to support flexibility in giving each of the 50 states in our nation different ways to meet minimum policy compliance.

The third policy was *decategorization* of federal programs that greatly reduced community input through advisory committees in federal programs addressing social and educational problems (Feldstein, 1994; Spring 2002). The chart for the fourth period identifies salient examples of court cases and/or legislation that have greatly impacted on the quality of living conditions of Latino and low-income communities. Each of the selected cases or legislation is briefly discussed:

TABLE 2.4 Salient Cases and Legislation 1980 to Present

Political Period	*Historical Events*	*Equity*	*U.S. Legal Cases & Legislation*
1980–Present	• Global economy & finances • NAFTA 1994 • Nuclear proliferation • Climate change • Iran • Afghanistan • September 11, 2001 • Anti-immigrant sentiment	• Decentralization policies • Decategorization of programs • Deregulation policies • Equal access • Equal benefits	• *University of California Regents v. Bakke,* 438 U.S. 265 (1978) • *Castañeda v. Pickard* 648 F.2d 989; 1981 (Fifth Circuit Court) • *Crawford et al. v. Board of Education of the City of Los Angeles* (No. 81–38., 458 U.S. 527, 1982) • *Plyler v. Doe,* 457 U.S. 202 (1982) • *Keyes v. School District #1* (1983) 413 U.S. 189 • California Proposition 63 (1986) • *Gómez v. Illinois State Board of Education* 1987, 614 F. Supp. 342 (E. D. Ill. 1987), affirmed 811 F.2d 1030 (7th Cir. 1987) • California Proposition 187 (1994) • California Proposition 209 (1996) • California Proposition 227 (1998) • No Child Left Behind (2002) • American with Disabilities Act (2004) • *Horne v. Flores* (2009) • Arizona S.B. 1070 (2010)

The push to *deregulate federal policy* is found among the early attacks centered on civil-rights-oriented services in education. In the case of *Northwest Arctic School District et al. v. Joseph A. Califano et al.* in 1978, a consent decree committed the U.S. Department of Education to publish for public comment official Title VI regulations in response to the *Lau* mandate of 1974. In August 1980, a proposed set of federal rules had two goals: to have non-English-speaking students learn English as quickly as possible and to receive instruction in required subjects in a language they could understand until they learned English. Under the Reagan administration the focus centered on three questions: (1) Who should control education—the federal government or the local government? (2) Should schools teach exclusively in English or allow the native language to be used? and (3) Who should pay for bilingual education programs—the federal government or local school districts? By 1981 the direction of federal policy to protect the rights of language minority students shifted; close to 500 *Lau* plans previously negotiated with the U.S. Office of Civil Rights were free to continue with those plans or to renegotiate new options with the Department of Education. Thus, this fourth period examines salient educational court cases and policies that have diminished the gains of civil rights legislation.

The impetus on deregulating federal policy in education, impacting the Latino and language minority communities of the nation, is found in the court case of *Castañeda v. Pickard* (1981). In *Castañeda*, Mexican-American children sued the Raymondville, Texas, school district, claiming that the district's failure to provide an adequate bilingual education program resulted in discrimination. The Fifth Circuit Court of Appeals in its ruling set a three-part test for determining whether a school district had taken appropriate actions to overcome the language barriers confronting language minority students. The court delineated a three-pronged test to establish the program's appropriateness, namely, a school district must demonstrate that (1) a program is based on an educational theory recognized as sound or, at least, as a legitimate experimental strategy; (2) the program is actually implemented with instructional practices, resources, and personnel necessary to transfer theory to reality, and (3) the program must not persist if it fails to produce results. Subsequent court cases, rather than a national policy, have consistently used the three-pronged test to determine compliance with the Equal Educational Opportunity Act of 1974. Since 1981, the "Castañeda test" has been used as the predominant criteria for meeting federal language guidelines in determining if equal educational access is provided to language minority students, such as *U.S. v. State of Texas* (1981), *Idaho Migrant Council v. Board of Education* (1981), *Keyes v. Denver School District* (1983), and *Gómez v. Illinois State Board of Education* (1987). Of importance, the *Keyes* (1983) court case centered on desegregation and as part of its remedy supported the use of bilingual education. In *Keyes*, the U.S. District Court found that a Denver public school district had failed to adequately implement a plan for language minority students—the second element of the "Castañeda test." At the same time, the movement to ensure the Americanization or assimilation of resident immigrants can be found in the passage of California's Proposition 63 (1986) requiring the state legislature and state officials to take all steps necessary to ensure that the role of English as the common language of the state is preserved and enhanced (MacKaye, 1990).

In the area of *social integration*, the court case of *Crawford et al. v. Board of Education of the City of Los Angeles* (1982) underlines the position towards school integration. This litigation began in 1963, when ethnically diverse students attending school in the Los Angeles Unified School District filed a class action in state court seeking desegregation of the district's schools. By 1976, the trial court had found de jure segregation and requested that reasonable steps be taken to alleviate segregation in the public schools through a plan for school desegregation. The plan was put into effect with mandatory student reassignment and busing, but by 1979 the trial court began considering alternatives. Nationwide, community sentiment against forced busing became the norm with volunteer ethnic integration becoming the approach to address the Brown 1954 decision to the present. According to the UCLA Civil Rights Project, the desegregation of U.S. public schools peaked in 1988; since then, schools have become more segregated because of changes in demographic residential patterns with continuing growth in suburbs and new communities (Badger, 2010).

Another educational tension *is the treatment of language minority students with disabilities* and their right to bilingual special education services. While the rights of language minority students with disabilities are protected by federal laws, under the Education for All Handicapped Children Act, Public Law 94–142 (1975) and the Individuals with Disabilities Education Act (2004), culturally and linguistically sensitive interventions have been lacking (Cummins, 2009). While these laws secure the rights of language minority students with disabilities to receive proper assessment, treatment, staffing, parent participation, due process, and evaluation of services—congruency between individual student rights and relevant and appropriate services for language minority students is significantly lacking.

In the arena of *actualizing the principle of equal access*, the period of 1980 to the present has explicit social tensions, specifically with regard to ethnically and linguistically diverse communities. One dominant tension is the treatment of immigrants and undocumented persons, especially children. In the court case of *Plyler v. Doe* (1982), the U.S. Supreme Court ruled that public schools were prohibited from denying immigrant students access to a public education. The Court affirmed that undocumented children have the same right to a free public education as U.S. citizens and permanent residents and are obligated, as are all other students, to attend school until they reach the age mandated by state law.

In reference to immigrant students receiving fair and adequate educational services, in the case of *Flores v. Arizona* (2000), the U.S. District Court cited the state for civil contempt for failing to adequately fund English language learner programs, in violation of the Equal Educational Opportunities Act, and rejected proposed legislation as inadequate to resolve the programs' deficiencies. With the passage of federal educational policy under No Child Left Behind in 2002, Arizona argued that the federal policy had sufficiently altered the foundations of the district court's original ruling and, therefore, relief was warranted. The federal district court of Arizona denied the motion. On appeal, the U.S. Court of Appeals for the Ninth Circuit, in the case of *Horne v. Flores* (2009), ruled in favor of Arizona, affirming that the state had fairly complied with the district court's original order.

In another case dealing with the *inadequacy of resources* to support the education of ethnically and linguistically diverse students, in *Williams v. State of California* (2004), San Francisco County students filed suit against the State of California and state education agencies, including the California Department of Education, on the basis that the agencies had failed to provide public school students with equal access to instructional materials, safe and decent school facilities, and qualified teachers. While the settlement has gained attention for improving California's schools for all students, it will take the continued action from all communities to make sure that the settlement's promise of educational equality actually takes place and is ongoing.

In the case of accessing quality education for ethnically and linguistically diverse low-income students, the nation's sociopolitical and economic climate had led to school districts debating the impact of a new English language learner program, the impact of No Child Left Behind, the impact of structural and managerial changes in its school system, and the impact of an increased state general education fund. These four issues have challenged the need for flexibility and what constitutes minimal compliance to meet the academic needs of ethnically and linguistically diverse students.

In terms of *immigrant students accessing higher education*, in the fall of 2010 the Dream Act was reintroduced. First proposed in 2001, the proposed legislation intended to give conditional green cards to undocumented immigrants if they graduated from high school and pursued a college education or military service. After a ten-year waiting period, they could obtain permanent residency if they met all the requirements, and they could eventually apply for citizenship. In December of 2010, the House of Representatives voted in favor of the Dream Act, while generating insufficient votes in the Senate to pass the bill that would offer a path to citizenship for hundreds of thousands of undocumented immigrant students who came to the country when they were children. By executive order, since 2012 President Obama enacted the DACA or the deferred action for childhood arrivals, which is being debated in the courts at the time of publication.

With regard to challenging undocumented students' access to college, in 2005, a national anti-immigrant group filed a lawsuit in California state court challenging the validity of AB 540. This AB 540 legislation provides a waiver of out-of-state tuition fees at California's public colleges and universities for students—regardless of immigration status—who have completed three years at a California high school and attained a high school diploma, or the equivalent. In support of undocumented students who are pursuing a college education, the California Supreme Court in the fall of 2010, under *Martinez v. Regents of the University of California*, ruled to uphold the California law known as AB 540.

In the area of *equal protection under the law*, in the case of undocumented persons seeking a better life, one frequently finds the U.S. Immigration and Customs Enforcement (ICE) driving close to local schools that have linguistically diverse students. The physical presence of ICE in low-income immigrant school communities has been documented since 1990 by the California Delegation Against Hate Violence based on human rights abuses by ICE agents and private citizens against migrants in the San Diego-Tijuana border area and in the Los Angeles county area (NNIRR, 2010). Marking the climate of the nation towards undocumented immigrants, in April of 2010, Arizona passed S.B. 1070, an anti-immigrant legislation requiring officials and agencies to comply and assist in the enforcement of federal immigration laws and establishing crimes involving transporting, harboring, or concealing undocumented persons. At least five states followed with the introduction of similar immigration legislation, including Pennsylvania, Minnesota, South Carolina, Rhode Island, and Mississippi.

Another campaign against immigrant communities is illustrated with the passage of *California Proposition 187 (Save Our State* [SOS] initiative) in 1994, that was designed to create a state-run citizenship screening system in order to prohibit undocumented immigrants from using health care, public education, and other social services in the United States. While the proposed law was initially passed by the voters through referendum on November 8, 1994, Judge Pfaelzer, U.S. District Court, ruled Proposition 187 to be unconstitutional.

In 2001, following the terrorist attacks of 9/11 (September 11th), Arab-Americans and others of Middle Eastern descent experienced a backlash in the United States, as hate crimes, discrimination, and bias increased. In 2004, the Minuteman Project began to organize anti-immigrant activists at the U.S./Mexico border, while immigrant rights supporters conducted counter-rallies in public opposition to the Minuteman Project's tactics and beliefs. In 2006, a significantly large number of Latino immigrants and their allies launched massive demonstrations nationwide in support of immigrant rights and to protest the growing resentment toward undocumented workers. Meantime, since 2006, the U.S. Congress continues to debate legislation that would criminalize undocumented immigrants with no action taken by Congress as of 2015.

As the *nation's ethnic and linguistic diversity increases*, one also finds other attacks on the right to equal representation and the principle of equal opportunity. Beginning with the dismantling of affirmative action in the case of *University of California Regents v. Bakke* (1978), the federal court ruled that a university may consider the race of an applicant in making admissions decisions, but may not use quotas. In the minority, Justice Marshall wrote a separate opinion supporting the use of quotas in affirmative action programs. In 1996, California Proposition 209 (named the California Civil Rights Initiative) was placed as a ballot initiative calling for the prohibition of public institutions from considering race, sex, or ethnicity as a basis for providing equitable representation in public employment, education, and public contracting. The proposition was approved in November 1996 with 54%

of the votes. In November of 2006, the state of Michigan passed a similar amendment, named the Michigan Civil Rights Initiative, as well as Nebraska (2008) and Colorado (2008). While Proposition 209 was challenged as unconstitutional, the Ninth Circuit affirmed the constitutionality of Proposition 209. The passage of Proposition 209 has had significant ramifications to the principle of equal access in a society that is seeking to take deliberate speed to undo past discriminatory practices.

In the area of *treatment of language minority students*, once again in California, Proposition 227 (English for the Children) was introduced by Ron Unz, a 1994 Republican gubernatorial primary candidate. The proposition was controversial because it was associated with the issues of language, race, immigration, poverty, and assimilation over multiculturalism. In 1998, the proposition passed with over 60% support. Although the research on its success is for the most part inconclusive, if not negative (Baker, 2006), the impact of Proposition 277 shifted the responsibility from school districts to offer some form of bilingual education, to the language minority parent to request bilingual education or an opt-in structured English language educational system, despite opposition from language education researchers (Baker, 2006).

In California, Proposition 227 did not end bilingual education, since one of the options for parents seeking a waiver was an alternative bilingual program. Arizona followed with Proposition 203 (English for the Children) in 2000 with a 63% approval of the voters and in content more restrictive than California Proposition 227, with its limits on "waivers" to the English-only rule to allow for bilingual program options. Massachusetts followed in 2002 with "Question 2 Initiative" with an estimated approval of 68%. However, in the same year Colorado (2002) voters gave Ron Unz and his anti-bilingual, English-immersion amendment (Amendment 31) its first defeat. More recently, as previously mentioned in the case of *Horne v. Flores* (2009), the U.S. Court of Appeals for the Ninth Circuit court ruling caused further diminished funding and program resources to address the educational needs of language minority students.

Lastly, on the *role of the federal government support to improve the education of Latinos and low-income students*, we can look to federal legislation for its present direction under No Child Left Behind (NCLB) signed by President George W. Bush in 2002. Historically, NCLB is another form of the Elementary and Secondary Education Act (ESEA) of 1965 that was legislated to focus on the inequality of school resources and improve the education of low-income students. The intent of NCLB was to reduce the achievement gap between low- and middle-income students, to "disaggregate" the average achievement scores of state accountability programs, and to expose student educational inequality over the past several decades.

Because test scores are the main determinant of accountability, NCLB has pushed the public school system to teach to the state norm tests (e.g., California Standards Test). Educational reform is presently based on improving only what tests measure and using the test scores as the deciding fate of students, teachers, principals, and schools. Furthermore, the Bilingual Education Act (1968) was replaced with Title III (under NCLB), focusing primarily on English and with bilingualism no longer the interest of the federal government. Under NCLB the achievement gap remains and the outcomes of NCLB can be summarized by the critique of Dianne Ravitch (2010) on NCLB, as she states:

> At the present time, public education is in peril. Efforts to reform public education are, ironically, diminishing its quality and endangering its very survival. We must turn our attention to improving schools, infusing them with the substance of genuine learning and reviving the conditions that make learning possible.
>
> *(p. 242)*

Conclusion

Now in the second decade of the 21st century, Latinos are the nation's largest culturally and ethnically diverse group and the number is expected to triple by the year 2050. Yet, the dream of *Brown v. Board of Education* (1954) for equal access, equal opportunity, and equal representation remains a dream to be realized.

In the face of egalitarian ideology, there is a call to reexamine our language, education, and social policies, given the persisting educational practices and economic and political inequalities among diverse ethnic and linguistic segments of society, especially with regard to its support for our youth in low-income communities (Kincheloe, 2008). We also need to question our nation's commitment to reexamine the values of social justice and democratic schooling, and their implications for the social, economic, political, and educational institutions of our society. This reexamination of values must encourage a renaissance of social justice in our country as we press forward to actualize equality, freedom, and democratic principles. In a world where over 80% of the peoples are non-Christian, speak a language other than English, and are non-Euro-American, our nation is fast becoming a nation made up of minorities, with 53 million Latinos according to the last census. Yet, despite our nation's democratic ideals we find that antidemocratic practices, such as racism, have been institutionalized via federal and state immigration laws (Hing, 2010).

As the focus of this chapter has documented, the Latino community has a long history of engagement in seeking fairness, inclusion, and equal access to the institutions of our society. Paulo Freire (1970) reminds us that sometimes we need to work with those in power and also we need to work through them. The ongoing educational and economic crisis impacting the Latino and low-income school communities will continue to be compounded by the national and global financial conditions that work against the collective good. We have the potential to strike back, to work with those who are serious about reforms that can benefit low-income communities; we can also hold accountable those who have worked against the actualization of the principle of equal access and equal benefits. Our search for answers and solutions to the problems facing the Latino community and our culturally and linguistically diverse society has profound implications within and across all societal sectors, both structurally and ideologically.

References

Alvarez v. Lemon Grove School District, Petition for Writ of Mandate No. 66625, February 13, 1931.
Arizona S.B. 1070, signed into law April 23, 2010.
Aspira v. Board of Education of New York City, U.S. Court of Appeals, New York, Consent Decree, 72 Cir. 400, (1974).
Baker, C. (2006). *Foundations of bilingual education & bilingualism* (4th ed.). Buffalo, NY: Multilingual Matters.
Badger, E. (December 7, 2010). Walking backward out the schoolhouse door: desegregation of public schools peaked about two decades ago, and no one at the federal level is doing much to reverse the decline. The Idea Lobby, *Miller-McCune Smart Journalism Real Solutions*.
Brown v. Board of Education of Topeka, Kansas, 347 U.G.S. 483 (1954).
California Proposition 187 (1994), submitted to the people in accordance with the provisions of Article II, Section 8 of the Constitution.
California Proposition 209 (1996), amended the California Constitution to include a new section (Section 31 of Article I).
California Proposition 227 (1998), adds sections to the Education Code; Section 1. Chapter 3 (commencing with Section 300) is added to Part 1 of the Education Code.
Castañeda v. Pickard 648 F.2nd 989 (1981).
Cintrón v. Brentwood 1977, 1978 (U.S. District Court, Eastern District of New York.
Civil Rights Act (Pub.L. 88–352, 78 Stat. 241, 1964).
Covarrubias v. San Diego Unified School District, Civ. No. 70–394-S, (S.D. Cal., Filed Feb. 1971).
Crawford et al. v. Board of Education of the City of Los Angeles (No. 81–38, 458 U.S. 527, 1982).
Cummins, J. (2009). Transformative multiliteracies pedagogy: School-based strategies for closing the achievement gap. *Multiple Voices for Ethnically Diverse Exceptional Learners, 11*(2), 38–56.
Delgado et al. v. Bastrop Independent School District of Bastrop County et al., No. 388 Civil District Court of the United States, Western District of Texas (1948).
Department of HEW, May 25, 1970 Memorandum (35 Fed. Reg. 11595).
Diana v. State Board of Education, C. A. N. C-70–37 R. F. P. (N.D. Cal., Filed February 3, 1970).
Education for All Handicapped Children Act, Public Law (94–142) was enacted by the United States Congress in 1975.
Elementary and Secondary Education Act (ESEA) (Pub.L. 89–10, 79 Stat. 27, 20 U.S.C. ch.70) 1965.
Equal Educational Opportunity Act (20 U.S.C. Sec. 1703 [f], 1974).
Feldstein, M., ed. (1994). American economic policy in the 1980's. *NBER* 1994, 371–72.

Figueroa, R. A. (1999). Special education for Latino students in the United States. *Bilingual Review, 24*, 147–59.
Flores v. Arizona, 160 F.Supp. 2d 1043 (D.Ariz. 2000).
Freire, P. (1970). *Pedagogy of the oppressed*. New York: Herder and Herder.
Gómez v. Illinois State Board of Education, 811 F. 2d 1030 (1987).
Guadalupe Organization, Inc. v. Tempe Elementary School District, 578 F. 2d. 1022 (1978).
Hernandez v. Texas, 347 U.S. 475 (1954).
Hing, B. O. (2010). *Ethical borders: NAFTA, glozabilzation, and Mexican migration*. Philadelphia: Temple University Press.
Horne v. Flores, United States Court of Appeals for the Ninth Circuit, Case No. 08–289 (2009).
Idaho Migrant Council v. Board of Education, 647 F. 2nd. 69 (1981).
Immigration and Nationality Act of 1965 (Hart-Celler Act, INS, Act of 1965, Pub.L. 89–236).
Independent School District v. Salvatierra (1930, 1931).
Individuals with Disabilities Education Act (IDEA) reauthorized and amended (2004), Parts 300 and 301 of Title 34 of the Code of Federal Regulations.
Jose Peter v. Ambach, 669 F. 2 D 865 (1982); 557 F. Supp. 1230 (1983).
Keyes v. Denver School District, 576 F. Supp. 1503 (1983).
Kincheloe, J. L. (2008). *Knowledge and critical pedagogy: An introduction*. Dordrecht, London: Springer.
Lau v. Nichols, 414 U.S. 563 (1974).
Lau Remedies. (1975). Task Force Findings Specifying Remedies Available for Eliminating Past Educational Practices Ruled Unlawful Under *Lau v. Nichols*. HEW Office for Civil Rights (OCR). Issued August 11, 1975.
Lopez v. Seccombe 71 F. Supp. 769 (S.D. Cal 1944).
MacKaye, S. (1990). D.A. California Proposition 63: Language attitudes reflected in the public debate. *The Annals of the American Academy of Political and Social Science, 508*, 1135–146.
Martinez v. Regents of the University of California rules to uphold the California law known as AB 540. The Court of Appeal, Third Appellate District, Case No. C054124 (2010).
Martinez v. Regents, No. CV 05–2064 (Cal. Super. Ct. Oct. 6, 2006).
Mendez v. Westminster, 161 F. 2d 774 (Ninth Cir. 1947). Retrieved December 24, 2010, from http://sshl.ucsd.edu/brown/Mendez.htm
NNIRR. (2010). *Episodes from the struggle for justice, equality, & dignity: A brief history of the last 15 years national network for immigrant and refugee rights*. National network for Immigrant and Refugee Rights. Retrieved December 28, 2010. http://www.nnirr.org/about/about_timeline.html
No Child Left Behind (January 8, 2002). Public Law 107–110—An act to close the achievement gap with accountability, flexibility, and choice, so that no child is left behind. Pub.L.107–110, 115 Stat. 1425.
Northwest Arctic School District et al. v. Joseph A. Califano et al. United States District Court for the District of Alaska, No. A-77–216 Civil, September 29, 1978.
Orozco, C. E. (2010). "Del Rio ISD V. Salvatierra," Handbook of Texas Online. Retrieved from http://www.tshaonline.org/handbook/online/articles/jrd02
Otero v. Mesa County Valley School District No. 51, 408 F. Supp. 162, (1975).
Pasadena City Bd. of Educ. v. Spangler, 427 U.S. 424 (1976).

Perez v. Lippold (aka Perez v. Sharp), 32 Cal. 2d 711, 198 P.2d 17 (1948).
Plessy v. Ferguson, 163 U.S. 537 (1896).
Plyler v. Doe, 457 U.S. 202 (1982).
Ravitch, D. (2010). *The death and life of the great American school system: How testing and choice are undermining education.* New York: Basic Books.
Rehabilitation Act of 1973, as amended, 29 U.S.C. § 794 (Section 504).
Rios v. Read, 73 F.R.D. 589, 598 (E.D.N.Y. 1977).
Serna v. Portales Municipal Schools, U.S. Court of Appeals, Tenth Circuit, 499 F. 2nd. ll47, (1974).
Spring, J. (2002). *Political agendas for education: From the religious right to the green party* (2nd ed.). Mahwah, NJ: Lawrence Erlbaum Associates.
Swann v. Charlotte-Mecklenburg Board of Education, 402 U.S. 1 (1971).
Title IX of the Education Amendments, United States Code Section 20 (1972).
United States v. State of Texas et al., 5 Cir., 447 F.2d 441 (1971).
University of California Regents v. Bakke, 438 U.S. 265 (1978).
U.S. v. State of Texas, U.S. District Court Eastern District of Texas, Tyler Division, Civil Action No. 5281, Pursuant to the Provisions of Rule 52, F.R. CIV. P (1981).
Williams v. State of California, Superior Court of the State of California, County of California, No.312236 (2004).

3

THE LEMON GROVE DESEGREGATION CASE

A Matter of Neglected History

Mike Madrid

> *Some Mexicans are very bright, but you cannot compare their brightest with the average white children.*
> —*A superintendent of schools circa 1940*

Introduction

After working in K–12 education for more than 30 years, I started a second career at the university level working with prospective elementary and secondary educators. At Chapman University in Orange, California, I have had the good fortune to research and investigate specific topics of the history and culture of people of Mexican descent, including the folklore of the southwest, the Latino achievement gap, as well as court cases such as Lemon Grove, which took place in 1931 in a community that lies to the east of San Diego, California.

While conducting research for a journal article I was preparing on *Mendez v. Westminster*, it became apparent to me that there have been many incidents—historical, social, and political—pertaining to people of Mexican descent that have received little or no attention, many of which occurred in California. I thought, "Why have we not heard of these incidents and, more importantly, why have they been excluded from our school texts?" The more I read and investigated, the more it became obvious that keeping these exciting, vibrant, and noteworthy stories and histories from the public eye serves only to perpetuate the marginalization of Mexican-Americans, thus rendering their experiences as insignificant, unheralded, and unimportant. That is, these neglected histories deserve to be showcased.

While reviewing the history and background of *Méndez*, a landmark decision that had an impact on desegregation not only in California, but also on a national scale, it also became obvious that in most cases, no one, single event effects social or political change. Of course, *Mendez v. Westminster* is an important historical and legal event, but it is only a single link in the chain of victories leading to the demise of de jure school segregation. As with *Méndez*, many of the cases and legislative actions that comprise the progression of events that contributed to the desegregation of California schools are matters of neglected history, such as *Ward v. Flood* (1874), the amendments to Political Code Section 1662 (1893), *Piper v. Big Pine School District* (1924), the failure of the passage of the Bliss Bill (1931), *Alvarez v. Lemon Grove* (1931), *Lopez v. Seccombe* (1944), and the Anderson Bill (1947).

Why Lemon Grove? The elements that characterize *Alvarez v. Lemon Grove*, which has come to be known as the Lemon Grove Incident, are the stuff from which epic historical dramas are made. The Lemon Grove case is a victory against separate school facilities, equal or otherwise, and it speaks volumes of the courage and tenacity of the parents who fought for their children's education. Moreover, the Lemon Grove case, albeit an item of neglected history that has yet to be incorporated into the school curriculum, is a momentous and symbolic historical civil rights event that is only one of countless and unique historical, political, and sociological elements that constitute the Mexican-American experience.

Mexican School Desegregation: A Different Racial Paradigm

In 1931, the Southern California community of Lemon Grove served as the unlikely stage for a dramatic and significant civil rights court case in which a group of courageous Mexican and Mexican-American parents and their children won a major victory in the battle against school segregation and the perfidious notion of separate-but-equal facilities. The case, the Lemon Grove Incident, was the nation's first recognized court-ordered school desegregation case. The case involved more than 70 children of Mexican descent who were summarily directed by their school principal to attend a hastily constructed, two-room segregated school, the caballeriza, the barn, which was situated in the Mexican side of town.

The Lemon Grove case is not well known and one could surmise that its most distinguishing characteristic is its obscurity. Similar to the post–World War II, landmark case of *Mendez v. Westminster*, the Lemon Grove matter could be characterized as an item of neglected history not only because of the public's ignorance, but also because of its absence from the public school curriculum (Madrid, 2007, p. 29). As with the Lemon Grove and Méndez cases, many important historical events pertaining to the Mexican-American experience are not taught in the public schools. For example, according to Bowman (2001), there were approximately 100 school desegregation and education-related cases that were heard during the 19th century, many of which pertained to Mexican-American civil rights, yet there is little mention of them in the history texts.

Many, if not most, of the better-known desegregation and civil rights issues have emerged from the Black experience. That is, events related to the Black civil rights movement generally are well known and rightfully are considered important aspects of U.S. history. In stark contrast to Black civil rights issues, many incidents pertaining to the Mexican-American struggle are neither familiar nor renowned. Why?

A Brown/White Paradigm

Matters of civil rights and school desegregation traditionally have been perceived within a Black/White context, which is problematic because it tends to marginalize the history of intolerance and bigotry leveled at Latinos, according to Bowman (2001). Unlike African-Americans, Latinos were not methodically enslaved. Rosales (2000) found that Blacks are presumed to be bona fide U.S. citizens, yet Mexican-Americans frequently are perceived within an immigrant context because of their historical, linguistic, and cultural ties with Mexico. People of Mexican descent frequently are viewed as foreigners, and the perception of the Mexican-American's foreignness is, in part, attributable to the great number of Latinos who are immigrants. The notion of foreignness often is intensified due to language issues, for example, Spanish speakers who need to learn English or need to improve their English. Furthermore, Bowman (2001) found that the notion of foreignness is a prominent characteristic of the English-only movement as reflected in its attacks on bilingual education, which are indicative of the enmity directed at those who speak Spanish.

People of Mexican descent frequently have been categorized as "White," although there have been many occasions when politicians sought to categorize them as "Indian." Yet the practice of classifying Mexican-Americans as "White" may have fostered the illusion that they have not been targets of discrimination and, indeed, have benefited as members of the dominant culture. Such is not the case for "These interpretations . . . threaten Latinos' pursuit of equality by assuming the existence of a level playing field where none exists" (Bowman, 2001, p. 15).

According to the U.S. Census Bureau (2004), as recently as the 2000 census, Latinos could categorize themselves as "White," which may seem a viable option because their choices were limited to "White," "Black or African-American," "American Indian and Alaska Native," "Asian," "Native Hawaiian or Other Pacific Islander," and "Some other race" (U.S. Census Bureau, 2004, p. 1). In other words, according to Bowman (2001), although Mexican-Americans may be any race, in actuality they tend to be identified not by what they are, but what they are not.

By bringing to light the neglected histories of Mexicans and Mexican-Americans, the general public, educators, and the chroniclers of history would realize school desegregation did not begin in Topeka, Kansas in 1954. As evidenced in *Mendez v. Westminster*, many of the legal arguments used by Thurgood Marshall and Earl Warren in Brown emanated from the experiences of Mexican-Americans who lived in the southwest. That is, much of the progress of school desegregation is based upon a Brown/White paradigm that includes the Lemon Grove case, which is extremely important in

> U.S. history, not solely because it occurred but because the community took court action and won the case that established the rights of their children to equal education, despite local, regional and national sentiment that favored not only segregation, but the actual deportation of the Mexican population in the United States. The case is a testimony of the . . . Mexican community's rights and their actions towards equality in education . . . for the Mexican population in California and the United States.
>
> *(Alvarez, 1986, p. 116)*

The Education of Children of Mexican Descent in the 1930s

During the early stages of the 20th century, people of Mexican descent comprised the dominant workforce in agriculture, mining, transportation, and construction. With respect to Lemon Grove, California, many of the families had emigrated from Baja California to the Lemon Grove and the general San Diego area, which offered jobs in agriculture, mining, and in packing houses. Despite the substantial Mexican presence in the local and national labor force, some of the White residents of Lemon Grove perceived Mexicans as inferior and, therefore, felt there would have been no value in educating the Mexicans.

In the early part of the 20th century, the brown-skinned Mexican immigrant frequently was regarded in a different manner than his light-skinned European counterpart. As an illustration, Kenneth L. Roberts, a journalist who had written favorably of the European immigrant, composed a less than complimentary depiction of Mexicans in a Saturday Evening Post article. According to Robert J. Alvarez (1986, p. 119), the Mexicans were described as "half-breeds" and the streets of Mexican immigrant communities were overcrowded with "shacks" belonging to people who were "illiterate," "diseased," and who possessed the "reckless prodigality of rabbits."

Due to the Mexican's alleged substandard nature, segregating Mexican children and children of Mexican descent was a legitimate and accepted practice. According to Bowman (2001), irrespective of an opinion expressed by the California Attorney General in 1929 that indicated segregation of Latinos could not be defended under California law, segregation continued to flourish. In California, the establishment of Mexican schools was commonplace. Cities such as Pasadena, Santa Ana, Ontario, Riverside, as well as Los Angeles featured separate educational facilities for children of Mexican descent. Furthermore, Bowman (2001) found in 1931 more than 80 percent of California school districts with significant Latino populations were segregated and many of the remaining 20 percent of the districts practiced some form of school segregation, which endured into the 1950s.

A traditional and common discriminatory practice was the establishment of Americanization schools. The Americanization projects were initiated in reaction to the influx of immigrants during the period that began at the turn of the century and continued into the 1930s. The limited Americanization curriculum featured cooking, hygiene, English, and civics. In addition to the substandard course of study, the Americanization and Mexican schools were characterized by inadequate equipment and resources, squalid buildings, and teaching staffs whose rate of compensation was substantially lower in comparison to the teachers of the White schools. Teaching in a Mexican or Americanization school was not a highly prized career goal insofar as a transfer to a White school would have been deemed a promotion.

The teaching staffs of the Americanization schools often held the opinion the Mexican student had limited ability and essentially only needed training for agriculture and domestic work. That is, Ruiz (2003) indicated the Americanization program generally prepared Mexican children and adolescents for jobs with low pay and low status.

During the Depression, in addition to substandard educational programs, Mexican and Mexican-American students had to contend with a pervasive anti-immigrant sentiment, which fostered the development of separate educational facilities for children of Mexican descent, despite many of them being U.S. citizens and proficient speakers of English. It should come as no surprise there were racist and anti-Mexican sentiments in Lemon Grove, too. For example, a Lemon Grove citizen who promoted the separation of the Mexican students from White children said if the Mexicans were to prevail in Lemon Grove, they would "slip" a bill through the legislature so they might be able to segregate the "greasers" (Alvarez, 1986, p. 123).

As previously indicated, the attempt to segregate Mexican children in California was supported by some politicians in the California legislature. As an illustration, in 1931 Assemblyman Bliss of Carpinteria introduced a bill that would have legalized the segregation of Mexican and Mexican-American students. The bill sought to classify Mexicans and Mexican-Americans as "Indian," a racial category for which separate schools legally could be established. The California Education Code, which was changed soon after the *Méndez* appeal in the late 1940s, originally allowed for the establishment of segregated schools for Japanese, Indian, Chinese, and Mongolian students. Fortunately, the Bliss bill failed and its demise perhaps was due in part to the racist nature of the Lemon Grove case.

Although the Bliss legislation was not successful, the racist and anti-Mexican sentiment prevailed throughout the southwest during the 1930s. The matriculation of Mexican children as well as Mexican-American children into separate and unequal schools persisted. Furthermore, many immigrant families, Mexican and otherwise, lived under the very real threat of deportation, an underhanded tactic that was used in Lemon Grove with some parents who refused to send their children to the Mexican school. According to Ruiz (2003), approximately

170,000 Latinos living in the United States were repatriated, that is they were deported to Mexico between 1931 and 1934. Many of those deported were U.S. citizens.

History and Trial

Case Background

In July of 1930, trustees of the Lemon Grove School District developed a plan to build a special school for the Mexican children, which received the support of the Chamber of Commerce, as well as the PTA. In August of 1930, the trustees held a special meeting because the "situation had reached emergency conditions," which according to the trustees included overcrowding, as well as purported "sanitary and moral" disorders that were engendered by Mexican children (Sanchez, 2004, p. 3).

There was no attempt to apprise the parents of the children who would be affected by the board's decision. It was apparent the board wished to delay a confrontation with the parents and avoid a controversy and therefore, they used the element of surprise. According to Robert Alvarez, Jr. (1986), the son of the plaintiff, the members of the board decided against any official notice so as not to commit themselves in writing.

On the 5th of January, 1931, the day when the Lemon Grove students returned to class following the Christmas break, Principal Jerome T. Green placed himself at the front doorway of the school to greet and admit the White students, and to inform the Mexican children they could not enter. He told the Mexican children their desks and personal effects had been transported to a new two-room school, which became to be known as the caballeriza, literally a place for horses.

The parents, of course, were angered and wanted their children to remain at their former school site, but had little power to do so. They had no way of countering the Chamber of Commerce's support of the segregation plan because they held no influential positions in the Chamber, the school board, or PTA. Although the parents seemingly were operating from a position of weakness, they were neither lacking in courage nor ignorant of their rights; they adamantly refused to send their children, numbering 70, to a school that resembled a barn and was characterized by an inferior instructional program. Only three children attended class at the new Mexican school.

The parents quickly organized neighborhood meetings. At one of the meetings they formed the Lemon Grove Neighbors Committee and solicited support from the community, as well as legal assistance. Initially, the leaders of the Lemon Grove Neighbors Committee sought guidance from Enrique Ferreira, the Mexican Counsel. Ferreira, whose legal power to intervene was quite limited, did arrange, however, for a pair of San Diego attorneys, Fred C. Noon and A. C. Brinkley, to serve as counsel.

To counter the parents' boycott of the caballeriza, the Lemon Grove board expelled students whose absences exceeded 20 days. A social worker also was quickly dispatched to meet with some of the parents who were receiving assistance from the county. The social worker's deployment was a blatant attempt to intimidate through bullying tactics and unveiled threats of deportation. Unfortunately, according to Mancilla (2004), in keeping with the anti-Mexican and anti-immigrant sentiments of the times, some Lemon Grove parents actually were repatriated (deported) to Mexico.

The Lawsuit

With the assistance of their attorneys Noon and Brinkley, the parents filed a suit, a Writ of Mandate, which characterized the board's action as an explicit attempt to segregate children on the basis of race. The Writ indicated 95 percent of the children who were segregated were born in the United States and, therefore, were entitled to the rights and privileges afforded to all citizens. Furthermore, the parents demanded a quick resolution to the matter to "prevent serious embarrassment and to determine the legal right under the laws of California, of children of Mexican parentage, nationality and or descent to attend the public schools of California on the basis of equality with other Americans" (Alvarez, 1986, p. 124).

The lawsuit was listed under the name of Roberto Alvarez, Jr., an exemplary student who spoke English quite well. At the time of the case, Roberto was 10 years old. In the mid-1980s during the production of Paul Espinosa's award-winning dramatic semi-documentary, *The Lemon Grove Incident*, one of Roberto's classmates jokingly indicated that Roberto was selected to carry the lawsuit not so much for his English-speaking competence, but for his good looks!

The suit was filed in the Superior Court of California in San Diego. The suit disputed the Lemon Grove trustees' authority to build and maintain a separate, segregated school for Mexican children and children of Mexican descent. Prior to the building of the new school, some children had been enrolled in special classes because of their lack of English proficiency, but the creation of the segregated facility was regarded by the parents as illegal and detrimental to the children, as well as a danger to the welfare of the Mexican community.

In addition to the battle that would take place in court, the parents opened a new front in the media seeking to enlighten the public and garner support. Newspaper articles appeared in Los Angeles as well as in Tijuana, Mexico. For example, research conducted by Sanchez (2004) revealed *La Opinión*, a prominent Spanish-language paper, featured a page-long article, "No Admiten los Niños Mexicanos" (Mexican Children Denied Admission). The article included a letter from Lemon Grove Neighbors Committee indicating the school board's action was not only blatantly racist, but also illegal because the board members sought to distinguish Mexican children from children of other nationalities and place them in a separate, inferior school.

The Trial and Decision

The case of the caballeriza was heard in the Superior Court of San Diego County on February 24, 1931. The presiding judge, Claude Chambers, quickly and boldly indicted each member of the Lemon Grove board for illegally segregating the children. Needless to add, the board members denied the allegations and rationalized their action on a pretense of improving educational opportunities for children of Mexican descent. They indicated the facility was an Americanization school in which the children's deficiencies would be addressed and corrected. According to Alvarez (1986), the board felt by sending the children to the segregated facility, the corruption of the White children would be lessened if not reversed. Furthermore, through the teaching of American customs, the repute of the Mexican children invariably would rise to the level of the White students.

The board members described the caballeriza as a new facility, certainly not barn-like, with a fully equipped playground that could accommodate nearly 80 pupils. They also indicated the school's locale was selected for reasons of safety. The caballeriza had been situated in the barrio, allegedly for the well-being of the children who no longer would be required to cross the busy main boulevard as they did while attending their former school, Lemon Grove Grammar School.

The board members also indicated the great majority of Mexican students, many of whom were older than their White counterparts in corresponding grades, had been deemed as lacking English proficiency and, therefore, required special attention. According to Mancilla (2004), the defendants argued the Mexican students' language, Spanish, was a tremendous handicap and a segregated school for Mexican children would protect them from unnecessary competition with the White students, thereby mitigating feelings of inferiority. As Alvarez (1986) indicated, the board members argued the building of the new school was not a racist attempt to segregate children, but a measure to provide the inferior Mexican students an instructional program that was better than they had received at their former school.

During the course of the trial many witnesses took the stand. Ten witnesses for the plaintiff decried the false generalizations regarding the students' academic skills, and much of the testimony dealt with the actions, comments, and attitudes of the school staff and board. The list of those who testified at the trial included the school's principal, Jerome T. Green, the president of the Chamber of Commerce, as well as teachers from the caballeriza.

When Judge Chambers asked if allowing Mexican children to mingle with White students would facilitate the acquisition of English, the board and members of the instructional staff failed to respond. When the plaintiff's counsel, Fred C. Noon, queried one of the teachers as to why the Mexican children were separated from the White children, the defendant stated segregation was not only preferred, but truly necessary for a program of personalized instruction. Furthermore, it was revealed during the course of the trial some of the Mexican children lived in the White neighborhood and some of the White children lived near the barrio. Therefore, the board's action did little to improve the welfare and safety of the children because some White as well as Mexican children had to cross the busy main boulevard to attend their respective schools.

On the 30th of March, 1931, Judge Chambers rendered his monumental decision. He ruled in favor of the plaintiff and refuted each claim made by the members of the Lemon Grove School Board. According to Leonel Sanchez (2004, p. 3), a writer for *The San Diego News Tribune,* Judge Chambers' ruling indicated the board could undeniably "separate a few children to offer 'special instruction,'" but "to separate all the Mexicans in one group can only be done by infringing the laws of the State of California."

The judge demanded an immediate reinstatement of the Mexican children in the main building school, or Lemon Grove Grammar School. Judge Chambers declared the separation of the Mexican children was a blatant act of segregation and, moreover, the Mexican children were entitled to attend Lemon Grove Grammar School on the basis of being equal to the White children.

The Significance of the Lemon Grove Decision

The case was not appealed. The members of the Lemon Grove PTA and the Chamber of Commerce considered supporting an appeal, but did not proceed. A considerable amount of money had been spent not only on the court case, but also on the development and construction of the school building and, therefore, there was general reluctance to risk further financial loss. Furthermore, according to Mancilla (2004), the members of the Chamber of Commerce wanted to reestablish a respectable image of Lemon Grove and feared additional negative publicity.

The case was never recorded in the minutes of the school board and the only reference to the incident appeared in the minutes of a board meeting that took place after the trial. The reference indicated everything would continue as it had prior to the 5th of January, the infamous day Principal Green stood in the doorway of Lemon Grove Grammar School and told the Mexican children they would have to attend class in the caballeriza. The Mexican school eventually was demolished; the site has become a parking lot, and Lemon Grove Grammar School has been transformed into a middle school.

The case received little or no attention in the media after Judge Chambers ruled in favor of the plaintiff. Higher courts never had an opportunity to review Chambers' decision. Unfortunately, beyond the city limits of Lemon Grove, California, the segregation of children of Mexican descent persisted. Americanization schools flourished throughout the southwest until they were abolished by significant court decisions rendered in the 1940s and, therefore, the Lemon Grove case appears as yet another item of neglected history. It also is somewhat surprising if not alarming that other Mexican communities did not regard the case as a precedent for assailing segregated schools.

Notwithstanding the case's low historical profile, the Lemon Grove matter, indeed, was and is significant. According to Alvarez (1986), the case serves as testimony to the Lemon Grove Mexican community who successfully used the legal system to protect the rights of their children, the great majority of whom were U.S. citizens. The case also serves as testimony to the courageous Latino parents who prevailed in a prominent civil rights case and overturned a blatant, pernicious discriminatory practice.

As unheralded as the Lemon Grove case was, the decision played a significant role in the defeat of the Bliss Bill. The Bliss legislation would have classified Mexicans as Indians, which would have facilitated the segregation of children of Mexican descent, according to the laws of the time. Had the Bliss Bill been enacted, it would have perpetuated the segregation of children in California schools based on race.

The Lemon Grove victory is a significant incident in the history and experience of Latinos in general and Mexican-Americans in particular. It is a Brown victory. It is a civil rights victory. There are those who would argue that maintaining a focus on specific racial, ethnic-based incidents only serves to perpetuate prejudice, bias, and racist attitudes, but as Bowman (2001, p. 20) eloquently stated, "Racism will not cease to exist merely because we ignore it."

For the foreseeable future, many incidents that comprise the Mexican-American experience probably will remain unheralded and their mention in the classrooms will be imperceptible, yet incidents such as the Lemon Grove case do, indeed, merit attention because they commemorate and dignify the Mexican-American experience. According to Bowman (2001), many Mexican-American events pertaining to social justice and civil rights tend to be neglected because they lack the acclaim that is characteristic of many African-American achievements. Furthermore, they do not fit into the Black/White paradigm, but the Lemon Grove Incident should only be viewed within a Brown/White context because to perceive it in any other manner summarily ignores the unique nature of the Mexican-American experience.

The Lemon Grove case does matter. The parents' victory in Judge Chambers' court should be regarded as a significant victory against racist practices foisted on U.S. citizens of Mexican descent and all people of color. The Lemon Grove case is a victory against separate school facilities, equal or otherwise, and it speaks volumes of the courage and tenacity of the parents who fought for their children's proper education. Moreover, the Lemon Grove case, albeit an item of neglected history that has yet to be incorporated into the school curriculum, is a momentous, symbolic, and significant historical civil rights event in the array of incidents and historical episodes that comprise the Mexican-American experience.

References

Alvarez, Jr., R. (1986, spring). The Lemon Grove incident: The nation's first successful desegregation court case. *The Journal of San Diego History, 32*(2), 116–135.

Bowman, K. (2001). The new face of school desegregation. *Duke Law Journal, 50*(1751). Retrieved February 1, 2007 from http://www.law.duke.edu/ journals/dlj/jctrl.html

Madrid, M. (2007, March). Neglected history: The Méndez desegregation case. *Multilingual Educator*, 29–35.

Mancilla, G. (2004, winter/spring). Against all odds: The Lemon Grove incident. *Concientizacion: A Journal of Chicana & Latina Experience and Thought, 1 & 2*. Retrieved March 26, 2007 from http://www.wooster.edu/ psychology/apa-crib.html

Rosales, R. (2000). *The Illusion of Inclusion*. Austin, TX: University of Texas Press.

Ruiz, V. (2003, fall). We always tell our children they are Americans. *The College Board Review, 200*, 21–27.

Sanchez, L. (2004, May 18). Before Brown. *The San Diego Union-Tribune*. Retrieved March 27, 2007 from http://signonsandiego.com/uniontrib/20040518news_1n18grove.html

U.S. Census Bureau. (2004). *We the people: Hispanics in the United States*. Washington, DC: Author. Retrieved February 1, 2007 from http://www.census.gov/prod/2004pubs/censr_18.pdf

4
THE MEANING OF MÉNDEZ

Sandra Robbie

I grew up in Westminster in Orange County, California, but I never heard of the Méndez case until I had children of my own. And when I heard of it, I knew it would be my life's work to see that our children didn't have to wait until they had children to learn about this story.

I was visiting my folks in Westminster, California, sitting at the very same table where as a child I used to sneak my grandma's fresh tortillas each time she'd return to the griddle. But this morning, I was simply alone in the kitchen, reading the Saturday paper. The smiling photo of a Latina grandma and her adult daughter reminded me of Arizona relatives, warm and familiar. I didn't even sense what was coming. The article started something like this:

> In 1944, there were two kinds of schools in Orange County: ones for whites and ones for Mexicans. When eight-year-old Sylvia Méndez and her brothers were turned away from the Seventeenth Street School in Westminster because they were Mexican, their parents filed a lawsuit. Méndez vs. Westminster eventually went to the Ninth Circuit Court of Appeals and won in 1947. Seven years before Brown vs. Board of Education, California became the first state to end legal school segregation. A middle school being built in Santa Ana will be named in honor of Gonzalo and Felicitas Méndez who led the historic civil rights case.
>
> *(Hickox, 1997)*

I leaned onto the table as the rumble in my brain took over my body and my eyes brimmed with fiery tears that refused to fall. I grew up in Westminster, how could I not know this? My eyes became white hot lasers that bored through the rest of the article revealing Orange County's not-too-distant history of segregated housing, swimming pools and movie theaters. And when it got to the part about Thurgood Marshall, then-Governor Earl Warren and their roles in the Mendez case . . . paving the way to Brown vs. Board of Education . . . in my mind I was shouting, "Does it get bigger than this? In our study of American Civil Rights, does it get bigger than Brown vs. Board of Education?" With the breath beaten from my body, I slumped in the chair as the kitchen walls spun around me.

It took a while for the confusion to settle and for the sunlight to break through in my mind. When I raised my eyes to the world around me, everything looked different. Not just the wooden chair or the vinyl tablecloth or the beige curtains . . . everything was different. My past, my present, my future all looked sharp, shiny and right somehow, for the very first time. It was like the final puzzle piece locking perfectly into place revealing the true full picture. Suddenly, everything made sense to me. *This* was the world that I lived in. Prejudice and generalizations existed everywhere and no one was immune to its pernicious influence. I was both victim and perpetrator yet I felt no blame, no sadness, no hurt. It was a truth that also delivered a calm awareness and relief that I finally understood what was really going on. The Méndez story resonated with a recent experience at the park when, as I watched my little boy dig in the sandbox, a blonde 2-year-old girl whom I'd never seen before came up and tugged my hand. She said, "Mommy, swing." I was a mommy, but I was not *her* mommy, but she didn't have a different category for that yet. I understood then exactly how people learn. It takes experience and constant attention to see the differences in people. But the world is just too big and everyone makes generalizations. It takes discipline to really see the differences sometimes . . . and often we fail. We are human that way. I was at peace for about a minute. Then came the aftershocks.

Like a fist to my face, the first emotion that came to me was anger. I was angry. How could I not know this? I grew up in Westminster. I was sitting in Westminster at that very moment. I attended school there, from kindergarten through high school graduation, and never once in all those years had any of my teachers or history books ever mentioned the segregation that happened there. The way my history books told it, the civil rights struggle was something that took place in the American South long ago and far away, to people different from us. That was a lie. The Civil Rights struggle included all of us. It was about people of all colors all across the country. That was the truth. Then the blows came again: a one-two punch of guilt and shame. It was shocking to learn of this history that stood in stark contrast to way my school books talked about school segregation as if it was solely a black and white story that played out in the American South.

The *Mendez v. Westminster* Story

In the summer of 1943, the sky was truly falling. News headlines screamed of war and destruction across Europe and delivered stories of fallen soldiers to heartbroken families here in America. In Orange County, California, amid the internment of over 100,000 Japanese Americans along the Pacific Coast, banker man Mr. Monroe approached his Mexican-American client, Gonzalo Méndez, with a business proposal.

"Gonzalo, remember when you told me about your dream? You grew up picking grapes and oranges, but one day, you hoped to be the boss and run your own ranch. Well, the Munemitsu family is being sent to an internment camp in Arizona. If they cannot find someone to lease their ranch while they are away, they will lose everything they own. Mr. Méndez, would you like to live your dream?" Gonzalo talked it over with his Puerto Rican wife, Felicitas, but neither of them needed much convincing. Soon they drove to Arizona to sign the lease, then sold their cantina in Santa Ana and moved with their extended family to run the ranch just one city over, in Westminster.

Gonzalo's sister, Aunt Sally, took all the children to enroll in the Westminster School. The children were amazed with the beautiful brick building but it was the swings and the grassy field that got their feet to running. They chased and laughed while Aunt Sally spoke with the school official. The children had no idea what happened when suddenly Aunt Sally scooped them up and hurried them back to the car.

"Gonzalo, they would not take your children at the school," Sally Vidaurri fumed. "They said my children could go, but your children would have to attend the Mexican School."

Aunt Sally had married a Mexican who was part French and so her children, Alice and Virginia, had light skin and light hair as well as a French last name. The Méndez children, Sylvia, Gonzalo, Jr. and Jerome, had dark skin, jet black hair and a Mexican last name reflecting their father's heritage. And though all the children were born in America and they all spoke English, the Westminster school officials refused to admit them.

Aunt Sally continued, "I told them if they would not accept your children, then my children will not stay . . . and we left."

"There must be a mistake, an awful mistake," Mr. Méndez said. "I will speak with the school tomorrow."

The next day, Mr. Méndez went to speak with the Westminster School. Their response was the same, so he went to the school district and eventually to the Orange County Department of Education but the answer was still the same, "No, we will not accept your children in our school. Your children must go to the Mexican school."

All the children rode the same bus to school but when they stepped off, the White children simply crossed the street to attend their beautiful brick school with swings and grass in the playground. The Mexican children turned to walk another half mile to their school in the barrio. Some folks called the school "The Chicken Coop" because the rickety wood building was located on a big dusty plot adjacent to a cow farm. Flies, the stench of manure, and an electric cattle fence surrounded their playground. Once, a little girl played too close and accidentally grasped the fence with her bare hand. The electric current gripped her back and she stood frozen and frightened, unable to free herself until the farmer could be found and the current was switched off.

And then there were the beaten-up, second-hand books, with curriculum geared not toward high school and college diplomas, but instead intended to keep the children working in the fields or as domestic help.

While the disparity between the two schools was vast, what really motivated Mr. Méndez to fight the segregation was the fact that he did not want his children to grow up with hate in their hearts for the children who went to the beautiful school. "I will fight this," he thought, "But how?" At the farm, produce truck driver Henry Rivera told Gonzalo, "I know of a lawyer who might help. He fought a case for another truck driver when they wouldn't let him buy a house in Fullerton. I bet he would help you. His name is David Marcus."

Sure enough, David Marcus would help, first by proposing that Mr. Méndez find other families to join him in a class action suit that would be more powerful than his case alone. So Mrs. Méndez took the reins in running the ranch while Gonzalo invested his time working with community members to help organize. On March 2, 1945, David Marcus filed the case with five families in four Orange County school districts on behalf of 5,000 children. The families of Méndez, Estrada, Guzmán, Palomino and Ramírez held that the school districts of Westminster, Santa Ana, Garden Grove and El Modena were unlawfully discriminating against their children. Marcus presented testimony from students, parents and school officials to show the pattern of discrimination in which children of Mexican descent were routinely sent to Mexican schools under the guise of teaching those students English and Americanizing them, when in fact the children were never tested and many were already fluent English-speakers. Marcus submitted as evidence a master's thesis written by one of the school superintendents that essentially stated that Mexican children were inferior intellectually, physically, and hygienically, and that they could never compete with Anglo children. This provided information on the prejudiced mindset of some school personnel who rationalized why they had good reasons for segregation. The final witness, social scientist Marie Hughes testified, "It is not in the best interests of children in America . . . to go to school together under segregated conditions . . . Children learn a language through hearing it and through having a motive, a reason, for using it." She cited a classical study that unequivocally proved that children learned language more rapidly and with greater facility when they were not segregated. And very importantly, Ms. Hughes stated, "Segregation, by its very nature, is a reminder constantly of inferiority, of not being wanted, of not being part of a community. Such an experience cannot possibly build the best personality or the sort of person who is most at home in the world . . ."

On February 18, 1946, when Judge Paul J. McCormick's delivered his decision in favor of the plaintiffs Méndez, Estrada, Guzmán, Palomino and Ramírez, for the first time in American history a federal court judge ruled that separate was not equal. The school districts appealed, and in the Ninth Circuit Court decision, the plaintiffs won again in 1947, but the judges took a step back from McCormick's ruling and instead determined that the Mexican-American children were discriminated against based on national origin, a violation of the 14th Amendment. Nonetheless, the NAACP contributed a friend of the court brief to the Méndez appeal. That brief was written by Robert L. Carter and overseen by Thurgood Marshall. In 2003, in a video interview, Carter told me that his Méndez brief later served as the model for the 1954 landmark Supreme Court decision Brown v. Board of Education. And though the Méndez case only applied to four school districts in Orange County, exactly two months after the appeal was won, then-California Governor Earl Warren signed the Anderson Bill, repealing the statutes that had allowed for the segregation of Asian American and Native Americans, and children with disabilities, making California the first state to end public school segregation. And though our history books always talk about Earl Warren and his role as one of the chief proponents for Japanese internment during WWII and for his role as the Supreme Court Chief Justice who led the 9–0 decision in Brown v. Board of Education, those books never mention Warren's role in ending school segregation in California seven years earlier.

Connecting Brown and Méndez

Jurisprudentially, Méndez is not mentioned even in the footnotes of Brown v. Board of Education, but the influence of this case in the mind of Earl Warren can be clearly seen when comparing the language of the two decisions. Hon. Frederick P. Aguirre contrasts the writings here:

- *Méndez:* "The evidence clearly shows that Spanish-speaking children are retarded in learning English by lack of exposure to its use because of segregation . . ." *Id.* at 549.
- *Brown:* "Segregation with the sanction of law therefore has a tendency to retard the educational and mental development of Negro children and to deprive them of some of the benefits they would receive in a racially integrated school system." *Id.* at 494–495.
- *Méndez:* "It is also established by the record that the methods of segregation prevalent in the defendant school districts foster antagonisms in the children and suggest inferiority among them where none exists." *Id.* at 549.
- *Brown:* "Segregation of white and colored children in public schools has a detrimental effect upon the colored children. The impact is greater when it has the sanction of the law; for the policy of separating the races is usually interpreted as denoting the inferiority of the Negro group." *Id.* at 494.
- *Méndez:* "The equal protection of the laws pertaining to the public school system in California is not provided by furnishing in separate schools the

same technical facilities, text books and courses of instruction to children of Mexican ancestry that are available to the other public school children regardless of their ancestry." *Id.* at 549.
- *Brown:* "We conclude that in the field of public education the doctrine of 'separate but equal' has no place. Separate education facilities are inherently unequal. Therefore, we hold that the plaintiffs . . . are deprived of the equal protection of the laws . . ." *Id.* at 495.
- *Méndez:* "A paramount requisite in the American system of public education is social equality. It must be open to all children by unified school association regardless of lineage." *Id.* at 549.

My Life's Passion

This Méndez history is so much more than a court case to me. What does Mendez v. Westminster mean to me? What is it about this case that gripped and shook me until it unmoored every thought I had, every belief I held, and then compelled me to tell others about it . . . for the past 13 years? How did this story convince me to go back to school and study TV production so I could eventually create a documentary intended to get Méndez into every classroom across the country? How did this story give me the courage to set the goal of seeing the Méndez history honored at the White House and taught in our schools, and then set out to find ways to make that happen and more? And though we have reached many Méndez milestones with White House celebrations, a U.S. postage stamp, parades, books, hundreds of presentations, and many, many news articles that seem to show Méndez is indeed on its way into America's collective awareness, why do I go on?

The core truth is this: Through learning the story of a humble yet courageous Mexican-American and Puerto Rican family, as a Latina, I found potential for my future self and a deep-abiding essence for which I didn't even realize I was hungering. The brave families of the Méndez case fought for equality for their children and for all the children because they believed in their inherent worth. For the first time in all my studies of American history, I finally found a story that told me that I, too, was worthy. The Méndez story showed me that I was a card-carrying member of a diverse and powerful community that cared for me and for my future.

These people fought for me before I was even born and delivered with their battle a promising picture of who I could be, too. All the puzzle pieces of my life got thrown up into the air and came back together to reveal a picture of American history where my family and my friends of all different colors made a difference that changed not just their community but our nation. This was the truth. I couldn't blink back the fact that, yes, their concern for my future made me worthy. And when you convince a child, even an adult child, that he or she has worth, you rub the genie from the lamp and spark the essential fuel for all change. And that magic ingredient is hope. Hope is the fuel that gets you up and out of bed every day. Hope is that fuel that allows you to create and pursue dreams and goals. Without hope, you are a ship without oars. Without hope, you have no direction or vision for your life. Without hope, there is no reason to make any personal change.

Méndez revealed to me an America built by diverse communities with care, courage and commitment to equality for us all. It showed me unequivocally that every voice truly matters and that I am not "apart" but rather "an essential part" of American and even world history. And though the past 13 years of my Méndez work have been marked with amazing achievements and nearly soul-crushing disappointments, I understand clearly that this history gave me hope, worthiness and belief in my ability to dream and reach for that dream. It is my biggest dream to see that the lessons of worthiness and hope in the Méndez story may inspire others, especially children, to envision possibilities for themselves that will bring meaning and fulfillment to their lives along with respect and peace for us all.

References

Brown v. Board of Education of Topeka, Kansas, 347 U.G.S. 483 (1954).

Hickox, K. (1997, January 24). Family's Landmark School Battle // Education: The Mendezes Are Honored by the O.C. Education Department for their 1945 Contribution to Civil-Rights Law. *Orange County Register*. Retrieved from http://search.proquest.com/docview/272898210?accountid=10051

Mendez v. Westminster, 161 F. 2d 774 (Ninth Cir. 1947).

5
MY RECOLLECTION OF A FAILED ATTEMPT TO RETURN THE SCHOOLS TO THE PUBLIC

Luis Fuentes

(NARRATED BY ANAIDA COLÓN-MUÑIZ)

I was born in East Harlem's "El Barrio,"[1] where only some of us somehow survived. After a stint with the Marine Corps, I got the G.I. Bill to push me through two teacher training colleges (White schools all, and at a time when no Blacks were allowed). I recall that my family moved out of Spanish Harlem and I spent my teenage years in the Red Hook housing projects of Brooklyn, among Jews, Blacks, Italian, Irish, Poles and Ukrainians, so we were basically all poor, working-class kids.

I relocated and began teaching in Savannah, Georgia, married a White woman there, had four kids, lived a White life (for example, my sons are named George—not Jorge, and Louis—nicknamed Buddy). Racial Georgia had never heard of a Puerto Rican, so they decided that I was Spanish. I just had a good tan, a "red-necked" tan. After Georgia came another teaching job in Miami. Five years later, life went sour. My wife and I split, I went broke, my kids stayed in Georgia and I came home to New York. I got a reading specialist job in the Farmingdale Schools in Long Island. The years down south had left me with a kind of broken, White-bred southern Spanish, but it was not just the language. Fifteen years in the Deep South had changed all that; I lived the double life of racial disguise. I had adopted the lifestyle of the South—talked, ate and acted that way. I saw one entire lifetime come and go as if it were another existence—with bankruptcy and divorce at the same time. This left me a hardened and insulated man, guarded, direct to the point of coarseness.

In July, 1967, the Ocean Hill-Brownsville Demonstration District[2] in Brooklyn—New York's largest borough—was getting underway, and the district needed a Puerto Rican to be the City's first Puerto Rican principal.

> The governing board appointed, over the objections of the UFT [United Federation of Teachers], five new principals: one white, two black, one

> Chinese, and the first Puerto Rican in the city. The Latino principal, Luis Fuentes, struggled to gain the support of the teachers, but, according to the CCHR [New York City Commission on Human Rights], he "quickly gained the respect of the students, parents, and the community." By establishing a rapport with Spanish-speaking parents, the principal served students for whom English was a second language. Parent participation increased dramatically as a result of his efforts.
>
> *(Pritchett, 2002, p. 230)*[3]

I had come forward with an impressive background of 15 years of professional teaching and administrative experience. Parents interviewed me and were impressed, so they hired me. This was the time of so-called *community control*[4] and so a lot was being done at the local district and school levels.

I came into a world I knew little about, a world with great tensions and politics: 1) a New York public school with an assistant principal awaiting his own promotion to principal, only to find that the school got someone who had never waited in their civil service "line" of seniority (me); 2) a teaching staff that had been dragged into an experiment that they did not want; and 3) a student body with a majority Black population, whose parents were sensitive to any programming efforts I might make on behalf of the substantial Puerto Rican minority. In the meantime, I was living in a White, Long Island suburb, and coming into a project that symbolized the rising racial consciousness and pride of Black and Brown people. My career in the New York City (NYC) schools began in the midst of these personal internal changes and the revolution of my own appointment as a principal and what that symbolized—a revolution I did not fully understand at the time.

The Ford Foundation, in a response to a proposal submitted by the NYC Board of Education, the United Federation of Teachers, and a city-wide coalition of parents and community organizations funded three separate experiments for the improvement of the public school in the big City: two bridges in lower Manhattan, Intermediate School (I.S.) 201 in Harlem and its feeder schools; and eight schools in Ocean Hill-Brownsville in Brooklyn (there's no ocean or hill).

Elections were held in each of the schools to select parent leaders (the voter turnout was greater than for the previous presidential election). The union was shocked that parents had gone ahead during the summer and filled the district's leadership position that the union had promised to another employee. That fall the UFT union (United Federation of Teachers) unsuccessfully challenged the parents' principal selection in court. I was in the middle of it all.

The union wanted the parents to support its program, the M.E.S. (More Effective Schools), which merely featured smaller class sizes. The parents had a bigger picture in mind than the size of classrooms. Parents wanted sensitive, culture-conscious and effective teachers, and suspension of city-wide testing, curriculum improvement, parent involvement and up-to-date books. They wanted the right to transfer ineffective teachers who couldn't or wouldn't give the taxpayers their money's worth.

One salient consequence of the experiment was a new bilingual program in the city. This was brought about by the parents of my new school, Public School (P.S.) 155 and the pressure that they put on me as NYC's first school principal of Puerto Rican descent. At first, I was reluctant to embrace the parents' idea, but then I realized that I needed to support them because this was their school and these were their children. I stepped forward.

Parent Action and Consequences

- Parents barred entry to P.S. 155, preventing contractors from getting in. They were upset that contractors had signed on as equal opportunity employers, yet all were White and did not include local workers from the community. The entry denial lasted three days (parents won).
- Teachers and parents joined forces to select books for the math and science areas. One class at each grade level (K–6) was identified as a bilingual class. Student selection to those classes was based on a limited English and parents' request (the school was 60% black, 33% Puerto Ricans, 7% other).
- Parents and teachers joined to develop a bilingual school handbook. Parents and other community personnel volunteered to teach Spanish and English to other parents Friday afternoons. The classes joined hands for social activities following the classes. Classes in art, weaving, sewing and cooking were made available.
- With the ethnic breakdown of the school, attention had to be focused on activities that promoted better human relations. District parents rented a truck and raided the city's bookstore to get books that had been ordered but not delivered by the opening of schools.
- Lunchroom leftovers were not dumped—at the end of the day parents and lunchroom workers cooperated in getting the food and milk to needy homes. The majority or 85% of the students qualified for free lunches. That meant that 15% were open targets for bullies and thugs on their way to school or in the schoolyard. Consequently we gave all lunches out for free.
- The Governing School Board encouraged parent support and the principals were encouraged to put parents' and teachers' ideas to work. They saw the bilingual program extending to the I.S. 55 School and publicity stated that they supported giving "voices" to the children. Reverend Oliver (chair of the board) stated "how does a child learn if instruction is given in a language other than the one he speaks?"

By 1968, some seven months after I became principal at Ocean Hill's P.S. 155, the parents and I had set up the City's first bilingual strand, or "sub school" within the school.[5] It consisted of at least seven full bilingual classes with bilingual teachers and paraprofessionals at every grade level in the school. Although there had been bilingual program experiments in other parts of the country, this was the first attempt in the City of New York as a part of the public schools' efforts to respond to the needs of the local community with regard to language and culture. Admission into the program was the voluntary decision of parents (not a mandate), and soon there were waiting lists for all of the classes. We recruited the paraprofessionals from the community and the teachers from Puerto Rico and the City of New York. The results were impressive, as far as we could tell, with the hiring of more community-based Black and Latino teachers and local non-certificated staff, a multicultural lunch program, and the first bilingual program within a New York City school. But, the Central Office didn't agree.

My recruitment efforts brought me into conflict with the Board of Examiners and their licensing procedures. These months of activity included repeated efforts by the professional teachers and supervisors' unions to overturn my appointment through court action claiming that I had not passed through Board of Examiners procedures. There was a city-wide chasm between the union and the community because Shanker decided to make this into a personal vendetta against me and the other community control advocates in our so-called experimental district. Rather than see it as a response to the community calling for more involvement, a more relevant and higher quality curriculum and a more effective pedagogy by teachers who understood and reflected the community, it was seen as a sort of mutiny within the school system, with us defying the powerful central City Board of Education. In my view, we were doing what we were asked to do in creating more community control by responding to the parents of the children in our school.

This led me to develop a philosophical stance that was revealed in a 1968 published interview. My spring interview was reported by Dr. Annette Rubinstein in her edited book, *Schools Against Children*,[6] where I described my own transformation and the impact that the Puerto Rican parents of that school had on me in Ocean Hill:

> It somehow seemed to me that the parents knew a lot more about what was happening than I did, in spite of the fact that I had been one of the children that they were talking about to me, having suffered the same sort of problems. But, somehow or other, I had removed myself to the extent that, all of a sudden, I became aware of the fact that I was more Anglo than Puerto Rican. In my thinking anyway, because I could never get away from the Puerto Rican label. I don't think that I would ever want to, but I never could anyway.

This interview was done a month and a half prior to the governing board's transfer of my school's pedagogical personnel. Here is an excerpt:

> I was a principal in 1951 in Georgia in a White rural school, and I didn't create any furor there. Here in New York it seems that everything is stacked

up against Luis Fuentes: he's not supposed to be successful, he's not supposed to exist; he's supposed to leave the establishment and their walls just the way they are. But, I have learned enough from working with other groups and with other establishments, too, to feather my nest in a different way. I'm more concerned with making sure that the right kind of jobs open up for us in education, and I have two motivations right now. That's to get as many bilingual teachers into the system as I possibly can, and to elevate as many of them as I can into principalships that are not occupied by Latinos. They're not occupied by Puerto Ricans who continue to constitute 25% of our student population.

Later, in a radio interview around the same time, I cited the following facts: "In this city, with over a million Puerto Rican citizens, there are less than 200 Puerto Rican professional educators of any kind employed by the public school system." I recruited in the *New York Times*, stating that P.S. 155 needed "10 bilingual teachers but that New York City needed 10,000."

By the spring interview, I understood the obstacles to this kind of change. I thought that it simply meant that we had to lift these rigid license requirements and bring in people that are bilingual, be they from Puerto Rico or Cuba, Santo Domino or Mexico, or be they from Project Seek, the factories or the hospitals where they were now working. I continued with my radio interview, "It is here where professional educators are working now, because they have an accent and can't pass an English exam, or because they aren't capable of writing in Dick and Jane sentences. They were told they couldn't be teachers in the system."

An example of this catch-22 is Antonia Pantoja, the founder of ASPIRA, Inc. An educator in Puerto Rico, she came to this country wanting to educate and work with Puerto Rican children. She was denied this opportunity, so she went to Columbia University and studied for a whole year in English, took the exam again and again, and failed. After flunking those two tries at getting a teacher's license in New York City, she returned to Columbia University where she was welcomed as a teacher of teachers. She was good enough to teach teachers, but not good enough to teach the children that she was most familiar with because of the cultural bias and institutionalized barriers inherent in the credentialing system. I could cite at least two dozen cases where individuals have been harassed at the Board of Examiners by questions such as, "Did you graduate from an accredited school?" (referring to the Catholic University of Puerto Rico), or "Are you an American citizen?" Of course, these educated people were not schooled in the fact that Puerto Ricans have been U.S. citizens since 1917. I was infuriated by this and questioned the entire scenario. If this is what our profession was turning into in order to deprive people of doing the job that they are best prepared to do, then we had better stop and look at ourselves.

I urged us to take a good look at the Board of Examiners. I also wanted us to validate that there was really a minority teacher shortage for which they were serious about recruiting, and not just a country club arrangement that permeated this downtown establishment, indiscriminately putting people aside who could communicate, educate and relate to the students in the schools. I urged the coalition of dissatisfied parents to insist on an end to the present teacher/student ethnic mismatch and xenophobia that existed in New York because I knew that the parents were the group that could wage that fight with the Board of Education.

Despite parents' demands, the city forced the experiment to end. To this day the racial, ethnic mismatch of the early '60s still exists, sometimes far exceeding that period's de facto segregation. Many personal sources comment that the schools under Bloomberg and Klein were worse than ever since they ran the city.

In 1972, I went on to become the first Puerto Rican superintendent in the New York City School system for Manhattan's District 1, but that too became a center of untested local power against the status quo. I continued to work towards achieving the goals set out in community control effort, despite the litigation challenges that I faced. I hope that someday, xenophobia will be conquered and that children need not give up their native language to acquire English. After all, two languages at their disposal are superior to having only one language exclusively, and that one being English. This is not to say that we shouldn't also consider how effective our teaching of English is and continue to improve it.

I paid dearly for my activism in New York. I engaged in a court fight that lasted over 20 years, but which I ultimately won. I got my doctorate and went to the University of Massachusetts at Amherst to become the director of their Bilingual Education Professions Program. There, I was better able to fulfill my dream.

I encouraged the credentialing of hundreds of bilingual teachers, psychologists and other education professionals. I oversaw the doctoral program, and chaired numerous dissertation committees. We also had a Title VII program to help fund doctoral students in their quest for higher education. These bilingual professionals have become the source of great contributions in education throughout the state and country, and in my mid-80s, this is an accomplishment of which I am very proud.

Notes

1. El Barrio in East Harlem is a neighborhood in New York City's Upper East Side also known as Spanish Harlem. There, significant numbers of Puerto Ricans and other immigrants settled in the 1930s and 40s. It had its heyday in the 1960s during the civil rights period when the Museo Del Barrio and other organizations were developed to try and address the many socioeconomic and educational issues that surfaced there as a result of poverty, cultural and linguistic mismatches, racism, oppression and high crime. Despite the challenges, there was the desire of a community to maintain a sense of cultural adherence and pride motivated them to engage in positive change for their residents. Many well-known Latin jazz musicians, artists, educators and political activists came from El Barrio.
2. Ocean Hill-Brownsville in Brooklyn was a highly politicized New York City school district during contentious times (1960s). It was formed in 1968 as a response to the

call for Community Control schools and districts. It was considered an experiment that failed because the power went to the local communities rather than the NYC central school board, which later fired teachers and administrators and took the power back, claiming that administrators like Luis Fuentes were violating the authority of the center school district.
3. Pritchett, W. (2002). *Brownsville, Brooklyn: Blacks, Jews, and the Changing Face of the Ghetto* (Historical Studies of Urban America). University of Chicago Press.
4. Community control was not what it seems to be from its name. All of the key funding and major decisions were still centrally controlled by the NYC Board of Education.
5. Podair, Gerald (Spring 1994). "White Values, 'Black' Values: The Ocean Hill-Brownsville Controversy and New York City Culture, 1965–1975." *Radical History Review* (59). Retrieved November 22, 2013.
6. To learn more about Annette Rubinstein see http://brechtforum.org/annette. Retrieved February 14, 2014.

6

THE BC 44, ETHNIC STUDIES, AND TRANSFORMATIVE EDUCATION

Sonia Nieto

"BC 44, we've come back to give you more!" The incessant chant reverberated in my ears as I looked out at the estimated crowd of 2,000 on the Brooklyn College quadrangle. It was April 23, 1974, a brilliant sunny but chilly day, and we had just returned to campus from a night spent sleeping on hard benches in a Brooklyn courthouse after being arrested for disorderly conduct. It was hard to believe that I was one of the "BC 44," an identity foreign to my upbringing and inclination. Yet, my early experiences as the child of working-class Puerto Rican [im]migrants, my training as a teacher, and my work with poor working-class, African-American, and immigrant children during years of great social unrest—all of these experiences serve as the backdrop to how I became one of the BC 44. And as unlikely as it might have seemed at first, they also help explain my social activism in the years to come.

    I certainly hadn't started out as a rebel. In fact, I had always been a "good girl" and a model student. The perpetual teacher's pet, I had loved school and everything associated with it. Compliant and industrious, my goal since childhood had been to attend college and study to become a teacher. Except for two cousins who had recently arrived from Puerto Rico to study at the university, teachers were the only people I met in my early years who had an advanced education. They were my models of education and accomplishment. My parents, arriving in New York City as part of the first wave of Puerto Rican [im]migrants* known as "los pioneros," raised my sister Lydia, my brother Freddy, and me to be "bien educados" in both the Latino sense of politeness and respect, and the American sense of formal education. Although both my parents were "bien educados"—respectful to everyone they met and dignified in their demeanor—neither had much schooling. Mami had gone through third year of high school in Ponce, quite an accomplishment for an orphaned girl from a humble family in the early years of the 20th century, and my father had to leave school in fourth grade to work in the fields and help care for his mother and many siblings after his father died. Papi came to the States in 1929 and immediately began working in a Jewish deli on Delancy Street in Manhattan. Mami came in 1934, a daring act for a single woman of 26, to live with an aunt and work at a candy factory. Each arrived by boat, at the time the only means of transportation from the island to the mainland. They met a few years later, married in 1941, and began building a family.

When I was 13, we moved from our ghetto neighborhood, a place where European immigrants, African-Americans, Puerto Ricans, and other Caribbeans co-existed fairly amicably. I perceived it as a "rich" neighborhood that was in reality barely a working-to-middle-class community of more established second and third generation immigrants, mostly Jewish, with smaller numbers of Irish and Italian Americans, in the same borough of Brooklyn. To me, it seemed a wealthy community because it was the first time I saw not tenement buildings and vacant lots, but private and semi-private homes and actual yards with flowers and shrubs. When we went to see the small two-family house on East 37th Street that would be our first and only home outside of our tenement apartments, I cried. I could not believe we would ever live in such splendor. In reality, though, it was a modest home with two fairly small apartments and a postage-sized backyard where my parents quickly planted tomatoes and other vegetables, as well as beautiful red roses.

It was only when we moved to East 37th Street that I became aware that, although I had been an exemplary student in my former schools, my ghetto education had ill prepared me for the rigors of the middle-class public school education I found in my new junior high school. There, my grades plummeted and I struggled for a couple of years to keep up with my peers. My high school years at Erasmus Hall High School, one of the most highly regarded public schools in the city, were a time of both social alienation and academic advancement. With 5,600 students and a graduating class of 1,500, the school had a handful of African-Americans and only three Puerto Ricans (my sister and I were two of them). At the same time, Erasmus Hall, a school imbued with a great sense of history as the first public school in New York City, was characterized by great academic rigor and implacable standards. I excelled in my studies, eventually making up for most of the gaps in my early education. Even though I felt lonely and socially isolated there, I am enormously grateful for the education I received at Erasmus. It is due to that experience, I am convinced, that I was able to pursue higher education and have the incredibly fulfilling future I would have.

My college education at the Brooklyn campus of St. John's University in New York, where I studied to be an elementary school teacher, followed. It was a commuter college, and Lydia (who graduated from Erasmus Hall a year before me) and I took the subway or city bus every day to our urban Brooklyn campus, an 11-story building with an adjacent library in what had formerly been a small apartment building, and two Quonset huts built during World War II that housed our cafeteria and lockers. It was hardly what would be characterized as a college campus today, but to me, it was heaven. It was the place where I became involved in every campus activity and where I came out of my shell and developed leadership skills to become president of organizations as diverse as the Spanish Club, the International Relations Club, and Delta Kappa Delta, a local sorority. After college, I had my first "going away" college experience when I went to Spain to study for a master's degree in Spanish and Hispanic Literature through New York University's Graduate Program in Madrid. I was there from 1965 to 1966, a year of unparalleled agitation and civil rights activity in the United States, to which I was fairly oblivious both because I was so far away from home and because of the sheltered nature of St. John's University. It had been a conservative place where the struggles around racial justice and civil rights had not really made an impact, and where the ensuing struggles around the Vietnam War had not yet begun.

I began my teaching career in a junior high school in Ocean Hill-Brownsville in Brooklyn in September 1966, right after returning from my year abroad in Spain. The contrast between the two environments could not have been more stark: Spain was still in the throes of what would become a 40-year-long Fascist regime where civil unrest was, for the most part, barely visible, but when it did surface, was harshly dealt with. To those not involved in these struggles, Spain was a quiet, peaceful, and orderly place to live and learn, and as an outsider, that was certainly my experience. On the other hand, New York City was in the midst of a community control movement, a civil rights struggle of huge proportions in urban education, where the United Federation of Teachers (UFT) was pitted against poor ghetto communities of color for control of the public schools. The unfortunate battle between the UFT, composed mainly of Jewish teachers on one side, and the Puerto Rican and African-American activists on the other, became not just a struggle for civil rights, but also an ugly reminder of our troubled ethnic and racial history. It was as a 22-year-old novice teacher that I was thrust into this brouhaha. I was also the only Puerto Rican teacher in the school and, in fact, the only Puerto Rican teacher most of the other staff members had ever met. It was a tumultuous time for me in many ways. I was a new and untested teacher in an environment of chaos and turmoil. I was also heartsick at being separated from Angel, the love of my life whom I had met in Spain during my studies. (This situation was resolved when I went back to Spain during that first Christmas vacation and we decided to get married right there and then.)

Having survived the first two years of teaching in Ocean Hill-Brownsville, I heard about a new school, an experimental bilingual school that was to open in the Bronx. I applied and was hired as a fourth-grade teacher to begin in September 1968. P.S. 25, the first completely bilingual school in the Northeast and only the second in the nation, provided the next chapter of my education as a teacher and a person. The school was one of five in the city (in a system of over 900 schools) to remain open during the teachers' strike of 1968. Solidly in support of parent and community rights, it stood nearly alone in opposition to the strong UFT. Unlike most other schools in the city, over half of my colleagues were Latinos and the rest were Whites or African-Americans—but regardless of ethnic background or race, everyone in the school was bilingual. Bilingualism was also a major goal for the student body, 85 percent of whom were Puerto Rican.

In terms of pedagogy and curriculum, cultural and ethnic pride and academic achievement were key principles that guided our work. Because at the time there were no curriculum guides that focused on Puerto Rican/Latino culture, we had to create our own curriculum and materials. By my third year at P.S. 25, the school had received a federal grant that included funds for curriculum development. I was selected, along with my friend and colleague Herminio Vargas, another fourth-grade teacher, as the two people to fill these positions. For the next two years, we worked hard to create curricula that were culturally relevant, rigorous, and bilingual. Hundreds of educators and community activists from around the country and beyond visited our school, which was at the time one of a handful of totally bilingual schools in the nation.

My education in the four years I was at P.S. 25 consisted of several significant lessons that were to remain with me throughout my career and that still guide my work: I learned that cultural and linguistic differences need not be disregarded but, on the contrary, can serve as a strong foundation for learning; that inequality was ineradicably etched in the history of public education in the United States; that education is always political (Paulo Freire's work, which I did not yet know, would put into words what I was learning); and that, in spite of the inequality that is embedded in our educational system, the role of teachers can be a transformative one for students. Looking back on what I learned at P.S. 25, I realize that all my professional work—my teaching, my research, and the books and articles I have written—has been based on these lessons.

After four years at P.S. 25, my colleague Herminio applied for a faculty position in the Puerto Rican Studies Department at Brooklyn College, and given our close working relationship over the previous four years, he encouraged me to do the same. The Department of Puerto Rican Studies was looking for faculty, he said, to staff a co-sponsored program with the College's School of Education for the preparation of bilingual teachers. Carmen Dinos, a Professor of Education, and the first Puerto Rican faculty member in the College, was instrumental in designing the program. Although I thought the chances were slim that I could get this job—after all, I did not have a doctorate, and my master's degree was in literature—I was excited about the possibility of working in higher education, something that had always been a dream of mine. I was thrilled to be offered the position and thus, at the age of 29, my adventure as a faculty member in ethnic studies, and my most intense political education, began.

The year was 1972, the height of political activity and civil unrest at colleges and universities throughout the nation. New York City had been a particularly active place for student activity, and CUNY (the City University of New York) colleges had been the site of much agitation on the part of Puerto Rican and

African-American students whose demands included ethnic studies programs and the hiring of faculty of color. Just two years earlier, the Puerto Rican Studies Department (PRSD) at Brooklyn College had been created out of this struggle. Headed by Josephine Nieves, a former Associate Assistant Secretary of the Employment and Training Administration of the Labor Department, the PRSD had grown to eight faculty members by the time Herminio and I were hired. Half of us were Nuyoricans, mostly from poor working-class communities, or long-term residents of the United States who had come as fairly young people from Puerto Rico. At the time, Nuyoricans with doctorates were hard to come by, so it was not surprising that most of us did not have a doctoral degree. For the most part, we viewed our work in ethnic studies as an extension of our commitment to the community's larger political struggles. The other half of our faculty were academics from the island, most of whom had been raised middle class, and although all had doctoral degrees, many of them saw their work in ethnic studies as a temporary and short-term stint in the States before returning to the island.

Josephine Nieves exemplified the aspirations and activism of the Nuyorican community. Born and raised in New York City as the daughter of a single mother who worked in a factory, she was a successful student whose studies in higher education culminated in advanced degrees in social work. A well-known community activist, she was a key player in initiating and developing a number of important organizations, such as the Puerto Rican Forum and ASPIRA. Her choice as Chairperson of the Department of Puerto Rican Studies was both a boon for the college (after all, she had been the highest-ranking Puerto Rican in President Lyndon Johnson's administration) and, given her activist past, a reassurance to students who were looking for something other than a typical academic leader removed from the concerns of the community. She saw Puerto Rican and other ethnic studies programs as having to chart a new course, one that would differ from traditional departments in a number of ways. Writing about the roots and challenges of Puerto Rican Studies over a decade letter, she expressed it this way:

> We sought a transformation in the nature of higher education itself. Not only had the university virtually excluded Puerto Rican students and faculty, it had also played a major role in distorting our history, and in so doing had misrepresented the history of the United States as well . . . Its emergence as a new academic area in higher education was not an isolated achievement. Rather, it was connected to the hard won gains of poor and minority communities across the United States, as well as the insurrections of third world peoples, including the movement for Puerto Rican independence.
>
> *(Nieves, 1987, p. 3)*

This was clearly a vastly different image of academia than I had been prepared for, one that changed how I viewed scholarly work, so-called objective research, and the "ivory tower" nature of the university, unsullied by the realities of the outside world. My political education began with my interview, where students and faculty members grilled me for three hours. The interview had as much to do with my training and experience as a bilingual teacher as with my commitment to the community and my views about the situation of Puerto Ricans both on the island and in New York. Everything about the department was imbued with a sense of urgency and struggle. We didn't have faculty meetings; we had "community meetings" in which faculty, staff, and students all had a voice and where decisions about the curriculum, hiring, and governance were discussed, debated, and decided. Meetings went on for hours and every interaction with the administration was viewed with suspicion. Needless to say, given the politics of the time, the department could also be a contentious place where political ideologies clashed with day-to-day realities.

It was within this context that our first major tussle with the administration began. When, toward the end of the 1972–1973 academic year, Josie Nieves declared her decision to leave her position as Department Chair, we quickly embarked on a plan for her replacement. Given the newness of the department, not to mention the scant respect enjoyed by the field of ethnic studies, we were certain that the central administration would want to control the Search Committee, which they did, by appointing three of the five members to a committee not from the Puerto Rican Studies Department, but from the School of Social Science. Nevertheless, although the Search Committee was not housed in our department, as it should have been, two of the members were friends of the department and therefore supportive of our goals. In turn, we appointed two members from the PRSD, and I was selected as one of them. The Search Committee decided on a plan of action, that is, how and where to advertise the position, what qualities we were looking for, how many candidates should be brought to campus, and so on. Meanwhile, in our community meetings, we were making our own plans. We knew that in order to be self-governing, we would need to hire someone who agreed with our goals and commitments. The best person, it seemed to us, was our own María Engracia Sánchez, the senior member of our department and a veteran of the bilingual education movement in New York City.

Having arrived in New York City as a new bride with a freshly minted bachelor's degree from the University of Puerto Rico, for two decades María had worked her way up from a teacher's aide to a supervisor of ESL teachers in the New York City Board of Education. One of her favorite sayings was that Puerto Rican teachers had gone "from SAT to RAT" (Substitute Auxiliary Teachers to Regular Auxiliary Teachers), not a great distance to travel in 20 years. Puerto Rican teachers were nearly invisible among the ranks of the 55,000 New York City public school teachers and María stood out as one of a handful that had advanced to an administrative position. With red hair and piercing green eyes, and nearly 20 years my senior, she was my mentor and role model. While she differed greatly from the young 18- to 21-year-old enthusiastic and sometimes impetuous students, she was nevertheless just as committed and, in her own way, as political, as they were.

She was also wise, and her wisdom was exactly what was needed in a leader for the Puerto Rican Studies Department. She was smart and strategic, as well as dignified and composed with the administration, and she was supportive of the students while also cooling the more hot-tempered among them. Nevertheless, in spite of her wisdom and experience, as far as the administration was concerned, María had several strikes against her: for one, she was an insider whose alliances were already clear and, for another, she did not yet have a doctoral degree, and the administration thought it unseemly that a department chair should not have a doctorate. (Although at the time of her appointment to the PRSD, Josie Nieves also did not have a doctorate, she was highly placed politically, and there was no question that she had the requisite administrative experience to lead the department. She did earn a doctorate a number of years later.)

The faculty and students had already signed a statement declaring our support for María. The Search Committee was not impressed with the other candidates who applied for the position. At the same time, it was clear that not many academics were anxious to apply to head a neophyte, politically active, and sometimes contentious department. While the central administration hoped that the position would attract a number of senior and highly respected academics, the candidates we attracted were for the most part fairly young and inexperienced, and almost all were from Puerto Rico and had little knowledge of the U.S.-based Puerto Rican community. It was not surprising that most of the candidates were from the island because, as mentioned before, at the time there were almost no Puerto Ricans in the continental United States with doctoral degrees. Also, salaries were double or triple those in Puerto Rico, which was very attractive to academics from the island. Thus, it was not unusual for island-based academics to spend a few years in Puerto Rican Studies Departments before returning home. Besides María E. Sánchez, only Elba Lugo, a faculty member in Language and Literature at a small college in Puerto Rico, was invited for an interview. It was clear from the beginning that Lugo was the administration's choice: she had a doctoral degree and she was an outsider who could be more easily controlled by the administration. The stage was set for a major battle.

The adversaries in this battle could not have been more different from one another. On one side, the central administration—President, Provost, Dean of the School of Social Sciences, and most of the established faculty members—were adamant that Brooklyn College remain the premier academic institution it had always been. Nearly tuition-free at the time, the CUNY colleges had been the pride of the city, educating the sons and daughters of both immigrants and more established residents for a century. Although all the four-year colleges in the system were rigorous, Brooklyn College stood out as one of the most difficult to get into, and the college of choice for most of the borough's working- and middle-class students. More than a decade earlier, I had been accepted as a freshman but had chosen instead to attend St. John's University, a private college that I perceived as both smaller and more welcoming. None of my high school classmates could understand how I could pass up a chance to attend the leading institution of higher education in the borough, something akin to rejecting the Harvard of Brooklyn. It was ironic, then, that I should end up at Brooklyn College as a young faculty member in what was by then a place that was changing quite radically in terms of politics and demographics from what it had been just a decade before.

On the other side of the battle lines were the largely Puerto Rican and African-American young people who, prior to 1968, had never seen the inside of the CUNY system. The civil rights and anti-war movements had radicalized these young people. Not only did they demand ethnic studies programs and African-American and Puerto Rican faculty and staff, but they also wanted an end to the Vietnam War, and the eradication of racism and the exploitation of the poor. Many, although not all, had socialist leanings and most were also in favor of Puerto Rican independence. I came into this situation as a young faculty member only slightly older than the students but worlds apart in terms of my sociopolitical understandings. While they had been brought up as teenagers in the highly politicized anti-war, civil rights, and community control movements of the mid-1960s, my teenage years in the 1950s had been quiet and nonpolitical.

Because of student protests in the late 1960s, the CUNY system had embarked on an Open Admissions policy in which any public school student in the city whose grades were adequate could attend one of the CUNY community colleges or four-year colleges. Although at the time there were a million Puerto Ricans living in New York City, the number of Puerto Rican students at CUNY colleges before 1968 had been infinitesimal. Along with Open Admissions came SEEK (Search for Excellence and Education through Knowledge), a counseling and academic support program for students who were underprepared for the rigors of university study. Most SEEK students were Latinos and African-Americans, and they changed the complexion of the college both figuratively and literally. For detractors of the policy, Open Admissions and SEEK were an abomination, an insult to the quality of academic excellence that had always characterized Brooklyn College. Ethnic Studies (at Brooklyn College, these consisted of Africana Studies and Puerto Rican Studies) were viewed in the same way.

By this time it was the fall of 1973 and I had been a faculty member in the Puerto Rican Studies Department for a year. It had been a year of countless meetings and strategy sessions, yet quiet compared to what was to come. We had locked horns with the administration on several issues: the creation and support of a bilingual day-care center, a bilingual program for the College's Spanish-speaking students, and a GED program for Spanish-speaking community residents, among others—and we had already occupied the President's Office at least once. But these were small battles in comparison to the struggle for self-determination of our department. The students, staff, and faculty were getting ready for what we knew would be a major struggle around the search for a new department chair. I had been selected by the department's faculty and students as our representative to the Faculty Senate, a body that consisted overwhelmingly of graying White males.

Not only was I one of the few women in the Faculty Senate, but I was also the only Puerto Rican (although there were a handful of other Latinos) and one of the youngest members of that august body. To say that I felt uncomfortable and alienated in the Faculty Senate is an understatement. I truly felt that I did not belong, although I tried my best to look as if I did.

In order to make our case to the general Brooklyn College community that we should have the right, a right enjoyed by every other department at the College, to select our own chairperson, we took several other actions. First, we asked to be placed on the Faculty Senate agenda and we drew up a statement to be read at the next meeting. As the only representative of the Puerto Rican Studies Department to the Faculty Senate, I was designated to read it. I still remember everything about that day: practicing the statement I was to read until I got it right, deciding what to wear (rather than the more informal jeans and sweater I tended to wear to work, I decided that my red suit seemed more appropriate), my nervousness as I stood there in front of hundreds of my colleagues, and my feeling that surely I must be the youngest person who had ever addressed this body. I no longer have the statement I read but I know it was fairly provocative for such an audience. I read it calmly and unhurriedly, and from the feedback we received from the small number of African-American and Latino faculty members in attendance, it was an important moment in defining our department as not only an academic entity, but a politically and community-oriented one as well.

Things came to a head late in that second year when the administration decided to hire Elba Lugo as the new department chair of the Puerto Rican Studies Department. As a member of the Search Committee, I had met and interviewed her, and she had met with our other faculty members, the students, and staff. Lugo had degrees in language and literature from the University of Puerto Rico and she had been Chair of the Hispanic Studies Department at the College of the Sacred Heart in Puerto Rico. Although highly trained in her field, it was clear to us that she knew little about Puerto Ricans on the mainland and that her "fit" with the field of Puerto Rican Studies was a poor one. In addition, she said that she was unaware of the situation in the Department, claiming she had never been briefed about it by the administration. Yet she was hired, despite the 3–2 vote of the Search Committee in favor of María E. Sánchez, a move that both faculty and students were certain reflected the administration's desire to control the department.

Elba Lugo came to campus to begin her new job on September 5, 1974. When the Dean of the School of Social Sciences, Bruce Birkenhead, brought her to the department so that she could move into her new office in Boylan Hall, they found the door blocked by students, who refused to let them enter. After several attempts, they decided instead to install her in an off-campus office a few blocks from the main campus. There, she held court mostly by herself, although we had a small number of students who served as "spies" and set up meetings with the ostensible purpose of talking with her about their programs of study or particular courses, but who really wanted to see what was happening in that office. In reporting back to us, they confirmed that she had little to do and that, in contrast to the noisy and hectic department office in which María E. Sánchez had been installed by us, Lugo's office was silent and empty. We imagined her there, arranging furniture, dictating memos about insignificant matters to her idle secretary, and staring out the window wondering if and when she would have some real work to do.

After President Kneller named Lugo to the position in spite of the Search Committee's recommendation, we began engaging in more radical actions: we picketed President Kneller's house, which was off campus in a quiet residential neighborhood; we staged numerous demonstrations on the quadrangle and in front of our building, Boylan Hall, in favor of María E. Sánchez's candidacy; we asked to meet with President Kneller and, when our request was refused, we occupied his office and remained there for a day or two until we won a concession to establish a Negotiating Committee and keep the lines of communication open. At the demonstrations, we asked a variety of people to speak—our own students and faculty, as well as sympathetic faculty and students from other departments—and we developed a series of chants, from the irreverent ("Kneller, you liar! We'll set your ass on fire!") to the more strident ("What do we want? Self-determination! When do we want it? NOW!"). We also traveled to hot spots at other universities around the city to support similar struggles. In fact, we used to joke that we could start a new business, "Rent-a-Demo," by simply loading our cars with bullhorns, poster paper, and markers. We had become veteran demonstrators.

I had been selected by the department to be a member of the Negotiating Committee, as was my colleague Tony Nadal, along with a couple of students and a faculty member from another department sympathetic to our cause. The administration, meanwhile, was involved in attempts to improve the public image of Brooklyn College, an image that had been sorely damaged by the negative publicity surrounding the entire incident of selecting a new chairperson for our department. Due to the numerous demonstrations and takeovers of the past year, representatives from the local New York City media—radio, television, and press—were frequently on campus. Needless to say, the administration had, as President Kneller mentioned at one of the Negotiating Committee meetings, "a PR problem." I remember saying, "Yes, it's a PR problem in both senses of the word!" and this provided one of the few laughs we could all share.

In addition to press releases from the college's point of view on what was happening in Puerto Rican Studies, the administration invited a highly respected group of Puerto Rican leaders to meet with them to help resolve the stalemate. Included among the group were the leaders of the preeminent Puerto Rican organizations and agencies in the city, as well as faculty from other universities. The administration also invited a representative from the federal Department of Justice to campus. Neither of these initiatives was successful, partly because we felt that the issue was a local one that needed a local solution, but primarily because there was little trust for outsiders, even for the Puerto Ricans among them. This was, after all, a time in which the saying "never trust anyone over 30" was in vogue, and both the Puerto Rican intelligentsia and the Justice Department were suspect because, to us, they represented old interests and old-fashioned ways of doing things. (I had just turned 30 myself, and although I was an insider, I imagined that I too might be in that questionable group to some degree.)

My own development paralleled that of the movement in general. Ever the Libra (my zodiac sign), I had been the peacemaker for as long I could remember. My character tended toward, and does to this day, the conciliatory more than the confrontational, and as a result, my personal inclinations were being severely tested. Although I would have favored working with the Puerto Rican elders, for example, I was clearly outvoted. It has always seemed ironic to me that the administration and, later, the court after we were arrested, placed culpability for "corrupting" the students on the shoulders of the faculty, but it was actually the other way around. A group of highly politicized students, along with Richie Perez, the most radical faculty member among us who had been a member of the Young Lords, ran the show. So, as I learned to be an activist, I also was brought along by the momentum, not always comfortably. I will always, however, value my experience at Brooklyn College because it helped shape who I am today.

In the midst of all the agitation and activism, education, both formal and informal, was taking place. Our courses were interdisciplinary in nature, straddling such disciplines as history, political science, economics, literature, sociology, the arts, and education. The classes themselves were energizing, even thrilling, because they were about us and our people, a unique experience for most of us. Students of all backgrounds were being educated through the courses. Although most of our students were Puerto Rican, we also had a good number of African-American and White students in our courses, and they learned a far different history than they had learned up to that point, one that included the experiences and perspectives of a previously invisible group. Faculty as well were learning a great deal. In preparing my courses, for example, I learned more of the history of Puerto Ricans both in Puerto Rico and in the United States than I had ever learned in school, or even at home. I learned how to develop course syllabi, how to search for creditable resources, and how to present information in ways that were engaging and that differed from the "chalk and talk" methods that many of us criticized. Non-classroom activities provided rich educational experiences as well, whether through our many meetings, writing press releases, strategizing our next actions, or learning how higher education worked. It was one of the most exhilarating times of my life.

Just as I had learned many things at P.S. 25, at Brooklyn College I learned valuable lessons as well. I learned, for example, to communicate persuasively to a large group, a skill that would serve me well in the years to come. Prior to my time there, I had never spoken before a group larger than a couple of dozen people, but on the Brooklyn College quadrangle, I addressed crowds of up to 2,000. I also learned that activism is necessary to confront social injustice and that, in the words of Frederick Douglass that we frequently repeated, "Power concedes nothing without a demand; it never has and it never will." Before this, I had not really thought much about power, but had only a vague understanding that most of life's decisions were made by others outside ourselves. I also learned that activism can take many forms, from petitions to takeovers, and from meetings to demonstrations. Although I was most comfortable with legal and socially sanctioned actions, I also learned that sometimes we need to work outside these more acceptable forms. Most of all, I learned to have courage.

Our final and most drastic action came about in my third year at Brooklyn College after Elba Lugo had been installed in her office for several months and there seemed to be no way out of the impasse. We started up with demonstrations and protests as soon as the fall 1974 semester started, but there was still no progress. On Friday, October 18, 1974 we took over the office of President Kneller, who was not on campus but sent word that he would meet with us the following Monday. That meeting failed to take place because Kneller refused to remove the security personnel and city policemen guarding his office (no doubt because of our previous takeover of his office the year before). As a result, we marched to the Registrar's Office, actually a suite of offices just down the hall from our departmental office and occupied it. We asked all the workers inside to leave, and setting up our "control center" in the largest office, we filled the offices with scores of students, faculty, and staff members. Outside the offices, a constant stream of supporters, mostly students, but others as well—including my husband Angel, the poet of the movement (see his poem, "El Arresto de los BC 44" at the end of this essay), and our 3-year-old daughter Alicia—demonstrated and chanted.

We worked hard to develop a multi-racial and multi-ethnic coalition by attracting students and faculty outside of ethnic studies to our cause. By this time, the demonstrations in the quad were an almost daily event, and our chant, "Blacks, Latins, Asians, Whites, for our rights we will fight!" reflected our broad alliances. Our on-campus supporters included numerous organizations (the Alumni Association, the Veterans' Organization, the Young Socialist Alliance, the Jewish Student Union, and the Student Assembly, among others), and these groups formed a Committee for Student Rights to manage the campus-wide activities of support. Ron Harrington, the President of Student Government, said that the issue was bigger than Elba Lugo and María Sanchez, and that it even went beyond ethnic studies. He said, "It's a matter of who runs Brooklyn College . . . does it exist for students and community, or for the personal empire of the administrator? This is only the beginning" (Newmark, 1974, p. 1). The editorial of the October 25, 1974 edition of *Kingsman*, the campus newspaper, expressed wholehearted support for the Department and for those arrested, mostly couched in terms of students' rights. It read, in part:

> Well, Kneller has really done it this time. No matter what the outcome of this affair is he has severely strained the already delicate relationship that now exists between himself and the students . . . We can't help but be bewildered

by Kneller's decision in this case. After all, the administration did appoint this search committee (which, incidentally had no student members), so why won't Kneller abide by its decision? To those arrested in the Thursday morning bust, we can only applaud your restraint throughout this highly emotional issue.

In addition, Lawrence Hyman, who was the grievance counselor of the Brooklyn College chapter of the Professional Staff Congress, a union representing most faculty members on campus, filed a grievance against Kneller on behalf of the Puerto Rican Studies Department.

Our off-campus supporters made their way to campus by subway, bus, and car, bringing food, blankets, and other provisions. There were dozens of community people, both Puerto Rican and non-Puerto Rican, who believed in our cause. A particularly memorable supporter was a Jewish woman in her 60s, an activist who had participated in many political struggles from the 1940s to the present, and who came to every demonstration, always standing right in front. The press was also there, and every evening we would watch the news on a television set brought into the Registrar's Office to see what was being said about us.

We stayed in the Registrar's Office for four days, taking turns to go home, shower, change and, on occasion, sleep. The days that we were in the Registrar's Office were eventful and chaotic, but at the same time extraordinarily organized. We held strategy sessions, composed press releases, cooked, cleaned, and even ironed. We wanted our takeover to be different from others that were taking place at around the same time in the city and the nation. We defined it as a "Puerto Rican style" takeover, characterized by working-class sensibilities, not the typical takeover that we defined as led by spoiled middle-class kids, the case in more privileged colleges and universities. For example, rather than trash the records in the Registrar's Office, as had happened in places such as Columbia University, we left the office in impeccable shape; even the newspapers commented that we left it better than we had found it. Professor Samuel Abrahamsen, of the Judaic Studies Department and Chairman of the Committee of Concerned Faculty, was invited to inspect the offices and after his visit said, "All equipment and all files are intact, and the Registrar's Office can be restored to its previous good shape in the matter of a half hour" (Newmark, 1974, p. 1).

The iron and the broom were our constant companions. Being primarily from poor and working-class families, the students knew that personal hygiene and appearance were a necessity, not an option. They refused to wear disheveled clothes, insisting on ironing even their jeans. We swept the floors daily and continually wiped down desks and filing cabinets. In spite of our organization, after a couple of days, the lack of sleep and the shared close quarters were hard to take.

We knew arrests were imminent. We organized for this as well, deciding who would be arrested, who would act as spokespersons for those inside and outside, and what actions to take after the arrests. My colleagues Tony Nadal and

Herminio Vargas and I agreed to be the faculty members arrested, along with 41 students, hence the name "BC 44." After three days, the administration sent word that they could no longer tolerate our occupation of the Registrar's Office and that the police would be called and arrests would be made. Twenty deputy sheriffs, accompanied by 25 armed police officers, arrested us at 4:30 a.m. on Thursday, October 24, 1974 (Newmark, 1974). As each of us exited the Registrar's Office, we raised our fists in defiance. The photo of me with my fist in the air made the first page of the *Kingsman* the following day.

We spent the night in a Brooklyn courthouse, sleeping on hard benches, as we waited for the judge to arrive. Geraldo Rivera, a lawyer long before he became a television celebrity, took an initial interest in our case, but it was Luis de Graf who became our attorney of record and represented us in court. De Graf, who passed away in 2007, subsequently had a distinguished career at the CUNY Law School for over 20 years. His involvement in the PRSD struggle was a major reason why the 2007 CUNY Law School commencement was dedicated to him, and Tony Nadal, one of the BC 44, delivered a moving eulogy at the event.

Although the judge who heard the case was quite stern, rather than send us to jail, he released us on our own recognizance, giving us 60-day suspended sentences. Little did we know that on the morning of our arrest, Ron Harrington, the BC Student Government President, had called for a massive student demonstration and boycott of classes to support the 200 students and faculty who had occupied the Registrar's Office and the 44 who had been arrested. We made our way back to campus, arriving before noon, not really knowing what to expect. We were greeted by a loud and raucous crowd of 2,000 supporters chanting "Sánchez, sí, Lugo, no!" to which we responded, just as loudly, "BC 44, we've come back to give you more!" The assembled crowd represented a vindication of our two years of struggle.

Although our struggle was not yet over, that day was the turning point for us. After this, it became clear that the administration's support of Elba Lugo was untenable because, as department chair in name only, she had been collecting a hefty salary for several months while doing nothing. More significant, we had succeeded in bringing to a halt the administration's plans to control the department and our chants of "Self-determination!" became a reality. Soon after our arrests, María E. Sánchez was named Acting Chair and, in 1976, she was appointed Chair of the Puerto Rican Studies Department, a position she held with distinction until 1989 when she retired. Several years after assuming the position, she successfully completed her doctoral degree. Through her skillful leadership, the department went from being a stepchild of the college to being a solidly respected academic program well integrated into the life of the academy. María was succeeded by Virginia Sánchez-Korrol, a renowned historian, and later, by Tony Nadal, one of the BC 44 and a long-time scholar of Puerto Rican Studies who remains Department Chair as of this writing. In the meantime, in recognition of the growing diversity within the Latino community in New York City, several years ago the department was renamed the Department of Puerto Rican and Latino Studies.

Thanks to subsequent hires in the following years, the Department of Puerto Rican and Latino Studies became known not only for its activism and community connections, but also for its scholarship and research. Nevertheless, without its beginnings through activism and struggle, this metamorphosis would not have been possible. In a book chapter written about a decade after this momentous struggle, María E. Sánchez and Antonio (Tony) Nadal reflected on the development of Puerto Rican Studies Departments:

> During the early years of their existence, these programs pioneered in the creation of a new interdisciplinary field of study and succeeded in representing the interests of a community of students, faculty, and alumni. In the process, these departments also struggled for autonomy, internal consolidation, and the elaboration of a philosophy and direction that grew out of this praxis.
>
> *(Sánchez & Nadal, 1987, p. x)*

In the same book, however, Josephine Nieves, the first chairperson of the Puerto Rican Studies Department, sounded a cautionary note about the development of the field:

> the institutionalization of Puerto Rican Studies has been both a victory and a defeat. A victory because we affirmed our right to space within the university, where our intellectual work can focus on the needs and concerns of our community. A defeat, because the very struggle for survival, while making us strong, also dissipated energies on goals that were short-term and disconnected to our primary purpose. The search for permanency and legitimacy reflected in the fight for faculty lines, tenure, and academic jurisdiction, tended to become ends in themselves rather than mechanisms to accomplish our objectives of autonomy, an alternate methodology, and ties to the community.
>
> *(Nieves, 1987, p. 8)*

As a result of institutionalization, bureaucratization, and the growing elitism in the programs, she was concerned that if Puerto Rican Studies forgot its roots in struggle and activism, it would differ little from more traditional academic programs. This is an important lesson for all of us who participated in the Latino civil rights movement, as well as for young people who benefited from those struggles.

And that is the story of how I came to be one of the BC 44. But the story is much more than a personal odyssey; it is most of all a chapter about the struggle that led to the establishment of ethnic studies departments at CUNY and throughout the nation. The times were ripe for social activism and change, and without this climate, advances in the education of marginalized Latino and African-American students would never have taken place. Just as important, the nature of the academy began to change, slowly but perceptibly, as previously marginalized content became core subject matter in colleges and universities around the country. For my part, this experience brought me a greater political clarity and a renewed commitment to social justice in my chosen field, education, a commitment that I have maintained to this day.

Acknowledgments

I am indebted to Professor and Department Chair of Puerto Rican and Latino Studies Tony Nadal, Dean of Students Milga Morales Nadal, and Deborah Norat, all of whom were active participants in the BC struggles of 1972–1975 and who read an earlier version of this chapter and helped fill in the blanks of my memory.

Note

* Roberto Marquez (1995) coined the term "[im]migrant" to reflect the unique status of Puerto Ricans who are neither migrants (those who migrate from one geographic region to another in the same political area) nor immigrants (who leave one nation state for another). As a territory controlled by the United States, Puerto Ricans, whether born in the continental United States, or in Puerto Rico, have been U.S. citizens since 1917.

References

Marquez, R. (1995). Sojourners, settlers, castaways, and creators: A recollection of Puerto Rico past and Puerto Ricans present. *Massachusetts Review, 36* (1), 94–118.
Newmark, I. (1974). Strike demanded by campus leaders, *Kingsman, 49* (6), 1.
Nieves, J. (1987). Puerto Rican studies: Roots and challenges. In M. E. Sánchez & A. M. Stevens-Arroyo (Eds.), *Toward a renaissance of Puerto Rican studies: Ethnic and area studies in university education* (pp. 3–12). Boulder, CO: Social Science Monographs and Highland Lakes, NJ: Atlantic Research and Publications, Inc.
Sánchez, M. E. & Nadal, A. (1987). Preface. In M. E. Sánchez & A. M. Stevens-Arroyo (Eds.), *Toward a renaissance of Puerto Rican studies: Ethnic and area studies in university education* (pp. ix-x). Boulder, CO: Social Science Monographs and Highland Lakes, NJ: Atlantic Research and Publications, Inc.

7

MEMOIRS OF EL CENTRO

The Impact of the Civil Rights Movement in Higher Education

Pedro Pedraza

Introduction

Although there were some Puerto Ricans in New York City in the 19th century it was not until the early 20th that a community was established: one in East Harlem (El Barrio) and another in Williamsburg, Brooklyn (known as *Los Sures*). In the 1940s the insular government of Puerto Rico instituted *"Manos a la Obra,"* a program to industrialize the Island. The program included the planned migration of a significant part of the labor force to the United States. As a result, these communities and others, now newly established throughout the city, experienced significant population growth. Migrants were drawn to an economy that still required cheap labor for manufacturing and services.

By the late 1960s problems accrued that had a devastating effect on the standard of living and, therefore, the well-being of the community. Low school completion rates, high incarceration rates, sub-standard housing, high unemployment and under-employment, all in concentration, with low political representation, had taken a heavy toll. While the inadequate health services and biased housing practices and criminal justice infrastructure of the city were wreaking havoc, the civil rights movement began to open up educational venues of upward social mobility.

In 1969, the City University of New York (CUNY), the fourth largest public university system in the country, embarked on a bold experiment when it instituted an "Open Admissions" Policy. Depending on grade point average (GPA) and/or test scores, students graduating from New York City's public school system were guaranteed a seat in any of CUNY's eight 4-year or ten 2-year colleges. This, along with CUNY's tradition of free tuition since the opening of its first campus, The Free Academy, in 1847 to provide access to higher education for the general public, resulted in a tremendous increase of enrollment of Puerto Rican students.

By 1971, there were more Puerto Rican students in the CUNY system than on the mainstay Rio Piedras campus of the University of Puerto Rico.

Equal access, however, did not equate to equal treatment. Along with other minority students, Puerto Ricans were soon protesting the lack of curricula that reflected their experiences, history, and culture. They demanded the creation of Puerto Rican Studies programs, and on the campus of Lehman College, they fought for the establishment of a research center focused on the U.S. Puerto Rican experience to fill the void that courses focused on the Island colony did not cover.

With the mobilization of many Puerto Rican professional, civic, political, and grassroots supporters, the students opened new academic programs in the CUNY system. By 1973, there were seven Puerto Rican Studies programs on different CUNY campuses. That same year, supported by a grant from the Ford Foundation and a commitment from the CUNY Board of Trustees (to win that initial five-year grant), El Centro de Estudios Puertorriqueños was established at CUNY.

The Beginning of El Centro

Although I was not part of the group that proposed and wrote the original proposal establishing the Centro, I became one of its original staff members shortly after its foundation in 1973. After having served 38 years as a research director, I retired in 2011. This essay is a partial personal account of how this institution came to be, and it is to a large extent also a story about my experiences and commitment to the struggle for social justice.

I actually found out about the Centro's existence by accident. One day in December 1972, I encountered Dr. Frank Bonilla, the founding director, in CUNY's Central Offices, then the Board of Higher Education [BHE]. During that year, I was employed as a research assistant in a study of the Open Admissions program conducted by Dr. David Lavin, a sociologist and one of my professors at Columbia University. I went to a CUNY central office to retrieve a paycheck that I was told had been belatedly issued for accrued time. At that point, I was employed as an instructor in Sociology at the Borough of Manhattan Community College (BMCC) and Frank was working temporarily from a desk out in a foyer area, having recently started as the director of a newly established Puerto Rican research institute, El Centro de Estudios Puertorriqueños (the Centro).

I knew Frank from an effort to create a Puerto Rican/Latino institute at Columbia University initiated by the Latin American Students Association (LASA) and the Puerto Rican Students Union (PRSU) in 1970. I had been a member of PRSU and had participated in founding a chapter of the organization at Columbia University a year before this initiative. PRSU itself started as a mass organization of the Young Lords (a radical community organization). When I joined PRSU, it had just opened a storefront at 138th Street and Brook Avenue in the heart of the South Bronx. Shortly after this opening it became independent of the Young Lords, an autonomy that was mutually agreed upon. One of PRSU's initiatives was to create a citywide Puerto Rican student organization composed of chapters at CUNY and private universities. The Columbia PRSU group joined with LASA in this effort, and as part of that initiative organized a potential board of directors. Frank was recruited from California, where he was teaching at Stanford, to serve as a board member and in this process, I got to know him.

In this chance encounter at the BHE, I told Frank about my interest in language issues. Frank explained to me that the Centro's governing board had decided to make language one of the areas of research and urged me to apply for a position at this new research institute.

The governing board, known as "la Directiva" was made up of members of the coalition that saw the Centro through from conception to implementation. It included students, community activists, organizers, progressive academics, and practitioners in various fields of social service, etc. The whole original research agenda of the Centro was developed by this board. This research agenda focused on certain issues that emerged as areas of concern due to the precarious position and condition of the community. To work on these problem areas five task forces were organized: 1) Puerto Rican ethnic studies—later to become higher education; 2) history of the Puerto Rican migration; 3) the criminal justice system and prisons; 4) culture in popular expression, visual and performing arts, and literature; and 5) language policy—the task force I coordinated in my position as a research director. We eventually dropped the area of criminal justice, and upon entering the 21st century, phased out the task force organizational structure of the Centro altogether. In my view, limited resources and an overly ambitious agenda had a profound impact on the development of the institution, especially with the demanding work involved in the participatory research approach we took.

The Centro was founded on the premise that the whole knowledge production endeavor needed to be carried out with the participation of the larger Puerto Rican community. Furthermore, in the actual implementation of this research agenda, the perspectives, knowledge, and experiences of community members (especially practitioners) needed to be integrated into the process of inquiry. The Centro's original concept to utilize the dialectic between theory and practice was principally aimed at bringing about progressive social change for improving the living conditions of a community and not simply to further academic careers and/or disciplinary advancement.

Using a Marxist Framework

The Centro's goal from its beginnings was to produce knowledge to both fill in gaps and correct misaligned, dubious, and harmful understandings, principally from a community perspective. A Marxist analytical framework was used to focus on the working class socioeconomic position of the U.S. mainland community. Politically, the Centro was unapologetically oriented towards self-determination and at that time favored an independence status for Puerto Rico.

In the actual research process, collective practices and principles were privileged and emulated to the best of our abilities, even though these were frequently at odds with a higher education institution that functioned on a totally different paradigm. This collective approach extended not only to writing, data gathering, analytical methods, literature searches, and decision making, but even to the sharing of less glamorous tasks such as clerical duties. In practice, this meant, for example, that I spent half a day per week relieving a member of the administrative unit from their clerical duties and half a day answering phone calls so that they could participate in academic activities.

Centro-wide there was a governing steering committee made of representatives of all sectors of the organization: administration, library, public service/relations, and researchers. The steering committee was responsible for policy directing and integrating all our efforts. Decisions were based on consensus. I also served on the steering committee (for over 30 years), participated in weekly staff meetings, and organized and directed my own task force, the Language Policy Task Force (LPTF), which included staff members and community representatives.

Initially, individual desks were not even assigned to avoid spatial relationships that reflected hierarchy. This was grounded in the idea that avoidance of hierarchical relationships in work practices, including space allocation, would make for a much more open knowledge production process and that the results of these equalitarian working relationships would be positively reflected in our final products. This particular practice, however, was quickly abandoned due to the impracticality of the logistical arrangements needed to implement the idea.

Reframing Scholarship Production

In order to recognize the whole collective process of knowledge creation, (and not just the individuals who did the actual writing) publications were only identified by task force and not by individual researchers. This practice was eventually modified in response to the reality of the academy's criteria for the role of authorship in evaluations. In our publication procedures we followed a rigorous review process. The process entailed first a task force review and then a Centro-wide review committee made up of staff members from other task forces. This was a prerequisite for approving the release of any manuscript either as part of a task force's working paper series or any outside publication outlet. The purpose of this arrangement was to have all Centro members appraise each other's work to keep the language accessible for a wider audience (especially community), and, finally, to help maintain a sense of cohesion to our collective effort in relation to our mission.

To ensure a minimal common understanding of the Centro's mission and work we instituted staff-wide study known as political education (PE). These were collective study sessions in which all staff as participants were engaged in the discussions of history, theory, ideology, politics, and current events. As noted, an openness, or commitment, to the principle of self-determination at the national and local level was expected from each and every member of the collective.

Challenges of the Structure

Although they reflected our ideological commitment to equality, our attempts to embody egalitarian relationships across the organization often conflicted with the institutional and societal context in which we found ourselves. A good example of this tension was the issue of salary differences, over which we had very little control, since the University had job categories and pay scales fixed by contract and state regulations.

In an attempt to rectify this situation somewhat, a policy was agreed upon with the expectation that those in the relatively privileged position to earn extra income (such as honoraria) from University or Centro-related activities would donate those earnings to a Centro Staff Fund. This policy, it was also reasoned, would serve to eliminate, or at least minimize, the practice of entrepreneurial utilization of academic privilege. Frank on his part, for example, being the only staff person with an academic faculty appointment, earned a summer salary that he then donated to the staff fund to match our 11-month salary remuneration.

The Centro's Staff Fund was used to respond to requests that came from community groups and organizations which could not be attended to with our regular resources, for example, space, stationary, mailings, etc. As time passed by, we again found ourselves making adjustments to this policy. For example, those who earned the extra money that was to be donated to the fund were later expected to keep some of it to cover taxes and non-reimbursed expenses. The fund's use was also expanded to provide small loans to staff members for emergency purposes.

These types of contradictions often thwarted much of our intentions and required many adjustments for practical/functional reasons. Nonetheless, the need to reaffirm and support as much as possible the "collective" aspect of our organization, both in practice and spirit, was viewed as an essential ingredient to enhance our radical political/ideological stance of liberatory knowledge production for social justice.

In sum, we started to implement our research agenda armed with the scientific methodology of dialectical historical materialism (Marxism), the goal of producing knowledge for the benefit of and use by our community, and the cultivation of an organizational infrastructure and culture (or ideology) to facilitate that mission.

In order to not let our investigative efforts threaten our collective cohesion, we also encouraged research staff to be involved in at least one other area of work, or to develop interdisciplinary projects with members of other task forces or community organizations. For example, I became interested in the work of the culture task force. Thus, via some academic networks outside the Centro, I was able to support that task force's work by obtaining a grant from the Smithsonian Institution to hold a folk arts festival. It was to commemorate (ironically) the U.S.

bicentennial. We made of this an all-day event celebrating our traditional popular culture with community performers in theatre, music, poetry, and dance, celebrating our performing arts heritage and cultural resources.

On another occasion I participated in a visual arts/history project where artists of Taller Boricua produced the Portafolio Proletariado with the Centro's collaboration. This was a portfolio of illustrious leaders of the Puerto Rican working class, feminists, and union movements. The portraits were all silkscreen representations. I came to learn our practitioners were considered among the best in Latin America. I assisted in the actual production and printing process, which was regarded by my artistic colleagues as a non-artistic contribution in the spirit of collaboration.

The Language Policy Task Force

Like other candidates for Centro's positions, I was interviewed by a mixed group of students, activists, and academics, who decided to offer me a position to lead the Language Policy Task Force (LPTF). Since I was about to begin my second semester teaching at BMCC, I could not start immediately. However, I was actually an anomaly to the Centro design. The organizational arrangement of each task force consisted of a committee of community stakeholders, which established the research agenda and directed the investigations of a senior researcher, who in turn had a research assistant under his direction. When hired to direct the Language Policy Task Force (LPTF) in the early 70s, I was neither a research assistant nor a full-fledged seasoned academician, but a doctoral student. The Centro staff understood, however, that part of its responsibility was to provide young scholars and other members of the community the opportunity to develop their skills through study and praxis. Indeed, our motto was "Luchar es Aprender, Aprender es Luchar."

The Struggle for Language Rights

This was a time when bilingual education was gaining a foothold as an instructional remedy for the failure of the school system to educate language minority students and I had some evaluative research experience with these programs. There were Title VII funded bilingual ("experimental") programs in the Bronx and East Harlem. Besides, as part of the "National question" the language question was hotly debated within the Puerto Rican left, namely the independence and radical movements, in which I had participated. It was a time, where the "true" identity of the New York-based Puerto Rican socio-historical-cultural formation we called a community, now entering into a third and fourth generation, was called into question.

Concurrently, in the LPTF committee of the Centro *Directiva*, educational concerns and language/identity issues were emerging as the questions to be asked, therefore directing the research to address sociopolitical areas that also had educational implications. In the group, there were folks who came from East Harlem and who offered their assistance if we made "El Barrio" our unit of analysis. Along with "Los Sures" in Brooklyn, East Harlem contained one of the oldest (established in the late 19th century) Puerto Rican communities in the city, and at the time it was still one of the largest, most homogeneous, and clearly geographically defined communities.

In addition, as a result of the now famous School Wars of the late 1960s with the decentralization of the New York City school system, East Harlem came to encompass school district #4, after a protracted struggle to create the district took place. In 1972, after the second round of school board elections, the first school district ever in the history of the city, and probably the nation, that was controlled by Puerto Ricans came into being. This Puerto Rican-controlled school board knew they had to take dramatic action to improve the academic outcomes of the schools. Their first order of business was the search for and appointment of a new superintendent attuned to its objective for the improvement of academic outcomes.

In 1969, while still a graduate student at Columbia, I was able to get a part-time job with Mobicentrics, a Puerto Rican-owned company that had obtained a federal contract to evaluate Title VII bilingual programs in the Bronx, N.Y. I got to spend a lot of time at The Rafael Hernandez Bilingual Mini-school on Jerome Avenue, where I developed a good relationship with the principal Anthony Alvarado. I was impressed with Alvarado's leadership as an educator and decided to recommend him for the position of superintendent of District 4 years later by introducing him to board member Margarita Lopez. After interviewing him, she arranged an interview with the full board, who appointed him. As a new superintendent, one of Alvarado's first actions was to institute district-wide reading and math programs. Shortly thereafter, circa 1975, District 4's school board passed a vote to make it one of the city's first bilingual districts. The LPTF produced its first publication: "A Language Policy for Puerto Ricans in the U.S."[1] Alvarado asked me to condense our findings into one page so that he could use it to get as close to a unanimous vote on the school board declaring a bilingual policy for the district and so that he could go after more Title VII funds (the district had two programs that time).

At the Centro we also produced a step-by-step community guide to help Puerto Rican communities steer through the maze that a lawsuit for bilingual education against any school district would entail. We had realized the need for such a guide after our experience with the ASPIRA consent decree. The lawsuit against the New York City School system had been initiated by the Puerto Rican Legal Defense and Education Fund (PRLDEF) on behalf of ASPIRA Inc., seeking appropriate educational services to non-English-speaking Puerto Rican students. At a crucial point in the case, the Board of Education lawyers showed a willingness to end the litigation with a consent decree (an admission of fault and responsibility without the guilt). The judge seized the opportunity to end the case and instructed ASPIRA to come in the next day with a plan of exactly what ASPIRA wanted the school system to implement.

The director of ASPIRA, Mario Anglada, called on Frank and other academics such as Sylvia Rivera, a psychologist, and Rafael Ramirez, an anthropologist (both from Puerto Rico), to assist ASPIRA in completing this task. Frank asked me to participate. We were put up in a downtown hotel, where we worked all night long to design a plan of action for the NYC Board of Education to address the needs of who today are called English Language Learners (ELL) students.

We tried to get ASPIRA's lawyers, Richard Hiller and Herbert Teitelbaum from PRLDEF, to endorse a language maintenance program policy. In other words, we proposed that instruction in Spanish should continue beyond the acquisition of English, with literacy in both languages as the goal. We argued that eventually foreign language competence would be a requirement for high school graduation and college admission. I argued even further that the proposed policy was not a true language maintenance policy unless it was made available to any Puerto Rican student regardless of their level of competence in English. Only then it would be an instrument for maintaining Spanish as the vernacular of their community if they desired—the same as it is in their homeland. This was all within their rights as U.S. citizens in either locale, particularly since the U.S. Constitution does not recognize a declared official language with special exclusionary privileges.

The lawyers would have no part of an effort to expand the concept or definition of the education right recognized in the Lau Supreme Court decision (1974), requiring that instruction in public education should be in a language comprehensible to students. According to the lawyers, this was an equal treatment under law violation; an individual right, not a group right, which wasn't being recognized by the schools and which was protected under the Constitution. I argued that this separation from the social-cultural context for any individual U.S. citizen (in terms of his/her well-being) was bogus. The lawyers feared losing the case. They countered that settling for the surer, tried and true, more restricted approach would at least gain some remedial action for a greater number of students. In the end their counsel prevailed and ASPIRA opted for a transitional bilingual education policy in fear of no policy change at all.

Engaging in Community Research

By the second or third year of our work, the LPTF's advisory committee started suggesting, and then requesting, that we initiate some studies to help unravel and address the more essential, complex questions related to our sociocultural existence, that is, our identity. Specifically, they requested the LPTF to carry out empirical studies to find evidence about the little understood phenomena called Spanglish—the use of Spanish and English spoken in the community as well as the mixing of the two—which was used to stereotype members of the community.

By then, we had initiated a small study of children in a first grade bilingual classroom looking into their English acquisition by strapping small recorders with microphones onto them, while we observed them during various activities. We discovered and noted some very interesting patterns among Spanish-dominant children. Namely, we noted that in their egocentric speech, especially during play time, they would use a lot more English than they would in actual social interaction. This demonstrated to us the importance of play and the use of the imagination for the language acquisition of young children. This confirmed Vygotskyian[2] ideas about egocentric speech as a social phenomenon and its role in relation to thought and child development. It seems that this egocentric play for the children was a safe place to try new forms of expression before taking the leap into using their new skills in the unimagined world. Although the teacher found these observations useful for understanding her pupils' language development we never published these initial explorations. However, they primed us for the larger, more complex, empirical studies being called for by our constituents.

Then, the LPTF embarked upon what became a series of sociolinguistic, ethnographic, and attitudinal studies of everyday language use in a regular block/neighborhood in East Harlem. We traced out the social networks through which daily life in El Barrio was actuated. We documented the language use in different contexts, recorded actual performance in these settings, and asked community members about their beliefs and thoughts concerning who they were and their daily practices. We did the first study with an adult and adolescent sample and then with a children's sample over the course of three years. We continued with a second look at our data to utilize its richness for analysis that we did not attempt in our first studies. We mainly used content analysis and discourse practices for ways in which cultural norms can cross over linguistic code (language) differences, that is, how through communication one can personify being Puerto Rican in Spanish, or in English, or in both. Our attitudinal studies demonstrated that the El Barrio community had no trouble accepting that members had various abilities in the two languages, including limited Spanish fluency.

The results of these studies, which were published in different articles and presented in various venues, challenged many misconceptions about the linguistic repertoire of the community and its self-definition. A good example of this was an international conference on bilingualism some years later organized by the Ateneo Puertorriqueño (a sort of academy of arts and sciences organization). I presented at this conference and dared to claim that one can be Puerto Rican even with limited or no Spanish fluency. This created a controversy on the Island that my colleague, Alicia Pousada (then a faculty member at the University of Puerto Rico who was involved in the Centro research), documented for me by sending newspaper clippings of the polemics around national identity that ensued.

I experienced challenges to this more flexible view of Puerto Rican identity from scholars who I assumed to be allies because of our similar stance on Puerto Rican independence. For example, I was challenged by a co-presenter, Dr. Aida

Negrón de Montilla, whose work on the Americanization of the Puerto Rican school system I admired. In contrast, I received support or at least tolerance on my views from an unexpected source, the Puerto Rican linguist Ruben del Rosario. He asked to speak to me after the session to tell me that, although he couldn't agree or accept all that I said, I had forced him to reconsider many of his ideas and thinking about these issues of language and Puerto Rican identity.

Community Engagement

The small group from East Harlem within the Language Policy committee of la Directiva was led by Gloria Quiñones, the director of the Bilingual Institute of an adult education program in East Harlem. She helped us decide on the neighborhood we would choose for the 24/7 observations needed to document the very active street life of the community, especially during warm weather months. It was my belief that the linguistic repertoire of the community had to be sampled to give a true picture of its universe of social interactions and this could only be done by direct participation and observation. The Centro rented a space in a tenement building in "El Barrio" to serve as a field office, or base of operations for this work, and because of my collaboration with the culture task force, it became the site for a Centro-sponsored drumming workshop in the community organized by Francia Luban. She had what was then considered the crazy idea that girls should be included in the drumming class, with woman *congueras* (playing the conga drum).

And still even with all this community activity, something unexpected was lost along the way—the direct involvement of the community in the research process. Frank was very concerned about this situation and frustrated by our inability to keep this sort of activity with the community's involvement in Centro work at a high level. Eventually, la Directiva folded and Frank took it as the loss of one of our founding pillars. In a conversation with an active board member, I asked for an explanation for why. He answered that la Directiva thought they had accomplished their job, which was establishing and organizing the Centro, and setting us up for the task at hand: the actual research. La Directiva had come to regard us as professionals hired to accomplish the established goals. Having done their part, the responsibility to fulfill the mission was now in our hands, with only occasional checking in for accountability purposes.

Growth into Various Areas

In terms of the LPTF, the work on discourse analysis led us to address questions about the pedagogy of literacy, which, in turn, took us to work on the issue of school failure, and later on to expand our participation in school reform processes at all levels. This, I must admit, was not by design, but a gradual process of backing into the field of education from a language policy position. Still, we attempted to resurrect the collective paradigm for research whenever possible due to its potential to effect social change. An example of this was our participation in the creation and development of the Puerto Rican/Latino Education Roundtable in 1984.

The Puerto Rican/Latino Education Roundtable was a consortium of groups and individuals representing different constituencies and actors in our community who engaged the public school system in one way or another for the purpose of influencing local school system policies. It was the precursor of the National Latino/a Education Research and Policy Project (NLERAP), a similar effort at the national level that was later undertaken in the 1990s.

In 1982 the Centro organized a staff retreat to critically reflect on the first ten years of its experience utilizing Marxist theory in analyzing our community's social condition and grounded in the ideology of collective/participatory research practice. We concluded that the Centro made a major contribution placing the understanding of the Puerto Rican migration to New York City in the context of the Island's economic history. For example, it reflected on the capitalist development of Puerto Rico following the U.S. conquest in 1898. However, in coming to terms with the ensuing lived experiences of that community in the neighborhoods and streets of U.S. cities, given the expropriation of labor value and exploitation, and in comprehending the struggles of daily survival given the complexity of life in the modern metropolis, the work done was still limited. It was also concluded that besides the parameters of social class, the issues of gender, race, culture, and language are powerful determinants that influence our oppressed reality. These forces had to be critically examined and included in our understandings of the perpetuation of inequality. That retreat for me was a watermark, a turning point from this first phase of our inquiries into the next in our liberatory knowledge quest.

In the ensuing decade this broadening of perspective also lay the groundwork for coalescing with other similarly situated groups, particularly other Latinos in the United States, and expanding internationally, particularly the Caribbean. The IUPLR (Inter-University Program for Latino Research) and our Caribbean exchange program were an indirect result of this shift.

This essay is a personal and general account of how a community responded to an opportunity to construct a vehicle for self-representation. In the spirit of the civil rights movement of the time, we used that opening to challenge the rules of the political games as they existed, and still exist in academia. We did this for the benefit of a community and the goal of social justice. A lot still remains undone even from the perspective of that original agenda, such as a history of the New York Puerto Rican community. The community remains mired in ever more complex and seemingly intractable structures and practices of inequality. Even our understanding of the daily life of families in increasingly pan-Latino communities is limited, hampering the development of intervention strategies to assist great numbers of marginalized youth. While our ability to track and document the internal U.S. expansion and migration of our Puerto Rican community is excellent, the interdisciplinary theoretical framework and conceptual tools that could produce new insights and solutions to bolster our ability to solve problems remains elusive. Are our eyes still on the prize?

Notes

1. Centro Working Papers: Language Policy and the Puerto Rican Community 1 (1977 8), Language Policy Task Force. © The Research Foundation of the City of New York. (Reprinted from: Volume V January–August 1978 Numbers 1 and 2. The Bilingual Review/La revista bilingüe. Dept. of Foreign Languages, York College, CUNY. Jamaica, New York, 11451)
2. Vygotskyan reference on egocentric speech as a social phenomenon and its role in relation to thought and child development found in Vygotsky, L. S., (1986) In: Kozulin, A. (Ed.), *Thought and Language*. Cambridge, MA: MIT Press; and Miller, P. H. (2002). *Theories of Developmental Psychology*, 4th ed. (pp. 367–407; Vygotsky's Socio-Cultural Approach). New York: Worth.

8

THE 1968 LOS ANGELES CHICANO WALKOUT

Herman Sillas

Background

Southeast Los Angeles was home from the time I was born. My father spoke Spanish and my mother was bilingual, so . . . we spoke Spanish at home. Then one day, before I was in school, my father announced that we would only speak English at home. He had been denied promotion to lead man at work, because he couldn't speak English well enough. From that day forward, English became our official language. I placed Spanish words in the rear of my memory.

Later, I believe it was in the first grade, I had a teacher who every day would pick an alphabet letter and call upon each of us to say a word beginning with that letter. When called upon, we stood up and had to give her a word that had not already been submitted. On this particular day, she picked "C." No problem, I thought. But since I sat at the back and others had given words I had in mind, I started worrying. My turn was nearing and I didn't have a word to give her. Then one came to mind! It was a great word.

"Herman."

I stood up.

"Do you have a word?"

"Yes Ma'am," I answered with pride.

"What is it?"

"Chancla."

"What?"

"Chancla," I said again louder. The class laughed.

"What is it?" she asked.

"You know. You wear it on your feet in the morning," I said with some annoyance.

"Oh. You mean a slipper."

I had never heard "slipper" before. "No. A chancla," I answered defiantly.

"How do you spell it?"

"I dunno."

By this time the class, which was all Anglo, was really laughing. My teacher in a no-nonsense voice said, "There is no such word. Give me another word."

I don't remember what I did. I don't think I gave her another word because I knew a chancla when I saw one. And my mother had two of them. I had even been spanked with them. But I did learn one thing: Spanish words weren't worth anything in school. In time I would forget most of them.

I left home in 1958 as a third-year UCLA law student. I had taken Spanish in undergrad but viewed it as a waste of time. I wanted to be like the rest of the college students and they spoke English and many times used words I didn't know.

I had cousins that lived in East Los Angeles and visited them regularly as a child with my folks. Spanish was heard everywhere. It was a different neighborhood than mine. By the time I left home, my neighborhood was predominately Black. Seven years later, when the 1965 Watts Riots erupted, my parents still lived in southeast Los Angeles. Watts was thirty blocks from my parents' home. On the riots' second day, my fearful parents fled from looters and fires that were getting dangerously close. The National Guard ultimately was called in to quash the uprising. Lives and property had been lost. Fires had reduced structures to ashes over the four-day period. My parents' house remained standing, but its location appeal had vanished and so had its value. Los Angeles African-Americans had made their presence and plight known to the nation in a very dramatic fashion. They no longer would accept being second-class citizens in Los Angeles. I identified with what they were saying having grown up among them. There had been only one Black student in our law class and only three Mexican-Americans. The lack of representation of minorities in the legal profession was my motivating factor to go to law school. I had a burning desire to help the suppressed.

Local government officials were nervous after the Watts Riots and attempted to respond to a growing demand list from the newfound voice of the Black community. Meanwhile, these same officials recognized that the increasing Mexican-American community also had legitimate concerns. High on the list were education and police brutality.

Law enforcement had a different perspective. Since the Watts Riots, its ability to act promptly and protect property and life was in question. Police leaders wondered privately if the Mexican-American community would hit the streets as the Blacks did. Could local law enforcement fight a two-front battle, one from the east where most Mexican-Americans lived and one from the southeast where a majority of Blacks lived?

These concerns caused the Los Angeles County Human Relations Commission to call an emergency meeting of the County's Mexican-American leadership, such as it was. As a young lawyer, I was invited to attend. I did not consider myself a leader, but because of my profession and the limited number of Mexican-American lawyers at the time, I suspected this was my credential for the invitation. Hundreds of Mexican-Americans attended the evening meeting. I had never seen that many Mexican-Americans at one gathering. An education committee had been in existence for some time and reported to the body that evening. It was a grim report. The drop-out rate of Mexican-American students in East Los Angeles schools was nearly 50%. Members of the committee contended that teachers ignored Mexican-American students and that the Los Angeles Unified School District (LAUSD) didn't seem to care.

It was in this setting that I heard Marcus Deleon, a LAUSD teacher, who served as the chairman of the education committee. His booming voice articulated the problems facing Mexican-American students. He spoke of assimilation and the stripping of their culture by insensitive teachers and administrators. Our children felt unwanted as a result. As he spoke, I realized that he had described my school journey. When he finished, I asked for a meeting to explore what he had described.

At our subsequent meeting, he brought a chart and explained biculturalism, a new term for me. I realized I had subconsciously suppressed my heritage, in an effort to be accepted in the Anglo culture. He went on to explain how Anglo teachers for the most part were ignorant of other cultures and didn't care. Consequently, non-Anglo students felt out of place. Then I recalled my first grade experience. Listening to Marcus opened a new world for me.

My Journey with Mexican-American Educators and Students

I began meeting with Mexican-American educators and learned of their efforts to bring about change to address the needs of their students. Some teachers felt that LAUSD administrators were willing to listen to suggestions. Phil Montez, an outspoken educator, and others asked me to incorporate their group, the Association of Mexican-American Educators (AMAE). They had become a new voice in the educational arena advocating change to address the needs of Mexican-American students. East Los Angeles schools were shabby, needed repairs, and lacked Spanish-speaking counselors and teachers. AMAE's suggestions addressed these needs and called for changes in the curriculum.

LAUSD administrators were threatened by AMAE's presence and positions. The thought of Mexican-American teachers meeting in homes to develop strategies for change did not set well with their bosses. Meetings with school administrators brought few concessions. LAUSD's opposition stiffened and was supported by a majority of teachers who urged the retention of the status quo. AMAE members became frustrated but continued to press forward. In their meetings they began to believe that something more was needed to cause the changes they advocated. I attended some of their meetings and conferences and became a supporter of their position.

One of the accomplishments brought about by Mexican-American teachers was the establishment of a program to identify at-risk students. Students identified by their teachers were invited to attend a weekend seminar at Camp Hess near Malibu. Mexican-American professionals were invited to address and encourage students to finish school. I recall speaking at several such gatherings and seeing the eager student faces thirsty for direction. Here the students learned that "White" schools had better facilities than the schools they attended. They also came to grips with exploring their identity. A sense of pride of their heritage was now a part of them as they left the camp to return to their campuses. Their newfound identity consisting of a Mexican heritage and the concept of Americans' rights caused them to see themselves differently. They were neither "American" nor "Mexican" but were unique individuals made of parts from two cultures. Ultimately, many began calling themselves "Chicanos."

It was not long before Chicanos began to question the inferior education they were receiving and sought knowledge about the contributions to this country of their Mexican ancestors. Eventually the students produced a request list to the LAUSD administration.[1] The lack of response spoke volumes to the students. They turned to Sal Castro, a Lincoln High School teacher they could trust, for direction and counsel.

He had begun to feel that the LAUSD was only giving lip service and had no intention of committing itself to an all-out effort to address the special needs of Mexican-American students. He knew that his advocacy made him a marked man within the system. He was being watched by the administration eagerly waiting for him to commit an infraction no matter how slight. Still, he felt compelled to continue his advocacy for better education for his students. He concluded that the students needed to strike if any real change was to occur. The more he thought about it, the clearer the picture became. Castro also recognized that his involvement in such an act would jeopardize his teaching credential. He concluded that having a credential but failing to address the needs of his students was worse than having no credential at all. He also recognized that on this decision he would be alone. Castro's colleagues were not prepared to take such a drastic step. The decisions were clear for him: work with the students, educate the community, and lead a walkout.[2]

It is of importance to note that at this time the Black Panther Party was very visible in California. The organization was viewed by law enforcement as a dangerous militant and criminal unit. Its members wore black berets. Among the Mexican-American students who had attended Camp Hess were those who decided to wear berets also, but brown ones. They called themselves the Brown Berets and in public took on a military appearance. Their leader, David Sanchez, was referred to as the "Prime Minister." The press made note of the Brown Berets' appearance and made reference to the Black Panthers, implying that the Brown Berets were similar. Both spoke of their respective heritage with pride, but beyond that there were no similarities. This becomes of some importance when the conduct of law enforcement is subsequently examined during the walkout.

The Walkout

Commencing on March 6, 1968, Sal Castro and thousands of students from Lincoln High School, Belmont, Roosevelt, Wilson, and Garfield walked out from their respective schools in a peaceful demonstration demanding equal education. The walkouts lasted three days and in the height of the demonstration as many as four thousand young Chicanos joined the march. Brown Berets were visible at the walkouts. Law enforcement had been alerted and on the second day, violence erupted at some schools. LAPD's reaction was to pummel the students, boys and girls, with clubs. This police action was never shown on TV at the time, but students returned to their homes and some to hospitals battered and bruised.

The debates in the Mexican-American households that had taken place between parents and demonstrating students before the walkouts ceased when parents saw their battered children. Parents became incensed at the reaction of law enforcement. The elders took up the demands of their children. A community that had once been viewed as timid by L.A. administration now became vocal and supportive of their Chicanos. Castro became a spokesperson and urged other Mexican-American organizations to support the students. On May 14, 1968, in a radio broadcast, he outlined the history of the walkouts and how college students helped make signs and monitored the walkouts.

The voice for change from the Mexican-American community became louder and stronger. Julian Nava, the first Mexican-American to sit on LAUSD's Board, lobbied his colleagues on the Board to address the issues raised by the community and students. Equal education became the theme within the Mexican-American community. Mexican-Americans began to act and exercise the rights guaranteed to other Americans. It was a new feeling. What they did not know was that among the students that had attended the student meetings before the walkout was an undercover policeman posing as a student.

The Indictment of the ELA 13

It was clear that the walkouts had become the spark that ignited a complacent community. The youth with one teacher who was willing to put everything on the line moved people from their couches to school board meetings.

The walkouts also caused law enforcement to act. Misdemeanor complaints filed against leaders of the walkout were subsequently dismissed by the Los Angeles County District Attorney's Office, who had gone to the Grand Jury seeking the issuance of a Grand Jury Indictment. After listening to the testimony of the undercover police officer and other evidence submitted by the District Attorney's Office, the Grand Jury issued a Felony Indictment against Sal Castro and 12 other defendants.[3] They became referred to in the community and in the press as the "ELA 13."

Section 16701 of the California Education Code at that time read, "Any person who willfully disturbs a public school . . . is guilty of a misdemeanor, and punishable by a fine of not less than ten dollars ($10.00) nor more than one hundred dollars ($100.00)." But the defendants were charged with a *conspiracy* to violate section 16701 and a *conspiracy* to disturb the peace. The alleged conspiracy made their conduct a felony. Conviction could bring prison time. The felony indictment was a clear message from the establishment that it would not tolerate this type of conduct. The reaction among the activists within the Mexican-American community was one of disbelief. It also caused some to shy away from further involvement. The heroes of the walkout were now accused felons. Law enforcement did not intend to fight two fronts, particularly one led by a bunch of school kids. The felony indictments had the effect on the Mexican-American community that the establishment wanted.

The Legal Defense Team

As a young lawyer trying to develop a practice I was attending community meetings practically every evening. Some were held in my office, others in homes or restaurants. Sal Castro and I would run into each other at these meetings. Activism was contagious. After the walkouts, meetings increased in number and length as an energized community began to focus on addressing poverty, unemployment, poor housing, lack of preschool, and police brutality.

It was at such a meeting in my offices that Sal Castro asked me to represent him in the pending felony indictment. My law partner, Jose Mariano Castillo, graciously agreed that it was something I had to do. My reasons for going to law school were being fulfilled.

The American Civil Liberties Union (ACLU) had taken on the defense of some of the defendants. ACLU's counsel was the learned A. L. Wirin and Fred Okrand. Both were well-known constitutional attorneys. They were assisted by Paul M. Posner and Herbert E. Selwyn. Also part of the team were Neil Herring and Ralph M. Segura. The other attorney on the defense team was Oscar Acosta, a Chicano activist attorney.[4]

At the first attorneys' meeting, strategies were explored and all agreed to work cooperatively with each other, even though we represented individual clients. Castro was the only teacher. The other defendants were college students or community activists. Our approach was to attack the indictment as an overreach by government that infringed upon our clients' freedom of speech. It was our intent to never have the defendants face trial. Each attorney took on individual assignments for our overall defense. We viewed that our strongest argument was that the indictment infringed on the right of free speech. Since the case had been submitted to a Grand Jury, the defendants had not heard the testimony against them. When we received the grand jury transcript, we read, for the first time, the testimony of the undercover Mexican-American police officer.

The Court Battle and Victory

As I read the undercover officer's testimony and description of the discussions that took place among the defendants, I laughed. The conversations described were discussions I heard every time Mexican-Americans gathered. The topic always included the injustices all around us and bringing changes. How could that be a conspiracy to commit a crime? My task was to strike from the Grand Jury transcript inflammatory language used by witnesses that was nonfactual but would have prejudiced the Grand Jury. I also realized that these Chicano discussions were falling on Anglo ears who had never heard such discussions in their lives. I mused that they may have been threatening to an insensitive and closed mind.

One of the more interesting motions to dismiss the indictment was the one filed by Oscar Acosta on behalf of all defendants contending that the Grand Jury was unconstitutionally constituted in that no Mexican-Americans served on the Grand Jury and had been intentionally excluded. Acosta had assembled data that established that no Spanish-surnamed individuals had been selected to the Grand Jury for the last 20 some years.

The process for selecting Grand Jury members at that time was that each Superior Court judge submitted two names for the Grand Jury. The names were placed in a bowl and pulled out by the Court Clerk similar to pulling out a raffle ticket. The trial Court allowed Acosta to subpoena Superior Court Judges, place them under oath, and question them as to their selections over the past years. None of them had ever submitted a Mexican-American. Among the questions Acosta asked was, "Do you know any Mexican-Americans?" Most answered they did not. Those who answered, yes, testified that the only Mexican-American they knew was their gardener or housekeeper. The judges testified they never asked those individuals because they didn't feel they were qualified to serve. Although this motion was ultimately denied, the next year, Los Angeles Superior Court Judges were reaching out to find "qualified" Mexican-Americans to submit to the Court Clerk for service on the Grand Jury.

Our motion to quash the indictment on a variety of grounds, including that Education Code section 16701 was unconstitutionally vague and that a prosecution for conspiracy to violate the misdemeanors had a chilling effect on free speech, was also denied by the trial court as were all our other motions to dismiss.

We then filed a Petition for a Writ of Prohibition with the Court of Appeals, requesting a Restraining Order preventing the trial Court from proceeding with any further prosecution of the defendants, since their rights under the constitution were being violated. After reviewing our Petition and arguments, on July 17, 1970, Justice P. Kraus rendered the majority opinion stating that Education Code section 16701 was too vague and unconstitutional, *Castro v. Superior Court, 9 Cal. App. 3rd 675 (1970)*.[5] The court also found the section so broad that it had a chilling effect upon the exercise of First Amendment rights.[6] The threat of going to prison had been removed and our clients would face no further charges! I knew I had chosen the right profession.

Aftermath

The decision was received with great joy in the Mexican community and the ELA 13 were proclaimed heroes. LAUSD established a Mexican-American Advisory Committee to give the school board and administrators input as to how to service the Mexican-American students. Efforts were made to hire Mexican-American teachers and bilingual teachers with skills in Spanish and English. Legislation was introduced to establish a bilingual credential for teachers who were bilingual. Schools would be required to have bilingual teachers if the student population had significant numbers of students with limited English-speaking ability. Mexican-American organizations such as the Mexican-American Lawyers Club, the Council of Mexican-American Affairs, Mexican-American Legal Defense and Education Fund (MALDEF), American G.I. Forum, and others joined the voices of the parents. The effect on the Mexican-American community was that a new wave of enthusiasm filled the air as activists recruited more into their ranks. Middle-class Mexican-Americans began to support their youth demanding equal rights for Chicano students. It was now clear that there was another vocal minority community in Los Angeles. Coalition politics became a new path for Blacks and Chicanos in Los Angeles.

However, on August 29, 1970, less than six weeks after the Castro decision, Ruben Salazar, an *L.A. Times* columnist and news director of KMEX, a Spanish-speaking TV station, was killed by a sheriff's gas canister that was shot into a bar where he was seated. Salazar had been covering the August 29th Moratorium Demonstration against the Vietnam War in East L.A. Thousands of marchers showed up that day in the park. Violence erupted and law enforcement resorted to mass arrests and beatings. Ruben Salazar's writings had been the voice of the Mexican-American community that was read by Anglos as well as Mexican-Americans. Now he had been killed. The coroner's jury found that his death was a homicide but no one was ever prosecuted. The establishment still had ways to try and quiet the Mexican-American voice.

But activists continued, and more and more Mexican-Americans joined hands and entered new arenas where they had been excluded. More Mexican-Americans entered politics, became lawyers, judges, doctors, teachers, school officials, and elected officials. Unfortunately, the drop-out rate of Mexican-American students still hovers around 50%. In my alma mater, Fremont High School, the drop-out rate increased to 90%. The battle for equal education for all students continues and will continue until we get it right.

Moctezuma Esparza, one of the ELA 13, went on to graduate from UCLA and became a movie producer and director. His 2007 movie on HBO, *Walkouts*, brought to life the issues of the 1960s to a new generation, as his movie realistically portrayed the story of the walkouts. Recently, his movie was shown at the high school where one of my granddaughters, Eliana Vasquez, attended. Her teacher invited me to speak to her class. I looked around the room and it was filled with faces of all cultures and hues. I smiled at Eliana, and wondered what her generation would view as their issue. I know what my generation viewed as ours.

Notes

1. The requests were: 1. Class size will be reduced so that teachers can be more effective in the classroom and devote more time to each student. Team teaching approach will be used. 2. New high schools in the area to be built immediately. The present local schools should be renamed to help establish community identity. 3. Counselor/student ratios should be reduced. All counselors should be able to speak Spanish. 4. Library facilities should be expanded at all East L.A. high schools to meet minimum requirements. 5. The Industrial Arts program must be revitalized and modernized. 6. Open-air student eating areas should be made into roofed malls. 7. All buildings already condemned should be razed and new structures erected immediately. 8. All high school campuses will be open. Fences should be removed. 9. Entrances to all buildings and restrooms should be accessible to all students during school hours. 10. School janitorial services should be restricted to employees hired for that purpose. 11. The guidance program should be realistic, with newer and better methods developed. The present I.Q. tests will be abolished and valid student testing techniques developed in their place. 12. Teachers should become more aware of the social and economic problems of the community. 13. Proper emphasis should be given to student violations—just what is the punishment being given for? What is the standard penalty for a standard infraction of rules? Who settles disputes over rules and the punishment assigned?
2. The administration ultimately brought charges against him and I defended him at the administrative hearing. The panel sustained some of the charges and he was removed from the classroom for a period of time and relocated to the district's headquarters.
3. Moctezuma Esparza, Henry Gomez, Carlos Michael Montez, Carlos Munoz, Joe Angel Razo, Eliezer Loazado Risco, J. Patricio Sanchez, Richard Vigil, Frederic Bernard Lopez, Gilbert Cruz Olmeda, Ralph Luna Ramirez, and David John Sanchez.
4. He was a brilliant writer who would later author two classic Chicano books, *Brown Buffalo* and *Revolt of the Cockroach People*. His untimely and mysterious death cut short his career.
5. Referring to section 16701 the court stated, "The defined victim is a 'public school.' That presumably encompasses the buildings and grounds as such, which can surely be 'disturbed' by certain activities, as the occupants who are in the buildings and on the grounds for purposes to which these are devoted. The word 'disturb' itself may refer to conduct objectively disturbing as well as conduct disturbing to the victim, though objectively placid. The addition, in the statute, of the word 'willfully' merely implies a purpose or willingness to commit the act and although it does not require an evil intent, it implies that the person knows what he is doing, intends to do what he is doing and is a free agent (cites omitted). Literally it is thus apparent that the United States Supreme Court must have 'willfully disturbed' the public schools affected by its holding in *Brown v. Board of Education*, 347 U.S. 483 . . ."
6. Citing Landy v. Daley, 280 F. Supp. 968, which struck down a Chicago ordinance dealing with disorderly conduct, the Castro court borrowed the following language from that case to find section 16701 unconstitutional: "The legitimate exercise of freedom of speech, press or expression frequently interrupts a state of peace or quiet or interferes with a planned, ordered or regular procedure, state or habit. New ideas more often than not create disturbances, yet the very purpose of the First Amendment is to stimulate the creation and dissemination of new concepts. The prohibition against making or countenancing a disturbance would literally make it a crime to deliver an unpopular speech which results in a 'disturbance' or to stand by while someone else makes such a speech. This is clearly an invalid restriction of protected rights."

9

LA LUCHA SIGUE

An Interview with Dolores Huerta

Magaly Lavadenz and Anaida Colón-Muñiz

Dolores Huerta is an iconic figure in the civil rights efforts of Chicanos/Latinos, as well as for those of other immigrant and migrant workers and the union movement in general. We wanted to ensure that her perspective was included in this volume to share the incredible humanity behind this female champion of social justice and the issue of civil rights in the farm worker community. Accordingly, this chapter adds to the recognition of women leaders in the Latino civil rights movement, which is glaringly missing from American history books. The National Women's History Museum's (NWHM) biography of Huerta acknowledges her significant contributions to the nation: "Dolores Huerta would grow up to become one of the most influential labor activists of the 20th century."[1]

Born on April 10, 1930 in Dawson, New Mexico, Huerta's given name was Dolores Clara Fernández. First preparing for the field of education as a grammar school teacher, Dolores soon realized that for kids to learn we have to ensure their basic needs, "I quit because I couldn't stand seeing kids come to class hungry and needing shoes. I thought I could do more by organizing farm workers than by trying to teach their hungry children" (NWHM).[2]

As Latina educators we have been both inspired and moved by the passion and fearless leadership of Dolores Huerta, who is in our estimation perhaps the strongest Latina voice representing farm workers' civil rights and the rights of women and other underrepresented groups. She is someone who taught us how to fight against injustice through determination, collaboration and action. In solidarity with our "compadres and comadres" in the distant fields of Central and Northern California, hundreds and sometimes thousands of miles away from where we lived and worked, our kinship in "the elusive quest" (Moreno, 2010) for Latino and all farm worker civil rights motivated us and countless others to act in as simple and complex ways as boycotting grapes and grape products. Side-by-side with Filipino farm worker leaders such as Larry Itliong, Philip Vera Cruz,[3] and Mexican-American leader César Chávez,[4] Dolores Huerta mobilized Americans to demand basic worker wages and rights for those who suffered unbearable conditions, such as farm workers toiling the land as pesticides were sprayed over them by field airplanes while the hot sun beat their backs during their painstaking work.

> [Huerta] led the national table grape boycott in support of the farm workers strike, bringing the plight of farm workers to the forefront of the American consumer. The boycott was supported by an estimated 17 million Americans and led to the passage of the California Agricultural Labor Relations Act, the first law granting farm workers the right to collectively organize and bargain for better wages and working conditions.[5]

Few others in the United States wanted to do this painstaking and hazardous work, so thousands of farm workers have been brought over the years to these green concentration camps, lured by promises of honest work and a better future for their children. Poor immigrants in search of work from China, the Philippines, Mexico, Puerto Rico and the American South have followed crops to make a meager salary, toiling land that would never be theirs, subjected to illness and slave-like work conditions. With no contract, no union, no health plans, no security of any sort, poor migrant workers sweated to unfulfilled promises with their children along their side. Even prior to the Treaty of Guadalupe in the mid-1800s, Mexican and other farm workers (Chinese, Japanese, Filipino and Puerto Rican) in the United States have confronted an enormous challenge in attaining worker rights. Despite the most dire work conditions, and with no civil rights to speak of until they protested, farm workers have ironically served as the backbone to American agriculture and the dinner table, providing the basic food we enjoy every single day.

From the Classroom to the Fields and Beyond

After leaving the classroom in the early 1960s, Dolores Huerta left the Stockton Community Service Organization (CSO) with César Chávez to focus on their common interest of organizing farm workers to address their deplorable work conditions. She co-founded the National Farm Workers Association (primarily Mexican), which would later merge with the Agricultural Workers Organizing Committee (primarily Filipino) to become the United Farm Workers Organizing Committee. As an organizer, Dolores played a key role in the organization, and the organization made great inroads over the years. For example, she was key in the establishment of the Agricultural Labor Relations Act of 1975. This was the first U.S. law granting the right to collectively organize and bargain to farm workers in California.

A brief outline of her activism includes the following:

- 1955 — Helped organize the Stockton Chapter of the Community Service Organization (CSO), to fight for economic improvements for Latinos, fight segregation and police brutality and improve public services. Led voter registration drives and helped craft legislation.
- 1960 — Helped found the Agricultural Workers Association (AWA). Met fellow activist and labor leader César Chávez.
- 1962 — Huerta and Chávez founded the National Farm Workers Association (NFWA), a predecessor to the United Farm Workers Union (UFW).
- 1965 — Co-founded the UFW, for which Dolores Huerta served as Vice President until 1999.
- 1965 — Huerta helped Filipino and Mexican union leaders to organize the Delano Grape Strike of over 5,000 grape workers and coordinated a boycott of the California table grape industry, which led to a three-year contract about bargaining agreements between California and the UFW.
- 1967 — NFWA combined with the AWA to create the United Farm Workers Organizing Committee (UFWOC) for which Huerta negotiated contracts for workers and managed an entire hiring system to increase the number of available jobs. Huerta fought against the use of harmful pesticides and for unemployment and healthcare benefits.
- 1973 — Led a consumer boycott that resulted in the California Agricultural Labor Relations Act of 1975, so farm workers could form unions and bargain for better wages and working conditions.
- 1970s and 80s — worked as a lobbyist to improve workers' legislative representation.

Beginning in 1962 in Delano, California, their first attempt to unionize was called the National Farm Workers Association (NFWA), unveiling its iconic flag with a black eagle symbol during the first convention (UFW website). Later the United Farm Workers (UFW) was formed from a merger between the NFWA and the Filipino-American union efforts of the Agricultural Workers Organizing Committee (AWOK) to strike against the grape growers of Delano. This was an historic struggle, which expanded and lasted over five years, ultimately resulting in an international effort to support the grape farm workers, then lettuce, then citrus. By 1975 over 17 million sympathetic Americans were boycotting grapes, as well as lettuce and Gallo wine. Ultimately, the push was for the farm owners to sign contracts with the UFW and secure better pay and benefits (UFW website).

In 1972 the Arizona governor, Jack Williams, and legislature ignored the boycotts and signed a law banning the rights of farm workers. This began César's 25-day water fast, at which point Dolores is known to have rejected the notion that the Arizona laws couldn't be beaten. It was there that she coined the now famous slogan, "¡Si se puede!" to counter the prevailing pessimist attitudes and engender a rallying cry for social justice in Arizona.

Our Conversation with Dolores Huerta

After multiple attempts by the authors, the interview was conducted over a series of conversations between M. Lavadenz and Dolores Huerta both in person and over the telephone. While in Washington, DC during September 2012 at different conferences, a face-to-face meeting at that time wasn't possible due to the continual requests and invitations for her to speak nationally, locally and internationally. Without hesitation to respond to requests, we collected Dolores's articulate passion and recollections during our conversations. These revealed the historical and contemporary encounters that intertwine her advocacy and educational mission even into the 81st annual commemoration of her birth, which was being celebrated when we spoke. At a time when most octogenarians are well into retirement mode, Dolores's active commitment is to the poor and disenfranchised, understanding that they have the capacity and responsibility to improve their own lives.

A Woman Warrior

As the Dolores Huerta Foundation website states, she is "internationally recognized as a feminist, a farm worker advocate, a gay rights activist, and a labor leader, among other things. As a champion whose work transcends issue-specific movements, Dolores announced the launch of the 'Weaving Movements' campaign at her 80th birthday celebration on August 13, 2010 at a benefit concert supporting the Dolores Huerta Foundation" (www.doloreshuerta.org). The Foundation's work focuses on the intersectionality of issues that have evolved from the early days of the struggle for farm workers' rights.

From those times, Dolores faced challenges in receiving the appropriate levels of respect among the mostly male leadership. She was representing not only the men, but also the women and children who worked in the fields. But, that was a challenge she could meet. It is said that in one of her letters to César she joked, "Being a now (ahem) experienced lobbyist, I am able to speak on a man-to-man basis with other lobbyists" (Dolores Huerta Foundation website). As noted earlier, together they set out to speak in favor of improved working conditions and created what is now known as the United Farm Workers Union. Dolores by his side, César joined leaders from the Filipino-American Agricultural Organizing Committee, such as Andy Imutan, Larry Itliong and other activists. These individuals gave their lives to give shape to a movement that to this day continues to demand equity and justice for farm workers. Among other rights, they continue fighting against the use of dangerous pesticides and working in unbearable heat.[6]

As a woman, her approach can be compared to Gloria Anzaldua's *Haciendo Caras/Making Face, Making Soul* (1990). A devout Catholic, Dolores followed her spiritual commitments by actively engaging in advocacy to promote justice for the farm workers. As revealed through the selected timeline, Dolores's trajectory has been one of directly facing injustices and being unequivocally *in* the moments that required intervention, voice and presence. During the interview she states:

DH: We don't have ethnic studies; kids don't learn about themselves; we don't have women's studies so women don't know the contributions women have made to our society. We don't have a study on the labor movement. Most of the people, most of our people are working people and they have done a lot *for trade unions and labor unions, and [schools] don't teach about what trade unions have brought to our country* like minimum wage and the 8-hour day, unemployment insurance, safety standards, public education. The thing is that's what made it possible for our American workers. So our kids don't feel valued and they don't know what their parents have contributed to make this a (great) society. And kids really don't feel like they are worthy; they say they do not feel like they are valued; they are not valued. Their teachers are not valued and so our values are upside down. We have to kind of change that mentality to respect our teachers, to respect our students, and make them our priority. They have to be the priority of everything we do in our country.

Schools as Sites in the Quest for Social Justice

It was only through the mobilization of the farm workers, with the leadership of Dolores Huerta and César Chávez and the support of forward-thinking Americans all over the country, that the wealthy farm owners would finally accede to improved work conditions that would eventually include the elemental human right to a basic salary, rest breaks, fresh water, and the limiting of dangerous pesticides. Also through this effort, farm workers fought for improved schooling for their children and continue to make inroads. *La lucha sigue*, the struggle continues, because the United Farm Workers never cease to challenge unfair practices. Much has been gained but much is still required:

DH: Oh, there [are so many recollections] I don't know where we start. You know that we have a big teachers' strike going on right now in Chicago (at the time of the interview). I think that one of the biggest issues that we have is that our teachers are not being paid enough money. You can, you know, be a prison guard out of high school and make more money than as a teacher. And when you think about how our whole country depends on our educational system and our children are so dependent on our teachers, our teachers are not respected. They are trying to destroy the labor unions so, you know, this is one of the big issues we have because when we don't have the right teachers, teachers don't have the support they need, it is very, very hard for them to be able to teach our students, you know?

We can start there. To begin with not enough money for our school systems, but when you think about all the money we spend on defense, or some of these other areas that we could have saved up because we need some of that money that could have gone to our school systems.

Denouncing Schooling Conditions for (im)Migrant Children

In the schools, the evolution of migrant education and meeting the needs of "migrant children" who travelled with their parents from farm to farm, or canning factory to canning factory, seeking work for periods that would last only as long as that agricultural season, has also evolved as of supreme importance for Dolores Huerta. Simultaneously with much of the educational legislation during the civil rights era, the Elementary and Secondary Education Act of 1965 included the Migrant Education Programs, which were mandated to provide better schooling:

DH: [We need] high quality education programs for migratory children and [that] help ensure that migratory children who move among the states are not penalized in any manner by disparities among states in curriculum, graduation requirements, or state academic content and student academic achievement standards. Funds also ensure that migratory children not only are provided with appropriate education services (including supportive services) that address their special needs but also that such children receive full and appropriate opportunities to meet the same challenging state academic content and student academic achievement standards that all children are expected to meet.

As educators we know full well how many caring teachers struggle to meet the needs of migrant children who might only be with them for a few months, barely getting to know their classmates before they would be transported to another location to help their parents (Gonzalez, 2001). However, reflecting on her educational experiences as a Latina who grew up in a very diverse community, close to the realities of migrant families, she recalled the following:

DH: Well, in the early days of the movement, you know in those days we had the state of California. For example, when I went to school, we had smaller classrooms; we didn't have what kids have . . . there was more concentration on reading and math, [than] I think there is in today's world. We had social studies and history, which was also a part of our classes.

While somewhat sheltered from the hardships of migrant life, she became aware of the hardship that surrounded her. She continues . . .

DH: I remember that when I went to school . . . all the kids that I grew up around, immigrant kids who were immigrants from Italy, from Greece, from China, from Japan, from the Philippines. We had the Dustbowl kids, the Oakies, the Arkies as they used to call them. There was no PTA then. There were no parent organizations, but the kids all learned. They all learned because there was a big concentration not just on reading and writing, but our classes were also all very small.

Critical scholars such as Freire and Macedo (1987) have decried the dehumanizing actions that occur in schools manifested through oppressive political, social and economic strategies that result in negative educational consequences for poor children. Dolores Huerta, however, serves as a "restorer of humanity" (Freire, 1978). Through her legacy of activism throughout five decades, she describes the complex lives of Latino immigrant families and the hope that families have that public education will be a way out of poverty for their children.

DH: You didn't have the classes like teachers have today with 30 kids and 40 kids and in some of our college systems where you know the kids can't even get into classes that they need because the classes are not available because of the cutbacks in education. And uh, so, our whole value system has to be looked upon and say education has got to be first. Now I'm a community organizer with the Dolores Huerta Foundation of Community Organizing and all of our house meetings we have, we meet with parents, 6–8 parents, and we ask them: "What is the number one thing, what is the number one issue that you care about?" They all say that number one is healthcare and number two is education and the third is immigration. And these are the things that they worry about, the things that Latino families want to share. They come here because they want a better life for their children. Often times, with the poverty we have, the kids have to drop out of school to help their parents just to have enough money to pay the rent and to buy food and to buy the bare necessities. So, there are a lot of things that have an impact on our children and when our families are so poor that they have to work two to three jobs, then the kids do not get the kind of support at home that they need because the parents are not there.

Since the passage of California's voter-led initiative Proposition 227 in 1998, multiple researchers and data banks reveal that achievement gaps between English Learners and their native English-speaking peers have increased (Gold, 2006; Parrish et al., 2006)—the "miseducation" of English Learners in California and other states that have highly restrictive language and education policies that have limited parental access to bilingual education (McField & McField, 2014). Dolores also points out the following:

DH: The other thing is that, you know in terms of teacher quality in education, we know that our Latino children are a little far behind and we have so many of them that came to this country and didn't speak the English language and yet we didn't have the kind of Spanish-speaking classes for them. They are going to learn English eventually, it is inevitable, but they have to learn their other classes, their math and their sciences, you know, their history classes. They could have been taught to them in their native languages just so they wouldn't lose their native language but at the same time they wouldn't be learning their English language. So, getting rid of bilingual education and not providing it for these children also hurt us a lot. So, there are so many things that are wrong.

The miseducation and the ensuing damages incurred as a result of the English-only politics call for a revitalization of sound bilingual programs that are additive versus subtractive in nature. The bridge between home and school is nurtured through the ability of educators to communicate, respond and collaborate with parents.

The Need to Improve Schools' Understanding and Respect for Parents

Through this interview it became evident to us how strongly Dolores supports parents' right to choose quality programs for their children. She firmly believes that schools have a responsibility to respond to parents and this is a matter of social justice.

DH: I was trying to leave the impression before, like when I went to school during the Depression, the parents were busy trying to earn a living like my own mother. She had to work two jobs—she worked in a cannery by night and as a waitress by day. She was a single parent just trying to keep the roof over our heads so she really didn't have time to participate in my education. But the one thing she did was let me know that it was important for me to stay in school and it was important for me to go to college. A lot of times the tendency is to blame the parents—"it's your fault that your kids are not achieving"—but it's not the parents' fault.

You know my oldest son is a doctor; there is no way in the world I can help my son with his calculus, his trigonometry, his organic chemistry—the classes he had to take to be a doctor. The only thing I could do was to support my son, and just say, "I'm glad you're in school" and give him financial aid because he had to borrow money and work at nights in a store as a janitor to be able to pay for his education. All I could do was support him and say was, "adelante mi'jo". . . go ahead, and I think for a lot of parents, [schools] make them feel guilty, and maybe some of them don't know how to speak English, and even some of them don't even know how to read or write, you know? And that's [unfair].

In the following vignette, she notes how parents found the strength to move toward the firing of a principal who wanted to eliminate the breakfast program for poor children.

DH: We recently had one of our principals that took away our breakfast program. Well the parents got together and they got rid of that principal but they kept the breakfast program, okay? "Quitarle el alimento de la gente?!!" So let's just not make them feel guilty—we just say to them, "mira apóyalos." Take away from the video games, you know? And make them do their homework before they do anything. "Quitarlos de la television también." Just support them and set those guidelines for them, so we shouldn't make our parents feel guilty. A parent should know the difference between what they can do to support the kids and influence them to stay in school and make sure that they put their homework first and their video games second and the television. You know? And I think that's what would be good for parents to get involved in the school system. We have parents whose kids were suspended for no reason! And we as parents need to get involved in the schools.

The United States has reached a crisis point in the education of Latinos (Gándara & Contreras, 2009) with a history that documents the disproportional treatment and access to a fair and equitable education. This history is plagued with unequal treatment of Latino/a students, including greater punitive disciplinary treatments for student behavior amongst minority populations (Skiba, Horner, Chung, Rausch, May, & Tobin, 2011). The consequences of disproportional disciplinary treatment for Latino students was recounted by Dolores in the following scenario:

DH: There was one young woman and they suspended her for two weeks because she sat on a cafeteria table. *Óyeme*! So we had to go back to her school and say, "why are you suspending this girl for two weeks because she sat on a cafeteria table?" That's crazy. Give her detention. Keep them after school instead of putting them out of school or suspending them. You know, have them stay in school and have them do extra work, you know? Extra studying, "no los tiren a la calle." Don't throw them on the street because all they are going to do is get in trouble out there with other kids that are on the streets. So as parents, we have to go out there and fight to keep our kids in school. Recently we had an incident because at our organization the Dolores Huerta Foundation of Community Organizers (that's what we are concentrating on, our schools now), we had one parent that her son had been suspended so many times that she went to the school and did a sit-in and she said "I am not leaving this school—you can put me in jail if you want until you put my son back in school." And guess what? They did! So that is what we have to do because you know, I can understand that some of the teachers have so many kids in their classrooms and they don't have a system to help them in the classroom. They get frustrated and they don't have anybody to assist them in the classroom with the kids, you know? And we just have to get frustrated [we just have to say] don't expel our children. There are some schools—I visited a school in Los Angeles the other day. They have zero suspensions—zero! They do not kick the kids out of the school. They keep them in the school and that, and we as parents—we are working with a group called Families in Schools of Los Angeles.

At least three consequences of disproportionate discipline for Latino students, such as in the example provided by Dolores, are clearly identified: 1) removing students from the learning environment weakens their connection with schools; 2) research indicates that removing students through suspension or expulsion neither improves behavior nor increases school learning; and 3) exclusionary discipline practices place students who may be already at risk at greater risk.

DH: We have got to keep our kids in school. And the other day I wanted to say to all of the parents that were listening—please, we have to keep the public schools system. Don't buy into this, the whole movement today and right now to do Charter Schools because the Charter Schools are thinking of themselves. Statistically, they don't do any better than the public schools and when they do Charter Schools, they take the money out of our public school system and you know, give them to the Charter Schools, which are often like in my area where I live down in Bakersfield, California. The big Charter School that we have there is in one of our little communities [that] is the local grower. The local grower put up a Charter School instead of giving its workers more money and giving them better wages . . . of course then they start picking the kids that are the best achievers and denying entrance to the other ones, right? And they look good. But they are taking money out of the public school system, so we have to support our teachers and we have to support our students.

La Lucha Sigue—The Struggle Continues

Dolores Huerta, a notable octogenarian powerhouse, continues to act and encourage others to fuel the rights of the poor, the marginalized and the oppressed. She demonstrates through her life's work how one person can make a tremendous difference in improving humanity, and this is a lesson to us all. She is an illustrious example of how dedication and hard work, conviction and a belief in the rights of others can contribute to a better world.

It was under this aura that we joined in the cry of Dolores Huerta, *Si Se Puede—Yes We Can*—do better for farm workers; *yes we can*—demand more decent work conditions from the richest country in the world; *yes we can*—give the children a better chance to learn in the schools; *yes we can*, Dolores Huerta and César Chávez—support this cause, as it is also ours.

Notes

1. National Women's History Museum, retrieved February 23, 2014 from http://www.nwhm.org/education-resources/biography/biographies/dolores-fernandez-huerta/
2. Ibid.
3. Larry Dulay Itliong was a Filipino migrant worker and union organizer. Philip Vera Cruz was also a Filipino migrant worker and organizer in the Delano area. They were both members of the National Farm Labor Union and Agriculture Workers Organizing Committee before joining the National Farm Workers of America to form the United Farm Workers Union, where Vera Cruz became Vice President. Itliong eventually served as assistant director of the United Farm Workers under César Chávez and in 1970 he was appointed the United Farm Workers' national boycott coordinator. Along with other farm workers, they began the Delano strike to fight against reduced wages proposed by the growers. "It was this strike that eventually made the UFW, the farmworkers movement, and Cesar Chavez famous worldwide" (Scharlin & Villanueva, 1998, p. 203).
4. César Chávez was born in Yuma, Arizona. In 1929, his family moved to California to work as agricultural workers. Mexican immigrants, like Chávez's family, moved in to replace Asians that were formerly "California's primary source of agricultural labor." Chávez was influenced by his farm worker status. He was exposed to the ideas of labor unions, nonviolence resistance, and farm worker strikes. Because of the Bracero Program in 1942, millions of Mexican migrant workers came to the Southwest and were exploited. Chávez lead various strikes, boycotts, and fasts in the mid-1960s. In 1968, he held his first 25-day fast to support the UFW's national boycott, a movement for better wages and treatment of migrant workers. Chávez became a selfless martyr who was dedicated to justice (Etulain, 2002; Holmes, 2010; Wingett, 2009).
5. Legendary Labor Leader Dolores Huerta to speak at Mills College Convocation. Mills College Website Newsroom. Retrieved February 23, 2014 from http://www.mills.edu/news/2010/newsarticle08252010HuertaConvocation.php
6. http://www.ufw.org/_page.php?menu=research&inc=_page.php?menu=research&inc=history/01.html

References

Anzaldua, G. (1990). *Haciendo caras/making face, making soul: Creative and critical perspectives by women of color*. San Francisco, CA: Aunt Lute Press.

Etulain, R. W. (2002). *Cesar Chavez: A brief biography with documents* (The Bedford Series in History and Culture). New York, NY: Bedford.

Freire, P. (1978). *Pedagogy in process: The letters to Guinea-Bissau*. New York, NY: Seabury Press.
Freire, P., & Macedo. D. (1987). *Literacy: reading the word & the world*. Critical studies in education series. South Hadley, MA: Bergin & Garvey Publishers.
Gándara, P., & Contreras, F. (2009). *Latino education crisis: The consequences of failed social policies*. Cambridge, MA: Harvard University Press.
Gold, N. (2006) *Successful bilingual schools: Six effective programs in California*. San Diego: San Diego County Office of Education.
Gonzalez, N. (2001). *I am my language: Discourses of women and children in the borderlands*. Tucson, AZ: The University of Arizona Press.
Holmes, T. (2010). "The economic roots of Reaganism: Corporate conservatives, political economy, and the United Farm Workers Movement, 1965–1970." *Western Historical Quarterly, 41.1*, 55–80.
McField, G., & McField, D. (2014). "The consistent outcome of bilingual education programs: A meta-analysis of meta-analyses." In Grace McField (Ed.), *The miseducation of English learners* (pp. 267–299). Charlotte, NC: Information Age Publishing.
Moreno, J. (Ed.). (2010). *The elusive quest for equality: 150 years of Chicano/Chicana education*. Cambridge, MA: Harvard Educational Review.
Murphy, J. (2014, December 12). Teacher files rights complaints for pupils. *Democrat & Chronicle*. Retrieved March 23, 2015 from http://www.democratandchronicle.com/story/news/2014/12/12/rochester-teacher-alleges-discrimination/20301613/
Parrish, T., Merickel, A., Eaton, M., Pérez, M., Linquanti, R. , Farr, B., Socias, M., Spain, A., Speroni, C., Esra, P., Brock, L., & Delancy, D. (2006). Effects of the implementation of Proposition 227 on the education of English Learners, K–12: Findings from a five-year evaluation. Final Report for AB 56 and AB 1116 Evaluation Study. Palo Alto, CA: American Institutes for Research.
Scharlin, C., & Villanueva, L. (1998). *The fight in the fields: Cesar Chavez and the Farmworkers Movement*. Orlando, FL: Harvest/HBJ Books.
Skiba, R. J., Horner, R. H., Chung, C-G., Rausch, M. K., May, S. L., & Tobin, T. (2011). Race is not neutral: A national investigation of African American and Latino disproportionality in school discipline. *School Psychology Review, 40*(1), 85–107.
Wingett, Y. (2009, March 29) "Historic site hosts modern activism." *Arizona Republic* [Phoenix]. Retrieved November 6, 2012, from http://www.azcentral.com/arizonarepublic/local/articles/2009/03/29/20090329 chavez-santarita0329.html

10

I AM A CHICANA, I AM UNION, I AM AN ACTIVIST

The Struggle for Cultural, Educational, and Linguistic Justice

Theresa Montaño

I Was Union, before I Was Chicana

I was raised in a union family. My dad was a member of the Baker and Confectionary Workers of America, Local 37. I later discovered that my mother was also in the union. She met my dad when they both worked at Ms. Lee's pies in Los Angeles. Among my most precious possessions are their union cards.

I was union, before I was Chicana. As children, we learned never to eat grapes or cross a picket line. My father was quick to remind me that the little we had was thanks to the union. We were the only family on the block who owned our home and had health insurance. It was due to my father's involvement in the union that I developed a political conscience.

I was born a Mexican-American and became a Chicana. As a young woman, I worked with three other women to establish the first UMAS (United Mexican-American Students) chapter at Huntington Park High School. There is a photograph of us in the Huntington Park High School yearbook. In 1970, we joined thousands of young Angelenos in leading the high school walkouts. Among our demands was the call for bilingual instruction, the hiring of Chicano/a teachers and counselors, and the establishment of a Mexican-American Studies program. I recall that while we were engaged in our efforts to improve the schooling conditions for Mexican-American students, our teachers were simultaneously organizing United Teachers Los Angeles (UTLA). While the reasons we walked out of high school differed from our teachers' desire for union representation, my thirst for educational justice was fueled by my father's commitment to the union, my teachers' quest for union representation, and my involvement in the developing Chicano/a movement.

I made my decision to teach at that time. My decision to become a teacher was a political decision. The idea of teaching was inspired by a larger social movement that called for an end to an unjust war abroad and social and economic/educational justice here at home. I subscribed to Paulo Freire's principle that "education was a political act" (Freire, 1970).

> A political act aimed at fundamentally changing education by radically restructuring an educational system that had lied to us about our history, dishonored and disrespected our language and endeavored to confine our population at the lower end of the economic scale.
> *(Montaño, 2012, p.218)*

Community or Union: Selecting a Site of Activism

In 1979, I became a social studies teacher and a member of the union. I joined the California Federation of Teachers (CFT). The CFT was an affiliate of the American Federation of Teachers (AFT). As such, CFT was an affiliate of the American Federation of Labor and Congress of Industrial Organizations (AFL-CIO). I remained a member of the AFT for many years. Although I was a member of the union, I was not a union activist. I choose to enact my activist agenda in the community. I was a community activist. I worked with organizations such as the East Los Angeles Committee for Democratic Rights, the Chicano Moratorium Committee, the Committee to Elect Jesse Jackson for President, and others involved in improving the conditions in the Chicano/a community.

In 1984, I left Los Angeles to live in Denver, Colorado, where I taught at Merrill Middle School, gave birth to my son, raised a teenaged daughter, got married, and became a spokesperson for Coloradans for Language Freedom, a civil rights group challenging Colorado's English Only Initiative. As a spokesperson, I debated several Colorado legislators, right-wing demagogues, and testified before the civil rights commission about the continued marginalization of language minority students and Chicano/as. I consider bilingual education a democratic and civil right. It is about the preservation of language and culture. The support of primary language instruction is not simply an effective way to teach English. This is the perspective I brought to the work in Colorado and the view that I hold today.

As a Chicana, family is of primary importance. While I loved my activist work in Denver, I was incredibly homesick and in 1987 I returned to teaching in Los Angeles. Disillusioned with AFT president Al Shanker's view of bilingual education and his support of the Contras, I decided not to remain a member of the CFT.

In 1983, Shanker had supported the Bilingual Education Improvements Action, which in my opinion led to the beginning of the end of bilingual education in the United States (Shanker, 1983). Albert Shanker was one of the founding members of teacher unionism and while he was a staunch proponent of unionism, he was an opponent of bilingual instruction. On the question of bilingualism, Shanker once said, "I came to school not knowing one word of English and the teacher made fun of me and would not let me speak Yiddish. But maybe it was for the best. I learned English quickly because I had to" (Shanker, 1983). Criticizing bilingual education Shanker went on to say, "I am not sure the new way is better" (Latz Griffin, December 15, 1985). I could not in good conscience remain a member of the CFT. I had the good fortune of teaching in Los Angeles where the teachers' union, the United Teachers Los Angeles (UTLA), was affiliated with both the National Education Association (NEA) and the American Federation of Teachers (AFT). After speaking to my father about my reasons for leaving the AFL-CIO affiliated AFT/CFT, I rejoined as a member of the California Teachers Association (CTA), an affiliate of the National Education Association, a more bilingual-friendly union. In 1967, "the NEA sponsored a major conference on bilingual education and the needs of Spanish-speaking students. The NEA conference led directly to the passage of the 1968 Bilingual Education Act" (Holcomb, 2006). The official policy of the NEA was to support bilingual programs, including the use of the native language as means of instruction. In California, due in part to union support, in 1976 educational advocates were successful in passing the state's first bilingual education act, the Chacón-Moscone bill. Thanks to that bill, I became a secondary bilingual teacher at Robert Lewis Stevenson Middle School, where I taught in the "ESL building" (where the majority of English learners attended classes) and organized the school's first bilingual drama club. It was one of the most rewarding experiences of my life. I remember my students performing Luis Valdez's Los Vendidos before a packed auditorium. Students who previously displayed indifference to education enthusiastically performed in front of English-speaking and Spanish-speaking peers and teachers. The middle school students at Stevenson had established a convincing case for bilingual-bicultural education.

The Politics of Language

While the United States has never had an official national language policy, politics have influenced and driven educational practices in many states. Through compliance regulations, court mandates, and consent decrees, school districts have adopted language policies. These policies, in turn, impacted not only the quality of the instructional program, but decisions regarding the hiring, placement, and retention of educational personnel. As such, it is impossible to separate the politics of teacher unionism from the sociopolitical debate surrounding bilingual instruction. In California, the ideological battle appeared in United Teachers Los Angeles, where the English Only zealots would lead the effort to systematically dismantle bilingual instruction.

The short window of opportunity for the supporters of bilingual education lasted about 20 years (mid 1960s–early 1980s) (Montaño, Ulanoff, Quintanar-Sarellana, & Aoki, 2005; Cadiero-Kaplan, 2004; Crawford, 1999; Genzuk, 1988). For Chicanos/as, the turning point came when the U.S. Commission on Civil

Rights published a series of reports on the education of Mexican-American students and the walkouts by high school students in the southwest United States. During this time period, state legislatures and courts passed a series of measures that would require school districts to implement programs specifically designed and developed for students whose primary language was not English. *Lau v. Nichols* was the catalyst needed to force school districts to address the deficiencies in the instructional program offered to English learners. *Castañeda v. Pickard* initiated provisions that would require school districts to create programs based on sound educational theory, implement and evaluate said programs, and provide services and personnel that would eliminate the achievement gap between English language learners (ELL) and their English-speaking peers.

Interestingly, *Castañeda v. Pickard* ushered in the "dismissive period" in California in the late 1970s and 1980s. Karen Cadiero-Kaplan (2004) would argue that a prominent marker during this period would be the dispute over the language of instruction in the classroom. The resulting instruction eliminated any hope of ever implementing heritage language programs, shifting instead to programs focused on English language acquisition (transitional bilingual education, English language development, etc.). The stringent regulations placed upon school districts to hire qualified instructors served as the primary impetus for the anti-bilingual education forces to reserve the union's support of transitional bilingual education. These teachers felt their job security and positions in the union were threatened by the growth of the English learner population and the institutionalization of bilingual education.

After the passage of the Chacón-Moscone Bilingual-Bicultural Education Act (1976) and the Reauthorization of the federal Bilingual Education Act (1978), California began to issue the Bilingual Certificate of Competence (BCC). The BCC was granted to bilingual teachers who could prove competency in English and one other language, such as Spanish or Korean. Teachers were certified bilingual after passing a test or taking additional coursework at a university. Bilingual certificated teachers were placed in classrooms where the language of instruction was English and another language. Many of these teachers were placed in grades 1–3 and if there were English learners at beginning levels of English language proficiency, these teachers would be required to hold the BCC (Montaño, Ulanoff, Quintanar-Sarellana, & Aoki, 2005; Cadiero-Kaplan, 2004). The Language Development Specialist (LDS) was the compulsory certificate of instruction for any teacher teaching in a classroom where more than ten students were identified as English learners. The LDS credential did not require additional skills in a second language, but the idea that teachers would be required to understand second language theory and methodology angered many veteran teachers.

English Only and UTLA

As a member of UTLA, I remained active in Latino issues, particularly on issues regarding bilingual education and instruction for English learners. When I returned to Los Angeles, I was greeted by the first of several attempts to force UTLA to adopt an anti-bilingual initiative. The English-only forces within the union authored an anti-bilingual education referendum (Giordani, 1997; Gold, 1987; Imhoff, 1990; Montaño et al., 2005; Woo, 1987). LEAD's (Learning English Advocates Drive) action was motivated by self-interest. Their primary opposition was to the requirement that teachers in California have additional certification in English language development theory and pedagogy. The initiative was also an attempt to reverse the union's policy supporting a bilingual differential for bilingual teachers. The collective bargaining agreement between the union and the district provided a stipend for teachers who possessed bilingual certification or the Bilingual Certificate of Competence (BCC) and who taught in a bilingual classroom.

In 1987, pro-bilingual education forces and anti-bilingual education forces within UTLA engaged in an ideological battle that lasted over a decade. The LEAD referendum, authored by Sally Petersen, was initially supported by union leaders such as Wayne Johnson, who, according to Petersen, helped to author the initial referendum (Imhoff, 1990). Prior to this initiative drive, English-only advocates were vocal oppositionists on issues related to bilingual instruction, but their anger was directed to pro-bilingual forces at schools. LEAD forces did not have an organized presence in the union. In contrast to bilingual education union activists, LEAD was not involved in union governance and nor were they union activists. Those of us in UTLA who were bilingual education activists were enraged at the leadership's encouragement of anti-bilingual education forces and met with Wayne Johnson and the union leadership to express our disgust. Wayne Johnson assured us that he was not in support of the LEAD initiative and persuaded us to sponsor our own initiative. We did.

The LEAD forces emerged victorious in August 1987, when 78 percent of UTLA voters endorsed English immersion and rejected primary language instruction. The referendum simultaneously called for the elimination of the district's waiver program. The district waiver program required teachers to sign a promissory note that would waive the credentialing requirement until teachers attained the certificate required for teaching English learners. The union leadership tried to convince bilingual education activists that the vote was not a referendum against bilingual education but a question of job security for teachers who were afraid of reassignment due to the failure to meet the requirement. We knew better. However, the union needed bilingual teachers and the community. Wayne Johnson worked hard to keep us involved.

The LEAD forces would continue their attacks on bilingual education on a national level. In the summer of 1988, LEAD convinced the American Federation of Teachers to rescind its support of transitional bilingual education. However, it failed to persuade the delegates of the larger National Education Association. In fact, NEA passed a resolution supporting bilingual programs "where resources permitted" (Gold, 1987). Discouraged, I remained a member of UTLA, but my involvement in the union was peripheral. I retreated to my community and worked to elect Jesse Jackson to the presidency of the United States.

It wasn't until after the Jesse Jackson for President Campaign that I really joined the activist ranks of UTLA. As the Southern California coordinator of Latinos for Jackson, I was a delegate to the Democratic Convention in 1988. After Jackson lost, UTLA was looking for a Jackson person in Northeast Los Angeles to lead its work on the Dukakis campaign. This was my entrance into UTLA politics. While the Jackson campaign was the impetus for my involvement, my primary role in UTLA was to advocate for English learners, bilingual education, and educational justice for Latino/a-Chicano/a students. The LEAD forces were not satisfied with changing union policy; their ultimate goal was to abolish bilingual education policy in the state of California.

Union Policy, Yes! Statewide Referendum, No!

The political climate affecting bilingual education pitted additive bilingualism against subtractive bilingualism. Additive bilingualism supports English plus the primary language, as well as biculturalism, and considers bilingualism an asset. Additive bilingualism can be juxtaposed with subtractive bilingualism, which calls for the total eradication of the primary language instruction, promotes assimilation and English-only instruction. It can be argued that "subtractive proponents arguably won the ideological battle, leading to program planning efforts that would replace a child's primary language with the dominant language, English" (Montano, Ulanoff, Quintanar-Sarellana, & Aoki, 2005, p. 107). The bilingual education proponents were at least victorious in seeing to it that a "qualified" teacher must have the knowledge and background in second language acquisition theory and methodology. Moreover, the development and success of the Eastman program in Los Angeles (a developmental, intensive, long-term bilingual program offered to English learners from first through sixth grade) still necessitated the hiring of a substantial number of bilingual instructors. The increasing numbers of English learners in Los Angeles demonstrated that EL certificated teachers were still essential, even in classrooms where the mode of instruction was English. Therefore, while LEAD was successful in securing the passage of UTLA policy supporting English Immersion as a means of instruction union policy, it did not remove the credentialing requirement.

The continued push for the appropriate certification of teachers, coupled with the idea that a bilingually certificated teacher teaching in a fully bilingual classroom (who was required to spend extra time after school with students and with additional certification) would receive a $5000 a year bonus, infuriated the LEAD forces. In 1989 LEAD spearheaded yet another initiative campaign. This time the initiative was directed at the elimination of the bilingual stipend. Whereas the previous initiative had been mostly symbolic, the subsequent initiative could potentially affect contract negotiations between the union and the district. The bilingual stipend was a negotiated issue.

The Teacher's Strike and the Battle against LEAD

Incensed over the possibility that we would lose the initiative drive, bilingual education activists, parents, teachers, and the community organized a demonstration against LEAD at the union headquarters. When asked whether the initiative would win, Wayne Johnson, UTLA president responded, "that he thought it stood 'a very good chance' of passage" (Enriquez, 1989, p. 1). This time, under the leadership of individuals such as Mark Meza-Overstreet, Lupe Quezada, Jose Govea, Alberto Valdivia and others, the bilingual education activists in the union fought back. UTLA leadership, fearing that they would not have the support of pro-bilingual education forces in the ensuing battle against the district, supported the activists in their battle against LEAD. Unity among the ranks of classroom teachers was important towards winning a good contract. Wayne Johnson called for a meeting of community activists, such as the Mothers of East Los Angeles, Association of Mexican-American Educators, and new activists like me. At the meeting, community and teachers asked Wayne Johnson to take a public stance against the initiative. Activists reminded Wayne Johnson and other UTLA leaders of the divisiveness the initiative was causing among the ranks. It was agreed that division was not what teachers needed when we were about to take an important strike vote. Johnson and the UTLA Board of Directors took a stance against the LEAD initiative.

In 1989, we went on strike and managed to call to question the validity of the second LEAD initiative on technicalities. But this did not stop the anti-bilingual forces. As those of us in the bilingual education community sought to strengthen ties between the union and the community, the xenophobic English-only activists continued to organize.

Moving the Union toward the "Debilingualization" of Teacher Quality

In 1987, Governor Deukmejian vetoed the extension of the bilingual education law advancing the "debilingualization" of public education in California (Mathews, 1987). As a result, classrooms in which there were ten or more EL students required instruction in two languages, leaving non-bilingual teachers without the assistance of a bilingual aide and forcing school districts to adopt instructional options that did not use the student's home language as the means of instruction. The systematic dismantling of bilingual programs in California was not done in isolation. Simultaneously throughout the United States, linguistic supremacy was prevalent and the deficit view of language as a problem (Ruiz, 1984) became the dominant discourse in the development of bilingual programs. The legitimatization of programs that focused primarily on the teaching of English officially became the mode of instruction. Bilingual education and civil rights activists who advocated for bilingual-bicultural education were silenced. However, in Los Angeles and other districts, the school boards thwarted these efforts and local educational agencies continued to develop programs that were transitional or developmental in nature. These programs supported the use of the primary language in instruction until the ELL acquired sufficient English language proficiency to function in an English-only instructional setting. In Los Angeles, teachers would still be required to hold an additional certification. Los Angeles used the credential guidelines as placement criteria and in the event of lay-offs, the possession of English language development EL certification was used to retain or transfer teachers. Teachers with bilingual certification were assigned to classrooms with beginning through intermediate ELL students and in which the primary language of the students was the language of instruction. Teachers with a Language Development Specialist (LDS) authorization or Cross-Cultural Language and Academic Development (CLAD) credential (which was adopted by the California Council on Teacher Credentialing [CCTC] in 1992 to replace the LDS) were officially recognized as qualified to teach ELLs in non-bilingual classrooms with ELL students.

LEAD continued to pressure union leaders to adopt a position against anti-bilingual education and eventually succeeded in pressuring the union to lobby for the passage of SB 1969 (Colvin, 1989). Those in union leadership such as Helen Bernstein held the position that as long as members of the Latino/a community supported bilingual education, she would consider SB 1969 a compromise bill. However, the pressure by LEAD advocates arguing that experience in the classroom should count for something convinced Helen to lobby for SB 1969. The result was the "grandfathering" of experienced teachers into English Language Development classrooms where the primary language would not be used to instruct English learners. SB 1969 required every teacher of English learners to participate in a mandated 45-hour professional development course. I was chosen to be one of the lead developers of this course for the Los Angeles Unified School District (LAUSD) and along with the language acquisition department in LAUSD, UTLA certified more than 1000 non-certificated teachers.

Proposition 227 and the Teachers Union

I was a member of the UTLA staff when I worked on SB 1969. I quickly became the "bilingual go-to person" in the union. I worked with UTLA in 1996 when the pro-bilingual education forces were finally victorious. In 1997, Stephanie Schwartz, a high school teacher at Granada Hills High School, authored another anti-bilingual certification initiative (Giordani, 1997). I became a union spokesperson against the initiative. In June 1997, 57 percent of UTLA voters voted against the initiative. That same year, the bilingual education committee would author an initiative re-affirming UTLA's commitment to ensuring that Los Angeles teachers would hold the appropriate certification and to uphold its support for bilingual education. This initiative would meet with voter approval. It was our hope that these two referendums would settle the debate. They did not, because "unfortunately, sometimes in the heat of ideological battles, voters sometimes lose their common sense" (Gabaldón, 2004 p. 98). The debate over bilingual education in the union continued, as it did throughout the nation.

In June 1998, California voters approved Proposition 227. Authored by businessman Ron Unz and elementary teacher Gloria Matta Tuchman, the measure called for all students classified as English learners to be placed in Structured English Immersion (SEI) classrooms where the instructional emphasis was English language instruction.

In the midst of the struggle against Proposition 227, labor unions were engaged in a battle for their very survival. Proposition 226 threatened to stifle the union's role in the political process. Regardless of the ideological debate among union members, the leadership of CTA and CFT were officially supportive of bilingual education. While many in the bilingual community could argue that UTLA and CTA would place greater emphasis on the debate of Proposition 227, my job was to focus on the defeat of it. In the end, CTA would contribute more money against Proposition 227 than any other individual or organization. While Univision's chair, A. Jerrold Perenchio, would donate a whopping 1.5 million dollars to the forces opposing Proposition 227, CTA gave almost 2.2 million dollars in monetary contributions (WestEd, 1997). UTLA would re-affirm its pro-bilingual education stance after the passage and I was assigned the role of union spokesperson on the implementation of Proposition 227. In 1997, once again, taking on the LEAD proponents, we challenged schools to secure parental waivers allowing schools to continue bilingual education programs. Unfortunately, principals and school districts quickly moved toward the implementation of Structured English Immersion (SEI) programs, thereby sacrificing a child's human right to linguistic and cultural identity to the domination of English only.

Is Certification Enough?

In the final analysis, there are several reasons why our efforts to defeat Proposition 227 failed, among them the increasing anti-Latino, anti-immigrant sentiment among the Californian voting populace. In spite of this climate, the union has remained an advocate of English learners. The alliance between bilingual advocates and the teachers union continues, in part, due to the advocates of English learners who are also union leaders. CTA has established the Language Acquisition Committee, an alliance with the California Association of Bilingual Education and Californians Together. In 2008, members of the language acquisition committee in CTA State Council (CTA decision-making body) fought for the adoption of a new policy language so that textbook publishers could develop instructional textbooks for English learners based on the language proficiency standards. Bilingual teachers and higher education members are also actively working with NEA to develop professional development seminars for teachers demonstrating successful methods for EL instruction. We have seen to it that the majority of California's teachers have the proper certification to teach English to our English learners. But, is this enough?

My political and professional career can be summed up as the negotiation between what is good for the Chicano/a-Latina/o community and what is good for the union. As minorities in a union dominated by members who speak the dominant language and are of the dominant culture, bilingual activists have worked hard to secure a position of support for bilingual instruction, symbolically. I believe that my experiences and ability to cross borders has helped me to negotiate and place our issues at the top of the union's agenda. I honestly believe that we have made some progress in education. Latino teachers represent almost 30 percent of the teachers in LAUSD and we have more students in college than ever before. However, the reality is that in the United States, home language, immigrant status, and race impact the quality of education that students receive. The inequities facing our students must be placed in this larger educational context. A context where budget cuts are commonplace and public education is becoming more and more privatized. A context where English learners are blamed for the failure of schools to meet the high-stakes goals placed upon them by misguided policies. A context where union busting is fashionable and where we find ourselves engaged in yet another political battle against those forces that wish to silence our political voice. The political context can be summed up as one where politicians and educational leaders have capitulated to the corporate agenda to produce a succession of submissive, docile, compliant English-only literate workers.

As we face the worst economic crisis since the Great Depression, instead of improving public education, policy makers have done very little to improve the educational standing of our students. The beliefs that the political landscape requires leaders who are visionary, who can assess and analyze the entire educational spectrum, who are not afraid to "question authority," and who can "work well with others" are the factors that influence my continued participation in union politics (Montaño, 2012). I believe that presence in the union has provided me a broad perspective on public education, and has made a difference in the union. As a member of the union, I will continue to challenge the implementation of neoliberal policies that seek to destroy our public education system, inside the union and in the broader educational context. I will aggressively challenge those in our union who reduce the importance of minority issues and concerns, who seek to dismantle the gains we have made in securing a place in the union, and who refuse to recognize that immigrant and language minority rights are the civil rights issues of the day. I will not stop until minority issues become synonymous with union issues.

As a Chicana union member, I will continue to make connections between union and bilingual education activists. However, the alliance must be reciprocal. Those of us in unions and advocating for bilingual students cannot continue to border cross alone. We need members of the bilingual community to also support the teachers union. We do not choose to be in unions only to represent the interest of our communities. We are unionists who happen to be Chicana/os and language minorities. As such, we strongly believe that the education policies that determine the quality of instruction our students receive also determine the quality of our working conditions. Union members believe education is a right and those rights extend to both workers and students. As our unions engage in the fierce battle to exist and be political, they must also be supported by the community. Language and ethnic minority unionist activists must continue to struggle within their unions and in their community to bring these forces together to advance the educational interests of the next generation. We should not be forced to choose between the union and our community, because we represent both.

References

Cadiero-Kaplan, K. (2004). *The literacy curriculum and bilingual education.* New York, NY: Peter Lang.

Colvin, R. (1989, June 18). A LEAD role in bilingual controversy: Teacher's emphasis on English puts her in the center of the storm. *The Los Angeles Times.* Retrieved April 18, 2012 from http://articles.latimes.com/print/1989–6–18/local/me-3811_1_bilingual-education

Crawford, J. (1999). *Bilingual education: History, politics, theory and practice.* 4th edition. Los Angeles, CA: Bilingual Education Services.

Enriquez, S. (1989, March 30). Bonuses threatened by bilingual policy rift. *The Los Angeles Times.* Retrieved April 19, 2012 from http://articles.latimes.com/print/1989–03–03/local/me-206_1_bilingual-teacher

Freire, P. (1970). *Pedagogy of the oppressed.* New York: Herder and Herder.

Gabaldón, S. (2004). My mother's Spanish. In W. Au (Ed.). *Rethinking multicultural education: Teaching for racial and cultural justice* (pp. 97–99). Milwaukee, WI: Rethinking Schools.

Genzuk, M. (1988). *An historical overview of bilingual education in the United States.* 2nd edition. Los Angeles, CA: Los Angeles Unified School District Office of Bilingual-ESL Instruction.

Giordani, S. (1997). UTLA to vote anew on support for mandated bilingual education. *Daily News.* The Free Library. Retrieved March 9, 2015 from http://www.thefreelibrary.com/UTLA+TO+VOTE+ANEW+ON+SUPPORT+FOR+MANDATED+BILINGUAL+EDUCATION.-a083872693

Gold, D. (1987, 9 September). Union votes down bilingual education. *Education Week.* Retrieved April 4, 2012 from http://www.edweek.org/ew/articles/a987/09/09/07200029.h07.html

Holcomb, S. (2006, 25 April). Answering the call: The history of NEA, Part 4. In 2006–2011 archives. Retrieved June 16, 2015 from http://www.nea.org/home/12372.htm.

Imhoff, G. (1990). *Learning in two languages: From conflict to consensus in the reorganization of schools.* New Brunswick, NJ: Transaction Publishers.

Latz Griffin, J. (1985, December 15). Bilingual education: Learning to deal with problems that are words apart. *The Chicago Tribune,* pp. 3 of 3.

Mathews, J. (1987, August 2). California veto a blow to bilingual education: Gov. Deukmejian blocks extension of the law. *The Washington Post,* pp. A3.

Montaño, T. (2012). De levantarse y seguir cayendo: Taking a critical stance in troubling times. In A. Darder (Ed.). *Culture and power in the classroom: Educational foundations for the schooling of bicultural students* (20th anniversary). New York, NY: Paradigm Publishers.

Montaño, T., Ulanoff, S. H., Quintanar-Sarellana, R., & Aoki, L. (2005). The Debilingualization of California's prospective bilingual teachers, *Social Justice*, Vol. 32 (Num. 3), 103–121.

National Education Association. (2012). *NEA advocacy on behalf of bilingual education and ELL students.* Unpublished manuscript.

Ruiz, R. (1984). Orientations in language planning. *NABE: Journal of the National Association of Bilingual Education,* Vol. 9 (Num. 3), 131–137.

Shanker, A. (1983, June 7). Testimony before the subcommittee on elementary, secondary and vocational education. U.S. House of representatives on H# 2682, the bilingual education improvements act of 1983, 1–7.

WestEd. (1997). Summary (1997): *California's Proposition 277 experiences.* Retrieved April 18, 2012 from http://www.wested.org/policy/pubs/prop227/main.htm

Woo, E. (1987, August 13). L.A. teachers favor policy of English immersion. *The Los Angeles Times.* Retrieved June 16, 2015 from http://articles.latimes.com/print/1987-08-13/news/mn-1318_1_bilingual-education

11

OPERATION CHICANO/A TEACHER

A School-Based Teacher Equity Recruitment and Retention Program

Marta E. Sanchez

Introduction

It was 1968, spring semester at Beaumont High School. I was soon to graduate and had no idea what I was going to do with my life. My cousins who were slightly financially better off than me said that we were going to attend college. For me, college was an unfamiliar concept other than that it was school. It was a miracle that I was graduating high school and the thought of continuing school was not appealing. My grades were average and advisors were too busy counseling college-prep students. They did not see potential in Mexican students. I was a hard worker and thought that I would stay in Beaumont without a career. Both of my parents were immigrants from Mexico and most of my family worked as laborers in the hotel and food industry or as domestics. I figured that my life would mirror theirs. My days consisted of going to work as a maid at a local Jewish resort, babysitting and then partying at night. I had never taken school seriously and had a reputation for being somewhat of a disruptive student. In my mind, school was not something that I saw as a vehicle for success but rather a place to socialize. My immediate worry was always financial survival. I could say that my greatest role models were my mom who always supported education, my two cousins who insisted on college, my sister who had managed to work in a bank and my oldest brother who studied music at College of the Desert.

Well, I graduated, and thirty years later was recognized as the most educated in the Beaumont class of 1968. The timing of my graduation dovetailed with the onset of the great civil rights movement. High schools in cities surrounding Beaumont participated in the High School Walkouts. These smaller cities did not get as much notoriety as the high schools in Los Angeles. Nonetheless, these smaller cities were involved. I began to hear about opportunities for minorities from friends, and my cousins and I began to work our way through several community colleges. This was the way it was done by most poor and college-bound Mexicans. I needed a job and loved working with children so I applied as an English as a Second Language (ESL) teacher assistant.

Thus was born my passion for teaching and working with English Language Learners. No one, including those who had hired me, knew much about how to teach non-English-speaking students. My students were not only Mexican, but also Native Americans from the Hemet and San Jacinto areas. I worked hard to create meaningful activities for these children and I also found out that I was quite good at teaching. Every day became an inspiration and I knew that if I wanted to pursue a teaching career, I would have to take college seriously and study hard. After community college, I transferred to the University of California in Santa Barbara (UCSB), which had actively recruited me with offers of financial aid and Equal Educational Opportunity (EOP) grants. I was able to get into the university through Affirmative and Special Action Programs (without the basic admissions requirements). UCSB with its prototype, "El Plan de Santa Barbara," was the center of many Chicano Movement Activities. As a student at UCSB in 1969 and continuing into my professional life, I maintained a strong involvement with MEChA (Movimiento Estudiantil Chicano de Aztlan). I was also one of the founding directors of the first Bilingual Bicultural School, "La Escuelita Tiburcio Vásquez," in Santa Barbara. I had found my passion and was fully committed to the education of Latino children. I began to get politically involved and became more aware of the injustices that had plagued Chicanos for decades.

Fast forward from 1968: I have been in the field of education for over 40 years and have held many positions in schools of education. My love of teaching erased any of my early negative feelings toward school and motivated me to continue my education. I ended up with three education credentials, a Master of Arts Degree and my Ph.D. It has been a fulfilling profession. But, my role as the Director of the Operation Chicano/a Teacher (OCT) Program for 17 years was the most historically significant professional accomplishment I made with regard to civil rights.

Background

The following narrative is a personal account of the creation, operation and impact of the Operation Chicano/a Teacher Program, as well as its program components and its political evolution from the early 1970s to 1998. The account is based on my personal experience as the program director and program archives. I feel that this program warrants attention because it was the first educational equity program dedicated to the recruitment and retention of perspective Latino/a teachers in California. It successfully prepared thousands of Chicano/a teachers for Los Angeles and Ventura Counties at a time when there were relatively no Latino/a teachers or teacher candidates at California State University (CSU), Northridge.

It also helped to bolster the Chicano Studies department by providing enough students to create 16 faculty positions.

A Look Back at the History of Chicano/a Students

The educational history of Chicanos/as in this country is filled with discrimination and failure, despite the progress that has been made. It was not until the great civil rights turmoil of the 1960s and 1970s that higher education became attainable to Latinos. Elementary and secondary Mexican students typically attended segregated schools with substandard facilities. They were taught by teachers who were unaware of their language and culture and who often had low expectations based in societal myths.

Public attention turned to the educational neglect of Chicanos in the 1960s with student unrest that could be felt at universities and colleges all over the nation. Attention by both President Kennedy and later President Johnson spurred federal and state legislation. Progress was slow and legislation was riddled with terms implying that Latinos were culturally deprived. Programs such as Title I, designed to level the injustices, were compensatory in nature focusing on the "disadvantaged child." Even Bilingual Education programs were viewed by the public as compensatory rather than as enrichment programs. Those of us in the field of education knew that the only true disadvantage was the fact that schools did not recognize or honor the assets of bilingual and bicultural children. There existed a widespread belief that these children needed to be stripped of their heritage, language and culture to succeed.

Although the late 1960s and 1970s saw a rise in the number of Chicanos attending institutions of higher education, the educational attainments of Chicanos still lagged behind those of other minorities and Whites. Demographic trends reflected a large increase of Chicanos in the 1974 U.S. Census Data at 6.5 million, with the largest percentage of this population concentrated in Sunbelt Cities, particularly in Los Angeles and San Antonio. According to census data, the Hispanic population was young, with a median age of 22.1 in 1979. But the demographics revealed a dismal picture for the Chicanos. Carter (1970) and Ferrin et al. (1972) found dropout figures as high as 89 percent among Chicanos in the Southwest. In 1974 in California, there were 19,841 Chicano freshmen (7.6%) of the total freshmen population attending colleges or universities, but only 2,602 Chicanos in their senior year, or 3.4 percent of the overall senior population (Casso & Roman, 1976, p. 4). Additionally, 75 percent of those attending college were enrolled in two-year community colleges (Vela, 1977, p. 464). The large pool of Hispanics in the community college system did not necessarily translate to a significant number transferring to a four-year college or university.

Although the 1980s was named the decade of Hispanics, the educational attainment during this decade was just as bleak as those of previous times. In the report issued by the State Department of Education (1980), *The Status of Hispanics in*

California Public Education, a list of scathing statistics were reported regarding the educational attainment of Latinos, the increase in English Language Learners, the lack of Latino teachers and the absence of Latinos in policy making positions across the state.

In California, demographic changes focused on how the growth of Latino students in elementary and secondary schools doubled. There was a growing concern in the California State University System regarding Hispanics and higher education. In September of 1984, the Office of the Chancellor appointed a Commission on Hispanic Underrepresentation to research factors related to the participation of Hispanics in postsecondary education and make recommendations on the recruitment and retention of teachers. There existed a severe national shortage of qualified teachers from diverse backgrounds. Educational reforms and institutional university policy changes would have to be inaugurated to meet the needs of prospective Latino teachers.

The 1970s and 1980s showed an increasing decline in minorities attending institutions of higher education and the trend continued into the 1990s. The number of students in the California State University (CSU) system pursuing bilingual cross-cultural education decreased from a high of 2,317 in 1980–81 to 1,731 in 1983–84. The proportion of CSU students from minority groups who selected teaching as a career did not compare favorably with K–12 minority enrollments in schools. The California State University Commission on Hispanic Underrepresentation noted that while 40 percent of the K–12 student population were ethnic minorities, only 25 percent of the students in professional studies were ethnic minorities (Commission on Hispanic Underrepresentation, 1985). Sadly, stringent university entrance and credential requirements designed to produce what were deemed "quality teachers" proved to eliminate the most needed group of prospective teachers: qualified quality teachers who were culturally relevant in ways that were a reflection of the growing school population.

Operation Chicano Teacher

Established in 1973 by the Department of Chicano Studies in the School of Humanities, CSU, Northridge, Operation Chicano Teacher was the only program of its kind in the state of California. It was originally funded by the Ford Foundation through a proposal written by Dr. Rudy Acuña. Funding was triggered partially by a need for action to reply to the East Los Angeles school walkouts in 1968 and the U.S. Commission on Civil Rights Reports (1974, 1–6) about the education of Mexican-Americans in the Southwest. The information gathered in the sixth report, "Toward Quality Education for Mexican-Americans: Report VI, Mexican-American Education Study," confirmed the complaints of the students who participated in the walkouts, revealing devastating information about the treatment, academic performance, teacher force, curriculum and counseling of Chicano students in the Southwest.

The two following excerpts from the reports summarize the findings:

1. The findings of this report reflect more than inadequacy regarding the specific conditions and practices examined. They reflect a systematic failure of the educational process which not only ignores the educational needs of Chicano students but also suppresses their culture, stifles their hopes and ambitions. The Chicanos are the excluded students.
2. The process of exclusion is complex. Each component is strong. They create a situation which inevitably leads to the education failure. (p. 67)

Aside from the conditions mentioned in the reports, sufficient minorities were not attending colleges and universities and therefore not part of the perspective pool of teachers. Moreover, schools of education did not require teacher candidates to learn about the language and culture of the students in the schools despite the signs that Latinos were becoming the fastest-growing and youngest segment of the population.

The Operation Chicano Teacher Program was founded during the second year of the Chicano Studies Department at CSU, Northridge when it was the San Fernando Valley State College. Dr. Jorge Garcia initiated a partnership with Oxnard School Board member Rachel Wong and included Ventura County Schools. According to the proposal, "the program would attempt to recruit and prepare students to teach Chicano children in the school system." An essential aspect of the initial program, according to the proposal, was to provide "Chicano students interested in becoming teachers, with financial assistance and academic support services." The program would cover a three-year period commencing in September of 1973 and ending in June of 1976. Total financial commitment by the Ford Foundation for that period would be for $346,270. The bulk of all monies ($300K) would be allocated in the form of $1,000 stipends per year for the approximately 100 students participating during the life of this program. The following school year (1975–76) the program spent approximately $82,522 in student stipends and added another 23 students for a total of 82 students by the end of the fiscal year in June of 1976. Student recruitment and selection procedures were conducted by department faculty and staff. According to OCT Program reports, there were 75 students in the original group (1973). Surprisingly, almost half (47%) of the students had either withdrawn or had been terminated within two years or before the school year ended. Of this group, only 37 students completed the program—13 of those were in elementary and 24 in secondary education. In four years the program had a 50 percent success rate and spent approximately $9,359 per student to get the 37 students into teaching careers. It is important to point out that most of these students were the first in their families to attend college, had not attended college preparation courses of study in high school, and were ill prepared to attend college. The Ford Foundation had been eager to fund a program that recruited minorities into a university, and provided retention strategies and pre-professional training for prospective teachers. Unfortunately, after its initial years the program fluctuated and the Ford Foundation funding ended by 1978.

My Role with the OCT Program

In 1981, I was the Migrant Instructional Support Teacher for Santa Barbara County Schools. I received a call from Dr. Raul Ruiz, who was then the Chairperson for the CSU, Northridge Chicano Studies Department. He informed me that there was a new position open for Director of the Operation Chicano Teacher Program. I agreed to interview and was offered the position. The position included a lectureship in the Chicano Studies Department in the School of Humanities. Challenges quickly became evident. The OCT Program had lost its funding and was in desperate need of strong and creative leadership. Perhaps the most challenging part of the position was the inherent role of being a liaison between the Chicano Studies Department and the School of Education.

I found the program lacking in infrastructure and formalized procedures. Aside from the loss of funding, the social and political climate had changed. After my arrival in 1982, new state and federal programs had begun to provide state and federal funding to schools of education for the recruitment of minority teachers. The political atmosphere between the School of Education and Chicano Studies was strained. Chicano Studies had enjoyed the domain over all matters related to Chicano students. It was now forced to coordinate with the School of Education due to the shift in funding. The Chicano Studies Department and past OCT directors had waged turf wars with the School of Education regarding services and course offerings. The Chicano Studies Department was steadfast in its commitment to the special needs of Chicano students and resisted relinquishing their power. As the new director, I encountered unexpected problems and realized that I had walked into a very sensitive situation. My personal background as a first generation Mexican student and my professional experience fueled my ability to build partnerships between the School of Humanities and the School of Education to relieve some of the existing tension.

By 1984, the program had grown to serve over 300 students, and by the time the program was terminated in 1998, over 3,000 students had been served. These included undergraduates, multiple and single subject credential, Bilingual Emphasis, ESL certificate, Bilingual Specialist Credential and Master's Degree candidates in Education. Throughout this time, the only source of financial support provided by the School of Humanities was negotiated between the chair of the Chicano Studies Department and the Dean of the School of Humanities. Thankfully, my salary and a half-time program secretary were granted. The other source of funding came from the School of Education. As trust was built between our program administration and that of the School of Education, a partnership emerged with Dr. Dolores Escobar. She was a Mexican-American professor in the School of Education from 1962–84 who was also committed to prospective Latino teachers. She later became the Associate Dean in the School of Education and gave me significant assignments, such as the administrator of the Bilingual Teacher Corp Training Program funded under Assembly Bill 2817. This program provided financial support in the sum of $1,500 to teacher assistants who were pursuing Bilingual Emphasis Credentials. As legislation changed, the grant was extended to any student pursuing a career in Bilingual Education and became known as AB 2615. The Title VII fellowship program was also instituted two years after I took over the position. Dr. Escobar made sure that the OCT students were the principal recipients.

Later, the University appointed the Associate Dean of the School of Education as coordinator for Bilingual Education programs. This served to institutionalize the Bilingual Education Programs at CSU, Northridge. Dr. Hernandez (then Associate Dean of the College of Education) appointed me as the director of the Bilingual Education Task Force and Advisory Committee. This new authority provided support for OCT Program services in the form of alliances with other university groups. I became an expert on minority teacher recruitment and the program continued to develop at a time when there was a great demand for bilingual teachers (Sanchez, 1989).

The director position I held began as a lecturer rank but changed in 1984. The chairman of the Department of Chicano Studies recognized the importance of creating a tenure-track position, believing that this would help to institutionalize the program. Eventually, the program was terminated by the department, but by then I had become a tenured faculty member. This taught me a huge lesson—that programs often become the people who run them and vice-versa.

The Uniqueness of the OCT

The Operation Chicano Teacher program was composed of five essential components: recruitment, retention, training, financial assistance and the oral language exam administration. These approaches were ahead of their time, with culturally sensitive, compatible and relevant, and innovative practices. Perhaps the strongest and most unique factor was the program's ability to maintain credibility with students. As the director, I recognized the need to expose students to professional organizations. I founded the student organization Students United for Bilingual Education (SUBE), which was affiliated with the California Association for Bilingual Education. By reaching out to students on a personal level, I created strong ties with the student organization and sought out their assistance in all matters pertaining to recruitment and retention of students. I found the director was not only a role model, but also an academic model and mentor. I represented the link to their home culture because I shared their values, language, lifestyles and economic background. They recognized my efforts on their behalf as a strong student advocate. This was empowering for them and it encouraged them to raise their voices and participate in all facets of university life.

All of the program components were designed and executed with student involvement. Recruitment procedures were also planned and organized by the OCT Director in conjunction with SUBE. Two approaches were used. One included an outreach effort focused on the high schools and community colleges in the immediate service area, including Los Angeles and Ventura County. Home visitations were made and whole families were invited to the program. The second focused on intra-university efforts. Recruitment was coordinated with all other minority equity programs such as the EOP, Student Affirmative Action (SAA), and the Financial Aid Office. This ensured that the students received the appropriate information regarding the application process, financial assistance and program details to provide support at every level of their college life.

The OCT program maintained a strong relationship with the School of Education to bridge the undergraduate and graduate student experience. Credential advisors were invited to attend student meetings and provide informational sessions rather than have students attend the regular credential office informational sessions. All new recruits to the program were taken on tours to meet the School of Education faculty and program personnel. Seasoned OCT students, in turn, provided assistance to the School of Education faculty and staff.

Retention efforts included advisement and counseling for OCT students. The OCT office remained open until late in the evenings and became the hub of student activities and a home away from home. Having been a peer counselor in college, I recognized the value of this type of program. A peer counseling program was initiated and it provided students with guidance from students who had similar cultures, backgrounds and student experiences. Additionally, I was granted reassigned time as a Liberal Studies advisor. There I created OCT Program tags for student files. This alerted advisors when an OCT program student needed special intervention. It also served to communicate to the students that their progress would be monitored by both their academic major and the OCT programs.

Peer advisors were trained and scheduled all day and into the evening to offer support in class scheduling, choosing majors and academic issues. There was also a parent information component. As the director, I was often involved in student-parent interventions. As first generation students, most had parents who had never attended school. Parents expected students to comply with family responsibilities. Students would often ask if I would speak to their parents and explain why they were studying late or why they could not go home on weekends. As a result, we created parent information sessions to inform them about student activities and requirements. Parents felt comfortable calling the OCT office for information about their children. They were also welcome at all OCT functions.

The last programmatic feature was the training component. Just as my generation had been instrumental in promoting social change, I felt that it would be critical to train students to be future leaders and social change agents. While I admired the dedication teachers had to their classrooms, I firmly believed that prospective teachers also needed to see themselves as advocates for future generations.

As a member of professional organizations, I approached the leadership of the California Association for Bilingual Education (CABE), California Teachers Association (CTA) and the Association of Mexican-American Educators (AMAE). I was able to convince them that they needed a feeder population of students to secure their future membership. The OCT students became the first student chapters of all three organizations. In addition to the CABE/SUBE group, CTA also started SCTA (Student California Teachers Association) as the first student affiliate. AMAE incorporated our students into their general membership without hesitation because the leadership of AMAE happened to be alumni of OCT.

As a consequence, students learned the value of professional memberships, collegiality and received access to the latest developments in research, methodology and curriculum in education. They also attended the California Association of Teachers of English as a Second Language (CATESOL) and National Association of Bilingual Education conferences. I also involved the students at the district level. Student representation at the Bilingual Education Director's monthly meetings in Los Angeles Unified School District (LAUSD) became common. Students were part of the school district network and were given access to all workshops available through LAUSD and the Los Angeles County Office of Education. This exposure engaged students in professional practices, teaching them how to organize and collaborate with others. I am proud of the work we were able to undertake through the OCT program at Northridge. The program was discontinued but left an indelible mark on schools in both the Los Angeles and Ventura County schools with teachers and administrators who graduated from the program between 1973 and 1998.

Sadly, I continue to see tremendous shortages of Latino/a teachers in our public schools despite the fact that Latino youth is the fastest-growing and youngest segment of our population. As a professor at Loyola Marymount, I continue to advocate for these types of programs. I believe that we can best support our children by providing them with a more diverse, high caliber teacher force that represents the many communities that exist in California. Increasing the number of quality Latino teachers, ensuring a relevant curriculum and providing instruction in a language in which children can be successful are ways to ensure educational civil rights for Latinos. Our job is not over until we can find support for more university programs such as OCT.

References

Arciniega, T. A. (1985, June). *Hispanics and higher education: A CSU imperative. Final Report: Commission on Hispanic Underrepresentation*. Long Beach, CA: Office of the Chancellor, California State University.
California State Department of Education. (1980). *The status of Hispanics in California public education*.
Carter, T. P. (1970). *Mexican-Americans in school: A history of educational neglect*. New York: College Entrance Examination Board.

Casso, H. J. & Roman, G. D. (1976). *Chicanos in higher education.* Albuquerque: University of New Mexico Press.

Commission on Hispanic Underrepresentation. (1985). *Hispanic Americans.* Long Beach: Office of the Chancellor, the California State University.

Ferrin, R. L. et al. (1972, July). *Access to college for Mexican-Americans in the Southwest. Higher Education Surveys Report No. 6.* New York: College Entrance Examination Board.

Sanchez, M. E. (1989). *Factors for academic success of minority students: A descriptive study of Operation Chicano Teacher Program.* Dissertation, UC Santa Barbara. Santa Barbara CA: University Microfilm International, Bell & Howell.

United States Department of Commerce. Bureau of the Census. (1974). *The Hispanic population in the United States: March 1986 and 1987, WV Vance Report.* Washington, DC: U.S. Government Printing Office.

United States Commission on Civil Rights. (1974, February). *Toward quality education for Mexican-Americans: Report 6: Mexican-American Education Study.* Washington, DC.

Vela, J. (1977). *A comparison of Chicano and Anglo perceptions of the higher education environment at the University of Wyoming.* Unpublished dissertation, University of Wyoming.

12

I DON'T SPEAK MY MOTHER'S TONGUE

Evangelina "Gigi" Brignoni

As long as I can remember, I always wanted to speak Spanish like a native speaker. However, it was not meant to be, since my Puerto Rican Spanish-speaking parents made a conscious effort to make English the home language. My parents believed that children who spoke Spanish were discriminated against, and placed in a low-achieving class, not with higher-ability students. They knew it was not fair, but for their own children's academic success, they made the ultimate sacrifice. In less than one generation, through misguided good intentions and societal pressures, Spanish was eradicated from the Brignoni household.

We grew up in the Bronx surrounded by a diversity of ethnic groups. Even though my parents made friends with everyone, they always gravitated to Puerto Ricans and other Spanish-speaking families. When I was around 3 years old, I recognized that my parents communicated in two languages. They spoke English to their children, some of their neighbors, and work colleagues. In contrast, my parents energetically conversed in Spanish with each other, my grandmother, and the relatives from Puerto Rico. I did not think much about it, because it was just the way things were.

Years later, I attended a parochial Catholic elementary school and became best friends with Evelyn Ramos. She was Puerto Rican, understood English, and spoke Spanish fluently. In fact, when they held parent-teacher conferences, she would attend them, and translate what the nuns said to her parents. I wanted to do that. I wanted to know what the nuns had to say about me before the report card got home. I had the grand idea that if I made up a language, the nuns would not be the wiser, and I could sit in and translate the meetings for my parents. I felt powerless knowing only English.

At home, I asked my dad to teach me Spanish. He accepted the challenge and started to teach me vocabulary for food, and then the body parts. I learned the basics: *leche* (milk), *agua* (water), *arroz* (rice), *habichuelas* (beans), *guineo* (banana), *cara* (face), *ojos* (eyes), *boca* (mouth), and *brazos* (arms), for example. My father knew I was a visual learner and wrote the words for me to read. He was proud of my progress and wrote this word down, *cuello* (neck). I read it wrong. I did not know that two l's together sounded like a y, and I did not read the 'ue' correctly. I read that word incorrectly and said, "*culo,*" which made my dad laugh hysterically (means *backside*). Apparently, that was an unmentionable body part, and so that was also the end of my private Spanish lessons.

This last experience left me feeling a little deflated. When was I ever going to acquire Spanish and speak like the other Puerto Ricans or Nuyoricans in my neighborhood? I knew that my next opportunity would be to take classes in a secondary school. I was looking forward to high school because rumor had it that they taught Spanish there.

My education in the Catholic elementary school went quite well. The nuns accidentally tracked me with the older peers who celebrated their birthdays in the first half of the year. They were college bound, while the other students whose birthdays fell in the summer and fall months were tracked in general education. I was born in August and according to the nuns' tracking system, I should have been with the general education peers. Luckily, I was with the other students, because I did extremely well each year and placed in the top 5 percent of the class. I did so well that I was awarded a four-year scholarship to an all girls' Catholic high school. I knew I would be taking a language class and I was going to ask for Spanish. Unfortunately, that was not to be because the nuns placed me in Latin I. All college prep students took Latin. My general education counterparts were taking Spanish or French, but I was forced to take Latin. I did well but I did not like it. How was Latin going to help me in the neighborhood?

Due to economics, my family moved to California the following year. They discussed at length whether we should attend the local Catholic schools or public school. I voted for public school since it would be less costly than sending all five school-age children to parochial school. After much deliberation, they agreed.

When it came time to enroll my sister and me in the local high school, I met with my counselor. She was impressed with my academic record and asked if I wanted to enroll in the Latin II class. I immediately asked, "I have a choice?" I politely said, "No, thank you. I would like to enroll in Spanish." The counselor agreed to my request. I felt transformed, liberated, vindicated, and delighted.

Mrs. Pérez, the Spanish teacher, taught me so much. I learned how to trill my r's. Mrs. Pérez asked us to practice sounding out the motor boat's engine noise. I always thought that motor boats sounded like, "Brrrrmm, brrrrmm." In Spanish, they went, "*rerrrr, rerrrr.*" The trilling of the r's took a long time to master, but I did it. In Spanish class, I learned that Paco was always asked how he was doing. "*¿Qué tal, Paco?*" "*¿Cómo estás?*" I learned how to say last names properly like *Jiménez* (He-meh-nez). In my English world, Jiménez was pronounced, Gym-Meh-Nez. Learning Spanish, the language of my parents, in a California high school added to my bicultural worldview. I identified myself as a Puerto Rican via all the family functions; I just never had the added gift of the Spanish language.

My Spanish vocabulary increased by leaps and bounds and conjugating verbs was not difficult, thanks to my Latin class. I knew I had a long way to go to become fluent so every year after that initial course, I always enrolled in Spanish language classes in high school and college. As an adult and a bilingual teacher to be, I attended immersion classes in Cuernavaca, Mexico. My Spanish acquisition took on more of a Mexican accent than a Puerto Rican one.

The above narrative highlights how society influenced my parents to deny their children's linguistic heritage. Linguistic rights are civil rights. To eradicate one's language in less than one generation also means that part of the culture is erased and those civil rights are not validated. Even though the Spanish language is a manifestation of colonization of Puerto Ricans by the Spaniards, it has been the native tongue of Puerto Ricans for over 500 years. It was the native tongue of my parents and grandmother.

As a child, I knew I lacked the gift of the Spanish language, and I wanted to recuperate it. The time and energy I spent recovering my parents' first language paid off. Those life experiences determined the journey I took in becoming a bilingual teacher, a university professor in bilingual education, and the coordinator of the first bilingual education endorsement in Nebraska.

When I became a bilingual teacher in 1978, the professors of my university had faith in my ability to become a more proficient biliterate educator. Forty years ago, the Supreme Court justices agreed with the Lau family and passed the famous Supreme Court judgment, *Lau v. Nichols*. The federal and state education departments had funding available to instruct future bilingual teachers. I was fortunate to be part of the state funding. During this time, not only did I learn pedagogically sound strategies for bilingual classes, I learned to advocate maintaining the first language in the home.

Bilingual education, in those days, promoted a parallel education, which meant that the grade level curriculum would be taught in the language of the child. I was reminded that the three goals for bilingual education students were: 1. they would be successful academically; 2. they would become proficient in English; and 3. they would have high self-esteem. These are lofty goals for any new educator, but quite doable. They became my mantra for a long time.

I hope this narrative of the difficulty I had in recuperating the mother tongue helps parents to understand what difficulties they may encounter when their children are older. I remember when my *abuela* was dying, she also had dementia. She saw demons and screamed in Spanish, "*Demonios.*" Of my seven siblings, I was the only who could rid the area of demons, because I could understand and speak Spanish. I did my best to clear the room of the demons that frightened her with my words, and my grandmother rested peacefully that afternoon.

I advocate on a daily basis the need to maintain home language while adding on a new language, which in the United States is English. Even though I am bilingual, I still feel insecure when talking to native Spanish speakers, thinking I am being judged for my limitations. I did not grow up learning the songs of Puerto Rico, the *bomba* and *las parrandas*—songs sung during Christmas. I also was unfamiliar with the folklore and traditions indigenous to a Boricua's life. It is said that language is culture; so, when the mother tongue is taken away, remember the culture is taken away, too.

I don't resent what my parents did regarding not speaking in Spanish. It is what it is. I speak my hybrid Spanish, my own version of Spanish-Spanish, Mexican-Spanish, and some hints of Puerto Rican-Spanish. I speak what I recuperated and I am still working on it.

Alas, however, I don't speak my mother's tongue.[1]

Note

1. Although this is written in the present tense when she was still a vibrant force in education, Gigi Brignoni succumbed to cancer in 2012 leaving a great void.

13
BECOMING ME IN THE WORLD

Anaida Colón-Muñiz

Dangerous Memories Define Me

Dangerous memories define me; I am who I am because of my past.
The moments that I have lived shape and give color to my life.
A little girl of five arrives in New York with summer dresses made of tulle and lace.
Getting ready for winter . . . Dressed in tulle and lace—
¡Qué frío!

Higher education was in my future, a few good teachers assured me; others doubted me.
But, I was inside *the dream*;
I couldn't see the dangerous memories that were surrounding me.
¿Qué pasa?

College opened my eyes—I saw my reflection in the injustice.
Saw my father in the worker's plight; Saw my mother in the racist commentaries.
Saw my future in the struggle for equality.
Latin American studies, civil rights, the protest against the war
What should I do with my life?
¿Qué hago?

Then came clarity . . . critical pedagogy, children are our future.
Don't stop teaching the children . . . they are our hope.
Keep on trying to change for the better . . . seeds of love . . . seeds of hope.
That's why I became a bilingual teacher.
¡La esperanza está en la educación![1]

Introduction

Like so many others, as a Spanish-speaking child in New York City's English-only schools in the 1950s and '60s I was denied the right to speak my native Spanish tongue in school until I could enroll in Spanish as a "foreign language" class in 7th grade. This school policy violated my civil right to be me in the world and to express myself in the language in which I was raised. My Puerto Rican culture was also continuously assaulted by the hidden curriculum in schools along with teacher innuendos, comments, and actions that eventually engendered rebellion from what Sharon Welch calls "dangerous memories" (1985). Stemming from liberation theology, the construct of dangerous memories describes how humans respond to conditions of oppression. As an example, oppressed-language minority children face enormous challenges in reconciling their private and public identities, especially when confronted by English-only schooling, where teachers may be insensitive to their cultural and linguistic heritages (Portes & Rivas, 2011). Under such conditions, children may respond at home and/or school with rejection, rebellion, or other manifestations of negative or confused self-identity.

Dangerous memories led many students to internalize a poor self-image, as designed and manifested by oppressive cultural forces. For me, these experiences interrupted my personal development, delaying me from becoming comfortable as a bilingual, multicultural person until late in my teen years, when I was finally able to rupture the bubble I was in. At that point I realized that I was someone capable of being the protagonist of my own life, acting on behalf of myself and my community—a proud Puerto Rican woman who could code-switch from one culture and language to the other without feeling questioned or chastised or sensing less of me. The oppressive acts I endured by "well-meaning" school personnel were denials of my civil rights as a child who was in the process of becoming fully human (Freire, 1970). Recalling my dangerous memories and gaining critical consciousness helped me to become more of *me*, so I could help my community. In this narrative I will share my experiences as an English learner, how I gained critical consciousness, and how I found my civil rights agency as a critical bilingual and multicultural educator.

Recalling Dangerous Memories

Arriving in New York in 1956, at 5 years of age, my ties with Puerto Rico were greatly severed, and while I had my three sisters and my parents as an intact family to remind me of who I was, my only other extended family in New York were my parents' *compadres*, Tio Pablo and Titi Laura, who had arrived in New York shortly before we did. My world had changed radically as I was removed from everything that had been familiar in Puerto Rico. The years that followed threw me into a chaotic system of schools that were in the midst of civil rights change—but as a child I couldn't understand what was going on. I went to four all-English schools between 1st and 6th grades—three Puerto Rican and Black "ghetto" schools and one White. During that period of six years my family had only moved once, so it was the system that made me "transient," not my family. By the time I was 12 years old, I had also attended two junior high schools. When I finally got to high school, the attendance zones had once again shifted for the purposes of integration in the late '60s. So, the predominantly Latino and Black populated high school that my sister attended would not be my assigned high school. I was redirected to a White school.

As I got to high school, the hegemonic forces were winning. My blind allegiance was mainly to the U.S. flag, even while White American youth were burning it in protest because of the Vietnam War. I knew in my heart that I was Puerto Rican; however, at the time, that was a subcategory to my sense of American-ness. The ASPIRA[2] youth organization and my family had done a lot to make me feel proud of my Puerto Rican heritage, but I had become a poster child for the school, exemplifying all the good things that could come from my willing integration as a Puerto Rican kid into the predominantly White American high school. On the other hand, there was always a small part of me that resisted that notion, especially as I became more in tune with the racism, linguicism, and cultural bias that later turned into violence in our urban areas.

At my high school I was part of a small minority of Black and Latino students who would be called to become part of the fabric of the school—even though our families didn't live in that community, and the community that the school was in generally did not want or like us very much. We came to understand that integration almost always was "us" integrating "them," and not the other way around. Despite the tensions that surrounded us, the administration did its best to keep us connected through school activities and clubs, and I did my best to fit in and take advantage of the opportunities that were being presented. I got into school leadership, was president of the ASPIRA Club at my school, and became active at the main Brooklyn ASPIRA Center downtown; plus I got involved in all sorts of extracurricular activities at my school. Things seemed to be going well for me and a few of my friends, but there were always those "other" high school kids who never seemed to fit in well and spent their time rebelling in one way or another or hanging around the handball courts. The disparities were clear.

Then the bubble burst, and by my junior year, we were in the midst of a race and gang riot that clearly sent the message that we were outsiders. The school was locked down and we were required to wait for our parents to pick us up, or we could not leave the school. I was able to go home with my friend's mom, because both my parents were working, but other kids were not as lucky. People got hurt. Our communities were split, and I felt caught in the middle. For me and many of my peers, things were never the same.

To add pain to injury, it was 1968, and the Vietnam War protests divided the country. It was also the time of youth's rebellion with the hippie movement, and the struggle for ethnic studies was in full gear. I wrote an essay entitled *A Citizen of Two Worlds*, for which I got a small recognition from a community group. And that was how I felt; I lived in two distinct worlds, one Puerto Rican and one ideally "American," both parts of me living in the midst of the changing times. I struggled to make sense of it because traditional schooling only exacerbated the tensions I experienced between my private and public dual identity. Fortunately, unlike Richard Rodriguez (1982), my hunger was for more of my roots, not less. As I dug deeper, I began to awaken.

By the time I got to college, that mental model of being uncritical of all things American had changed radically. My rose-colored glasses were torn off by the reality of historical truths that were finally revealed to me about the colonized history of Puerto Rico and Puerto Ricans and the subjugation of minorities in the United States (Acosta-Belén & Santiago, 2006). Until then, I can say that I had been under the fog of denying myself. I was usurped by a false pretense that I belonged to something greater—called the United States of America—a false consciousness (Freire, 1970; Lukács, 1971 [1920]) that enveloped my life until I gained the critical consciousness (Freire, 1970; Freire, 1976) that I needed to reclaim my right to be me.

Becoming Me: From False to Critical Consciousness

Sadly, English language submersion, cultural displacement, biases, bigotry, and the confusion that accompanied these experiences left a void in my memory that made it difficult for me to reconstruct my past. But, as I slowly came to understand the sociocultural conditions that were manifested in my life, I spent a good amount of time reconstructing my past: visiting Puerto Rico each year as a youth; spending time with and interviewing my family elders; reading, studying, and researching about my culture. As a Nuyorican[3] youth seeking justice, música de protesta, guerilla theatre, protest marches, and campaigns filled my itinerary. Today, my work with non-profits and critical bilingual multicultural teaching are the different ways that I have directed my passion and energy to foster civil rights in education.

The underlying pattern in my life was that, no matter what the hegemonic forces wanted me to be, I *was* different from the supposed norm. Despite internal strife, I eventually came to understand and affirm the beautiful essence of my Puerto Rican identity. I learned that I had a role in resisting the systems of oppression that seemed to invade communities like mine. Clearly, I rebelled throughout my college years in search of my "self," fighting for ethnic studies, participating in political manifestations, singing protest music, and acting. As I did so, I realized that my work had to be channeled into a place where it could make a positive difference within the social context that I resided in, and that angst became an intricate part of my life. My dangerous memories had become the source of my indignation to denounce the inequities I saw around me and to announce what I felt were more equitable conditions for educating and liberating children (Freire, 1985).

The fact is that while American education is equated as a mark of freedom, as Valenzuela (1999) points out, we learn all too painfully that it has been the vehicle for perpetuating inequality and incarcerating children's minds. Except for a few chosen poster children that are hoisted onto a pillar for all to see, there are far too many who don't benefit from the kinds of schooling experiences that should truly liberate them. Rather than becoming protagonists of their own lives, as Freire (1970) dreamed and taught us to envision, our youths sometimes find themselves living the lives of antagonists, shunned by society for one reason or another, and ultimately locked down by poverty, crime, desolation, or incarceration. It's no wonder that history repeats itself with each wave of immigrants, given similar assimilationist schooling experiences.

A significant number of Latino scholars, journalists, poets, novelists, and biographers—such as Anzaldúa (1999), Cofer (1990), Darder (1991/2012), Gonzalez (2001), Levins Morales (1998), Nieto (1992), Santana (2004), Santiago (2006), and Valenzuela (1999)—have documented stories similar to mine stemming from their dangerous memories, remnants of those experiences fostered by the devastating effects of an assimilationist colonizing hegemony (Gramsci, 1971; Macedo, Dendrinos, & Panayota, 2003). While these scholars have written prolifically about their experiences, it took me a lifetime to acquire the sense of voice needed to write about my personal trajectory.

Reflecting on Dangerous Memories and Hegemonic Forces

It is evident that I was a child during the civil rights era—but this is something that I didn't think about critically until much later on—perhaps because I grew up in the northeast and we were in the midst of it all, just following orders of where to go to school and what buses and trains to get to the White schools. And so, while I lived at the cusp of great changes in education, I found myself in between spaces of repression and those of opportunity and possibility.

At the time I was in school, there was no bilingual education to speak of, no multicultural education, and no special classes to learn English, or to prepare students as new arrivals for the rigors of higher education. It was all sink or swim, and I treaded water the whole time to keep myself afloat as best I could. I would be disingenuous if I didn't admit that it took its toll, even if on the outside I might be rendered one of the ones "who made it" by the intervention of a few good teachers. Watching *Leave it to Beaver* and *Father Knows Best* imprinted an indelible image of what and who we should become, how we should look, where we should live, and how our parents should be. There were endless contradictions in the books and pictures we had in school and the lives we came home to each afternoon. American hegemonic pressure forces children to become socialized into people significantly different from who they were nurtured to be by their families and home culture, all with the aim of serving a political outcome under the guise of Americanization (Giroux, 2000; Darder, 1991/2012; Macedo, Dendrinos, &

Panayota, 2003; Sleeter & Delgado Bernal, 2003; Freire, 1970; 1985; 1998). This systematic denial of people's rights to define and affirm themselves within their communities can prohibit them to adapt naturally to new sociocultural conditions they confront. Through what Freire noted as "dispensers of false generosity," we are led to believe that Americanization through public schooling is a benevolent process to help children of immigrants integrate into society in the best way possible. The issue comes in when kids are denied their humanity and sense of being in order to become a victim of this oppressive generosity that is "nourished by death, despair, and poverty" (Freire, 1970) and that creates what Macedo names "a colonial existence that is almost culturally schizophrenic: being present and yet not visible, being visible and yet not present, It is a condition that I painfully experienced in the United States, constantly juggling the power asymmetry of the two worlds, two cultures, and two languages" (Freire, 2000, p. 11).

Culturally sensitive and responsive (Gay, 2000; Ladson-Billings, 2001; Nieto, 1999; Nieto & Bode, 2008/2012) pedagogical approaches in schools, much akin to critical pedagogy, respect diverse backgrounds, and use practices that facilitate an adjustment to new linguistic and cultural situations, without sacrificing the home language and culture but rather enhancing it. It is with these approaches that children can thrive, adapt, learn to culturally and linguistically code-switch. Gay (2000) points out, "The validation, information, and pride it [culturally responsive teaching] generates are both psychologically and intellectually liberating" (p. 35). Similarly, this would call for teachers being trained to use culturally relevant pedagogy, "a pedagogy that empowers students intellectually, socially, emotionally, and politically by using cultural referents to impart knowledge, skills, and attitudes" (Ladson-Billings, 1994, p. 17–18).

While we might imagine that this is an expectation common in most American schools, according to Ardila-Rey (2008, p. 341), "Only a handful of states have developed policies or standards for teacher preparation and credentialing that address issues to diverse populations." And yet students stand to gain much from culturally sensitive approaches. Nieto (1992; Nieto & Bode, 2008/2012) affirms that the richness that every child brings to the classroom community includes his or her right to use and maintain his or her native language/s. These culturally sensitive approaches are all aligned to Freire's ideas:

> What I have said and re-said, untiringly, is that we must not bypass—spurning it as "good for nothing"—that which educands, be they children coming to school for the first time, or young people and adults at centers of popular education, bring with them in the way of an understanding of the world, in the most varied dimensions of their own practice in the social practice of which they are a part. Their speech, their way of counting and calculating, their ideas about the so-called other world, their religiousness, their knowledge about health, the body, sexuality, life, death, the power of the saints, magic spells, must all be respected.
>
> *(1994, p. 85)*

Denying children a healthy sense of being is a violation of human and civil rights, especially when they are routinely made to feel distanced, estranged, and alienated from their home language and culture and/or belittled because of their culturally distinct backgrounds, such as children still have experienced in many schools throughout the country (Berry, 1983; Padilla, 1991). These hegemonic forces are especially offensive when they are employed by way of policies and practices of educational institutions that claim to develop the social and academic well-being of children and families. In fact, this sort of feeling dis-connection could lead to a confused sense of being and hopelessness or desperation, such as we found in the case of the English-only poster child, Richard Rodriguez (1982).

Through a concerted effort by so called well-meaning educators and other public institutions, it converts children and their families into the "other" (SooHoo, 2006) in order to impose the dominant society's perception of what good Americans should be, with a total disregard to the funds of knowledge, talents, worldviews, and experiences that they bring from their home cultures (Moll, Amanti, Neff, & González, 1992).

Consequently, when I hear of the high drop-out rate among Latinos in one state or another, I imagine students dropping out of school not because of their own failure, but as a last-ditch effort to save themselves from personal and cultural assaults and annihilation. For how long can you be told that you know less, do less, don't have the capacity to know and do more, and will never be who you wish to be, before you jump off that suicidal train? No matter how painful it is to leave school after being brainwashed that it is the only way to get ahead, and no matter how hard you hit the ground when you leave that moving train, our schools sometimes drive Latino students to that point. And so they jump. We must change this course of action to really make school a space where all kids feel like they belong and where they can be realized.

Hope through Critical Multicultural/Bilingual Education

I find hope in a critical and transformative approach to bilingual education (Collier & Thomas, 2004; Bartolomé, 2000; 2004; Darder, 1991/2012; Garcia-Gonzalez, 2000; Jenks, Lee, & Kanpol, 2001; McLaren, 2006/2015; Reyes & Vallone, 2007; Shor, 1992), especially for children who are caught between two worlds. In 1974, when I was at Bank Street College completing a Master of Science degree in teaching, we formed a small group to study the work of Freire (1970), who had published his seminal book *Pedagogy of the Oppressed* just a few years earlier. As a result, my eyes were finally wide opened to the possibility of reaffirming the realities of our students and using their own lives as the content and point of departure for teaching and learning. It wasn't that the work of past progressive White educators we were studying (such as John Dewey) didn't have important pedagogical ideas, but Paulo Freire's work connected us with the reality that we lived every day in a politically charged schooling environment.

We recognized then that traditional public schooling had to be challenged with something more relevant to poor Puerto Rican and Black kids in the upper west side of Manhattan. As we pursued our teaching credentials, we met separately in between classes and assignments to begin developing curriculum that could be used in the schools where we were working. We took those lessons and internalized them; they became our new mental model for teaching and changing the world through a more critical approach to bilingual education.

For Freireans, a critical pedagogical approach starts with the student and teacher as the point of departure for teaching and learning. Ambrosio (2003) defines it as a "pedagogy that uses the personal knowledge and experiences of students to reflect critically on issues presented from a variety of perspectives" and, "creating learning experiences and opportunities that allow students from diverse cultural groups to see themselves in . . . curriculum, instructional practices, and classroom climate" (p. 34). The curriculum evolves from the work done together in the local school and community using the gifts, talents, and context in which children live. This leads them to not only become literate in reading the word, but to read the world—meaning to gain a critical consciousness of oppressive social, economic, and political conditions that prevent communities from realizing their potential, identifying and naming the problems, and doing something constructive to address them (Kincheloe, 2008; Sleeter, 1996; Sleeter & McLaren, 1995).

Along with others in critical bilingual multicultural education, it is still my strong belief that by gaining critical consciousness, both teachers and their students can transform the negative energy generated from abusive schooling experiences that promote destructive dangerous memories and redirect it into 1) political resilience, 2) resistance, and 3) agency (Giroux, 2000; Welch, 1985). These three elements all happen to be important ingredients for democratic activism. Teachers and their students can become agents of their own educational experiences with a better understanding of the history and politics of education, and engender the will to engage in reflection and action given critical consciousness.

My Role Today

The sense of purpose that I found in those early years in New York City schools has become the driving force guiding my advocacy and agency even today in my role as a teacher educator. I value the potential inherent in bilingual and multiculturalism and I believe that schools are places that should help to nurture these abilities for students not only to become proficient in two languages and competent multicultural beings (Banks, 1996; Bartolomé, 2000; Darder, 1991/2012; Nieto, 1992; Nieto, 2000; Nieto & Bode, 2008/2012;), but also to see the possibilities of taking charge of their own lives and changing their social condition through reflection and action. For this, teachers need to understand the phenomena of dangerous memories, ascertain their own critical consciousness, and use and advocate for critical bilingual multicultural education as a viable pedagogy for the civil right of Latino children in becoming themselves in the world, as I was able to become me.

Notes

1. This excerpt is from an *otherness* poem I wrote for a course on multicultural education. This *Otherness* assignment was developed for a course designed by Suzanne SooHoo, which I teach for the College of Educational Studies. See *Talking Leaves*, by SooHoo (2006).
2. ASPIRA: "In 1961, Dr. Antonia Pantoja and a group of Puerto Rican educators and professionals created ASPIRA (which means aspire in Spanish), to address the exceedingly high drop-out rate and low educational attainment of Puerto Rican youth. They were convinced that the only way to free the Puerto Rican community from poverty and to promote its full development was by focusing on the education of young people, and developing their leadership potential, self-esteem and pride in their cultural heritage." Retrieved January 10, 2014 from http://www.aspira.org/book/our-history
3. Nuyorican—a designation given to Puerto Ricans living in New York, its negative connotations shifting as Puerto Ricans claimed their right to a unique identity.

References

Acosta-Belén, E., & Santiago, C. E. (Eds.). (2006). *Puerto Ricans in the United States: A contemporary portrait*. Boulder: Lynne Rienner Publishers.

Ambrosio, J. (2003). We make the road by walking. In G. Gay (Ed.), *Becoming multicultural educators: Personal journey toward professional agency* (pp. 17–41). San Francisco: Jossey-Bass.

Anzaldúa, G. (1999). *Borderlands/la frontera: The new Mestiza* (2nd ed.). San Francisco: Aunt Lute Books.

Ardila-Rey, A. (2008). Language, culture, policy, and standards in teacher preparation. In M. E. Brisk (Ed.), *Language, culture, and community in teacher education* (pp. 331–351). Mahwah, NJ: Erlbaum.

Banks, J. A. (Ed.). (1996). *Multicultural education, transformative knowledge and action*. New York: Teachers College Press.

Bartolomé, L. I. (2000). Democratizing bilingualism: The role of critical teacher education. In Z. F. Beykont (Ed.), *Lifting every voice: Pedagogy and politics of bilingualism* (pp. 167–186). Cambridge, MA: Harvard Education Publishing Group.

Bartolomé, L. I. (2004). Critical pedagogy and teacher education: Radicalizing prospective teachers. *Teacher Education Quarterly*: Caddo Gap, *31*(1), 97–122.

Berry, J. W. (1983). Acculturation: A comparative analysis of alternative forms. In R. J. Samuda & S. L. Woods (Eds.), *Perspectives in immigrant and minority education* (pp. 65–78). Lanham, MD: University Press of America.

Cofer, J. O. (1990). *Silent dancing: A partial remembrance of a Puerto Rican childhood*. Houston, TX: Arte Público.

Collier, V. P., & Thomas, W. P. (2004). The Astounding Effectiveness of Dual Language Education for All. *NABE Journal of Research and Practice*, *2*(1). Winter 2004.

Darder, A. (1991). *Culture and power in the classroom*. New York: Bergin & Garvey.

Darder, A. (2012). *Culture and power in the classroom: A critical foundation for the education of bicultural students*. Boulder, CO: Paradigm Press.

Freire, P. (1970). *Pedagogy of the oppressed.* New York: Herder and Herder.
Freire, P. (1976). *Education for critical consciousness.* Seabury, England: Publishing Cooperative.
Freire, P. (1985). *The politics of education: Culture, power and liberation.* Westport, CT: Bergin & Garvey Publishers, Inc.
Freire, P. (1994). *Pedagogy of hope: Reliving pedagogy of the oppressed.* New York: Continuum Press.
Freire, P. (1998). *Teachers as cultural workers.* Boulder, CO: Westview Press.
Freire, P. (2000). *Pedagogy of the oppressed,* 30th Anniversary Edition. New York: Continuum.
Garcia-Gonzalez, R. (2000). Is it a dream? Critical pedagogy in bilingual, elementary classrooms. Paper presented at AERA, New Orleans, LA. April 24–28.
Gay, G. (2000). *Culturally responsive teaching: Theory, research, & practice.* New York: Teachers College Press.
Giroux, H. A. (2000). English only and the crisis of memory, culture, and democracy. In R. D. Gonzalez & I. Melis (Eds.), *History, theory, and policy* (pp. ix-xviii). Urbana, IL: National Council of Teachers of English.
Gonzalez, N. (2001). *I am my language: Discourses of women and children in the borderlands.* Tucson, AZ: The University of Arizona Press.
Gramsci, A. (1971). *Selections from the prison notebooks.* London: Lawrence and Wishart.
Jenks, C., Lee, J. O., & Kanpol, B. (2001). Approaches to multicultural education in preservice teacher education: Philosophical frameworks and models for teaching. *The Urban Review, 33*(2), 87–105.
Kincheloe, J. (2008). *Critical pedagogy primer.* New York: Peter Lang Publishing.
Ladson-Billings, G. (1994). *The Dreamkeepers: Successful teaching for African-American students.* San Francisco: Jossey-Bass.
Ladson-Billings, G. (2001). *Crossing over to Canaan: The journey of new teachers in diverse classrooms.* San Francisco: Jossey-Bass.
Levins Morales, A. (1998). *Remedios: Stories of earth and iron from the history of Puertorriqueñas.* Boston, MA: Beacon Press.
Lukács, G. (1971 [1920]). *History and class consciousness; studies in Marxist dialectics.* Cambridge, MA: MIT. Press.
Macedo, D., Dendrinos, B., & Panayota, G. (2003). *The hegemony of English.* Boulder, CO: Paradigm Publishers.
McLaren, P. (2006). *Life in schools: An introduction to critical pedagogy in the foundations of education.* New York: Longman.
McLaren, P. (2015). *Life in schools: An introduction to critical pedagogy in the foundations of education,* 6th edition. Boulder, CO: Paradigm Publishers.
Moll, L. C., Amanti, C., Neff, D., & González, N. (1992). Funds of knowledge for teaching: Using a qualitative approach to connect homes and classrooms. *Theory into Practice, 31*(2), 132–141.
Nieto, S. (1992). *Affirming diversity: The sociopolitical context of multicultural education.* New York: Longman.
Nieto, S. (1999). *The light in their eyes: Creating multicultural learning communities.* New York: Teachers College Press.
Nieto, S. (2000). Placing equity front and center: Some thoughts on transforming teacher education for a new century. *Journal of Teacher Education, 51*(3), 180–187.
Nieto, S., & Bode, P. (2012, 2008). *Affirming diversity: The sociopolitical context of multicultural education,* 5th & 6th editions. New York: Allyn & Bacon.
Padilla, A. (1991). The English-Only movement myths, reality, and implications for psychology. *American Psychologist,* American Psychological Association, Inc., *46*(2), 120–130.

Portes, A., & Rivas, A. (2011). The adaptation of migrant children. *The Future of Children, 21*(1). Retrieved April 15, 2011 from http://futureofchildren.org/futureofchildren/about/

Reyes, A., & Vallone, T. (2007). Toward an expanded understanding of two-way bilingual immersion education: Constructing identity through a critical, additive bilingual/bicultural pedagogy. *Multicultural Perspectives, 9*(3), 3–11.

Rodriguez, R. (1982). *Hunger from memory: The education of Richard Rodriguez, an autobiography.* New York: Bantum Books.

Santana, O. (Ed.). (2004). *Tongue-tied: The lives of multilingual children in public education.* Oxford, England: Rowman and Littlefield.

Santiago, E. (2006). *When I was Puerto Rican: A memoir.* New York: Vintage.

Shor, I. (1992). *Empowering education: Critical teaching for social change.* Chicago: University of Chicago Press.

Sleeter, C. E. (1996). *Multicultural education as social activism.* New York: SUNY Press.

Sleeter, C. E., & Delgado Bernal, D. (2003). Critical pedagogy, critical race theory, and antiracist education: Their implications for multicultural education. In J. A. Banks & C. M. Banks (Eds.), *Handbook of research on multicultural education,* 2nd ed. (pp. 240–260). Jossey Bass.

Sleeter, C. E., & McLaren, P. (Eds.). (1995). *Multicultural education and critical pedagogy: The politics of difference.* New York: SUNY Press.

SooHoo, S. (2006). *Talking leaves: Narratives of difference.* Cresskill, NJ: Hampton Press.

Valenzuela, A. (1999). *Subtractive schooling: US-Mexican youth and the politics of caring.* New York: State University of New York Press.

Welch, S. D. (1985). *Communities of resistance and solidarity: A feminist theology of liberation.* New York, NY: Orbis.

14

PROPOSITION 227 AND THE LOSS OF EDUCATIONAL RIGHTS

A Personal Perspective and Quest for Equitable Educational Programs for English Learners

María S. Quezada

What is it like to grow up in California if you are a person of color and your first language is other than English? As an individual who came to this country from Mexico at the age of 5, I can tell you that experience has left deep scars, lapses of memory, and gaps in my education. I can remember the pain of feeling and being seen as "different" and the frustration I felt when the little English I had learned did not always help me in school. School was not a place for me to be successful in those early, critically important years. This unpleasant experience led me to become an advocate for the children in our schools facing similar circumstances. I became a bilingual educator in the late 1970s, right after the landmark *Lau v. Nichols* Supreme Court decision on behalf of English learners. I remember attending an annual California Association for Bilingual Education conference where Edward Steinman, the lawyer who litigated the case before the U. S Supreme Court and won, spoke of the importance of that decision—a truly inspirational speech that motivated me to continue what I knew in my heart was the right thing to do. I shared and understood firsthand the opinion of the court, "There is no equality of treatment by providing students with the same facilities, textbooks, teachers and curriculum, for students who do not understand English are effectively foreclosed from any meaningful education" (Lau v. Nichols, 1974).

In my bilingual classroom I saw how children, just like me, could have a different educational experience. As I went from being a bilingual teacher in the classroom and moved to coordinating bilingual programs at the district level, I could not only see students in many great bilingual classrooms learning English and learning content, but children who had a chance to meet with success because they understood what they were learning and the language of the teacher. Their language and what they brought to school was of value. Those early years as a bilingual educator were filled with hope for ensuring that students met with academic success, learned English to higher proficiency levels, and kept a strong connection to their families and culture by maintaining their first language. What was different than when I was a child going through school was the students in my class and many bilingual classrooms learned and felt good about themselves, and this gave me energy to know that what I had to give was important.

During the 35 plus years of my educational career, bilingual programs were always held to a different standard and criticism about them was always present—it was evident that this was mostly due to the population of students we served. The increase in the immigrant population and the number of English learners in our schools and the lack of resources and teachers exacerbated the challenge facing schools. It became quite clear that sooner or later we were in for unsettling times. The first attack was Proposition 63, which passed in 1986, amending the state constitution to declare English the official language of California, calling for English to be the common language of the state. MacKaye (1990) states, "The appearance of Proposition 63 on the political horizon brought language into public parlance, allowing us the opportunity to explore American language ideology." Language attitudes of the general population on both sides of the issue were highly charged. Every time that federal legislation for bilingual education was up for reauthorization, editorials and letters to the editor gave life to those language attitudes and questioned, once again, the whole notion of having languages other than English in the classroom, which in California was against the law until 1967.[1]

California nativism (spurred on by being the state with the most immigrants and English learners in the schools) once again reared its ugly head in 1994 when Proposition 187, the "*Save Our State* (SOS)" initiative sought to establish a state-run citizenship screening system and prohibit so called, "illegal aliens" [or undocumented residents] from using health care, public education, and other social services in California (Mailman, 1995). While the voters passed the initiative, it was challenged in a legal suit and found unconstitutional by a federal court in 1999. It was evident that some California residents were concerned about the costs of illegal immigration and the increase of the Latino population in California, while other residents saw this as discriminatory and racist. On the heels of Proposition 187 came Proposition 209, also known as the California Civil Rights Initiative. It passed in November 1996 and amended the state constitution to prohibit public institutions from considering race, sex, or ethnicity in the public sector. Two years later on June 2, 1998 California's voters passed Proposition 227, also known as the "English for the Children" initiative mandating students in California's schools be taught "overwhelmingly" in English unless parents signed a yearly waiver for alternative bilingual instruction.

Gendzel (2009), writing about anti-immigrant sentiment states, "Like Proposition 187, Propositions 209 and 227 were seen as thinly veiled attempts by native-born whites to punish non-white immigrants for having gained statewide demographic ascendancy" (p.76). He goes on to describe this initiative trend in California by stating,

> Props. 187, 209, and 227 were not just a spasmodic backlash against recent demographic trends; rather, they were the culmination of 150 years of nativist politics in California. From the earliest days of statehood, anti-immigrant laws directed against Latin Americans and Asian Americans have enjoyed broad support from the California electorate—which has always been, and still remains, predominantly white and native-born.
>
> *(p. 76)*

Each of these initiatives was directed at vulnerable people including the 1.5 million (25%) of the student population in California classified as English learners. According to Gendzel (2009), the initiatives "provoked worldwide denunciation of California voters for their hard-hearted inhumanity." At the federal level, in opposition to the Proposition 227 initiative, Secretary Riley stated, "that kind of extreme approach is likely to result in fewer kids learning English and fewer kids doing well in other academic subjects" (Peterson, 1998).

Proposition 227—A Tale of Distorted Facts

In 1996 I was elected president of the California Association for Bilingual Education (CABE) and took the oath of office in July 1997. During the first six months as president, CABE leadership began to hear that an initiative to dismantle bilingual education was looming in the horizon. There was a flurry of meetings and a coming together of advocates who had worked diligently since the early years of bilingual education to promote educational equity for English learners. As the deadline for the initiative to qualify for the ballot came closer, we knew that there was going to be an all-out attempt to once and for all undo the positive efforts we had achieved on behalf of English learners since the early years of bilingual education in 1968 with the passage of Title VII of the federal Elementary and Secondary Education Act. We knew that individuals with political capital and money were involved in paying for signatures to assure that the initiative would be on the ballot scheduled for June 1998.[2] To oppose the ballot initiative a political action committee, Citizens for an Educated America, was formed and an all-out battle was waged against what became Proposition 227.

As a bilingual educator it was frustrating to hear attacks on instructional programs that reached far too few English learners although they were demonstrating positive academic results (Ramirez et al., 1991; Green, 1998; Thomas and Collier, 2002). Less than 20% of English learners were in bilingual education programs because of the severe shortage of qualified bilingual teachers (Quezada, 1991). The educational failure of English-only programs, where over 75% of the English learners in California were enrolled, was used to malign and distort facts about English learners in well-implemented bilingual programs. It was hard to deal with the lack of integrity of those whose political and educational ideology trumped facts and research. Once again I felt as if I was a newly arrived immigrant and the attacks were pointedly directed at me, because I was one of the children who had to learn English and was admonished for speaking in Spanish. I found myself struggling to keep programs that gave English learners a chance to succeed.

As president of CABE, it was also the first time I had to deal with "talking points" used in the media and how they are used to convey a message (true or false) to wider audiences as well as the concept of "staying on message." Proponents of Proposition 227 had done their homework mainly because they had deep pockets with lots of money available to them. They had chosen "English for the Children" as their main message and that became a message that was difficult to counteract. Everyone wanted English learners to learn English, but the difference was in how this was done. The power, however, was in their ability to have a simple message and how often it was read or heard in television news and on the radio. How could you possibly refute the importance of learning English? It did not matter that many generations of children learning English submersed in an all English environment had not fared well and the drop-out rate illustrated the detrimental effects—not only educationally, but also psychosocially. In every attempt to discredit the opposing message and point out the fallacy of the claims made against bilingual education I once again felt the disconnect and shame of being different. I was defending students like me who, given the chance, are just as intelligent as other students in our schools. I wanted to scream—it was not only about learning English. I understood that this attack was not against bilingual education, but was against immigrant children and what they represented. It was a sad reminder that it did not matter if we reached the American dream and had the credentials and degrees supposedly needed to get ahead—we were still different and did not fit in "mainstream" America.

The "English Language Education for Immigrant Children" initiative included several key provisions. The first of these provisions called for replacing all current language acquisition programs with a singular, untested immersion methodology.[3] The "English for the Children" initiative campaign's stated intent was to end bilingual education in California. The Proposition 227 initiative stressed that "children should be taught English by being taught in English at school." "In California's schools, English should not be a foreign language," Governor Wilson, who supported the initiative said in a stinging veto message and a two-page statement endorsing Proposition 227 that aides said he crafted himself. "And yet it remains one for too many limited English proficient students because of the failure of bilingual programs" (Ingram, 1998).[4]

Throughout the 1997–1998 campaign, Ron Unz, the initiative's co-author, consistently stated that "Bilingual Education theories are not sound." He said, "Most research in favor of Bilingual Education is nonsense (not scientifically supported)"[5] and that "the National Research Council which reviewed research in favor of Bilingual Education concluded that the research was unreliable in both directions."[6] He felt that "previous research that supported the notion that it takes 7 years to learn the English language is nonsensical; this figure is wrong." He believed that "hard sciences—Biology and Neurobiology—prove that languages can be learned through immersion" (taken from a speech given by Unz in New York where he was seeking donations for his campaign, April 1998).[7] Advocates from Citizens for an Educated America were given talking points by political advisors based on information from the focus groups conducted. As I watched consultants talking to the various diverse background participants of the four large focus groups, I really understood the challenges we were facing because there were deep-seated negative beliefs about bilingual education and of course the children who participated in them. Watching through a two-way mirror the raw comments sickened me. These negative beliefs were not based on facts about the program or even personal experiences—just what they had heard and the animosity felt toward the children the programs were serving. The most astonishing finding for me was that it also came from minority focus group participants as well. It would have taken a course in bilingual education to set them straight—and in a campaign we were given no more than 30 seconds for a sound bite that would hopefully resonate with people!

Another responsibility I had as president of CABE during the campaign, along with many other bilingual education advocates, was to participate in debates against Unz and his co-author, Gloria Matta Tuckman, on television and on the radio. At each of these "debates" it was evident that the press was more interested in the "sensationalism" Unz and Tuckman created by making those outlandish, unsubstantiated claims about the best way to teach English. Unz, himself, never visited any well-implemented bilingual programs even though he stated that he had been interested in the programs for over ten years.[8] I had numerous interviews with reporters where I would explain the program yet the media, while given many leads to effective schools and research about bilingual education, chose to only restate the false claims made by Unz in their news stories. Facts were not checked and those false assumptions were never really challenged by the press. Since they were repeated often enough they became the "truth" during the campaign. Bruni (1998) stated,

> Mr. Unz said he succeeded because the current system was terribly flawed and voters needed only to be enlightened . . . "It's nice to be able to fix broken things, and there are a lot of broken things in California,' he [Unz] said. 'I certainly fixed bilingual education. I fixed it but good.'"[9]

It was a tough campaign that tugged at your heart when you heard the comments about English learners and their families. Afterwards, the campaign was criticized by individuals who did not want to face the fact that even when we were able to debate the merits of bilingual education programs, the electorate was against immigrants who were different and they were the ones that passed the initiative. Even Latinos, who now spoke English or never spoke Spanish, were against the bilingual program. I recall a group of Chicano veterans, who invited me to speak about the initiative, were adamantly against the program and they argued against the value of the programs. Finally one of their leaders stated, "I may not want to have this program for my children, but I don't have the right to take it away from parents who want this program for their children." With that the dialogue ended because that was the one true element of this campaign: people whose children were not affected by the proposition would be making choices for those children directly impacted by their vote.

Is Equity Possible Under Proposition 227?

The vagueness of the initiative and the political maneuvering on the part of the State Board of Education in 1998 over the implementation of the law (now Education Code 300) made for uncertainty and chaos. I attended a State Board meeting to testify against a change in the wording of the law. They wanted to change the language in the law that stated, "When there are 20 or more parent waivers at a grade level in a school a bilingual program is required" to eliminate "required" and instead use "where possible," which would have watered down the requirement. Unz also attended the board meeting to speak for the change—saying that it would be more in line with what he had intended to happen. He was unhappy that some districts were keeping their bilingual programs through the use of waivers. While there, he was treated like a hero with board members personally going up to him at the break to welcome him. What happened, however, was that CABE and Californians Together had done their homework (Californians Together is an offshoot of "Citizens for an Educated America," which organized after the passage of 227 with 6 organizations participating and has over 26 organizations as of 2015). I visited the Governor's office in Los Angeles and was given an opportunity to discuss the matter, and other advocates contacted legislative leaders to assist in presenting our side of the issue. Fortunately, we won that battle—and since then bilingual instruction has been required when there are 20 parent waivers at a grade level at each school. But, the war wasn't over, and Unz had a master plan to go national.

After the first year, the Unz camp had declared an early victory and lauded test results as a clear victory for their position. This supposed victory helped Unz introduce and pass two additional initiatives in Arizona and Massachusetts, even though Smith and Groves (1999) provided a different perspective by stating, "The pattern that emerges highlights the disappointment felt by those who had hoped for some spectacular sign that the state's intense focus on educational reform was already paying off." Among the findings of their analysis of the test scores they found:

> Language poses a far greater barrier to performance than poverty. Although negative effects of both are well-documented, the state's roughly 1.5 million students whose families were poor enough to be eligible for federal lunch subsidies scored better than its 900,000 who were limited in English ability

(low income students averaged 34th percentile while English learners averaged 24th).

(Smith & Groves, 1999)

The five-year study on the impact of Proposition 227 (Parrish et al., 2006) proved the assertion that the vagueness in the language of the initiative made it troublesome to implement. The State Board of Education and the Department of Education, as well as other educational agencies, struggled to provide regulations, guidelines, and technical assistance to school districts. Hardest hit were those districts that had fully operating bilingual education programs. These educators, knowing the benefits of their earlier bilingual programs, were now left to struggle to save their programs by any means possible, such as seeking charter status, parent waivers and/or general alternative waivers. Other educators, who were always opposed to bilingual education, were finally given permission to dismantle programs, and they did so almost immediately under the guise of following the "mandate of the people" (the initiative passed in June and implementation began in September 1998). There were also those districts that had to change very little because most of their programs were English-only even before the passage of Proposition 227 (Ramirez, 1999).

Dolson and Burnham-Massey (2011) in *Redesigning English-Medium Classrooms: Using Research to Enhance English Learner Achievement* state, "Effectively educating English learners continues to be one of the more elusive challenges facing public schools in the United States. Unfortunately, in California and several other states affected by ballot initiatives such as Proposition 227, the resulting legal and political fallout often interferes with the promotion of schooling practices grounded in solid research" (p. 1). The achievement gap between English-only students and English learners has not decreased, but increased according to assessment data from 2003 (when the Standardized Testing and Reporting [STAR] program was first implemented in California) to 2011. "Few if any educators and educational policy makers are satisfied with the mediocre scholastic outcomes experienced by language minority students" (p. 1), conclude Dolson and Burnham-Massey. In 2008 former Superintendent of Public Instruction, Jack O'Connell, in his yearly press release on the STAR achievement results, suggested that the academic achievement gap between ethno-linguistic minority students and other students, as represented by test scores, drop-out rates, and college admissions and completions, is the most persistent and pressing challenge facing public schools nationwide. This comment was made ten years after the passage of Proposition 227.

In an article for CABE's *Multilingual Educator*, I wrote, "A true test of the success of structured English immersion [and Proposition 227] will be when the 1998–1999 kindergarten class of English Learners reach the 4th or 5th grade and beyond—this will really show the impact and results of Unz' mean-spirited educational experiment" (Quezada, 1999). Sadly this prediction has come to pass. We now have "long-term English Learners" in our secondary schools. A report by Californians Together (Olson, 2010), *Reparable Harm*, brings to light the academic reality of students who "speak" English, but do not have the academic skills to pass academic English proficiency standards. These are students who are classified as English learners for more than six years and make up over 60% of English learners in secondary schools in California. This is the tragic outcome of educational policy resulting from a ballot initiative by a person without a background in education and who has the monetary resources to pass initiatives that today continue to impact 1.5 million students in California's schools. Many other students are affected in Arizona and Massachusetts where the initiative has even more restrictive language and where students are also failing. A sad truth is that no other instructional program available in California's schools has been designed by a ballot initiative—yet English learners and their families are subjected to a program that continues to fail many children.

One of the provisions of Proposition 227 was that the requirements in Education Code Section 305 could be waived by parents who have the legal right to apply for waivers. After 227, school districts have the ultimate authority to grant waivers or to offer programs. In a challenge to districts wanting a general waiver from the provisions of Proposition 227, *McLaughlin v. State Board of Education,* 75 Cal.App. 4th 196 (1999), the court ruled that school districts may not obtain wholesale waivers from the requirements of Proposition 227—as they could for other programs. The court ruled that only parents have the right under the initiative (Ed. Code Section 300 et seq.) to request that bilingual programs be continued. Even though the court ruled in favor of parent rights, in many school districts in California parents have given up asking for waivers that ultimately were not approved while others have struggled with district officials to keep their programs. Their request for alternative programs continues to be elusive and out of reach for their children. As this indicates, parents lost their power to choose bilingual programs for their children. The passage of Proposition 227 has restricted program options for parents, as was feared by opponents during the campaign. Most parents of English learners throughout the state encounter major barriers to enrolling their children in alternative (bilingual) programs. Schools/districts have exercised their power in a variety of ways. Some schools have fully explained parental rights for choosing educational programs for their children. Other schools/districts fail to inform parents or make alternative bilingual programs unavailable to parents at their school sites. Parents who selected the alternative program option find that they would have to move their children to other school sites when they chose this alternative program.

I am saddened by the impact of Proposition 227 in regard to parents, because they were sold on the idea that English is the answer to the challenges our English learners have to face in schools. I am often told, "parents are not seeking waivers." However, I know of too many English-speaking language minority students who are not making it and remain classified as English learners far more than the five to seven years research tells us is an average time for students to become fully proficient.

I also am frustrated when I see a dramatic increase in the number of two-way bilingual/dual language immersion programs where immigrant parents have to have a waiver for their children to participate while English speaking parents do not have to jump through those hoops to enroll their children. Too few English learners are participating (22% before 227 and less than 8% fifteen years later) in these or other bilingual programs. I ask myself—are these students being foreclosed of maintaining a high level of English and their home languages and ultimately not qualifying for the new California State Seal of Biliteracy (Californians Together, 2011) that so many advocates fought to get for our students? Will they have an opportunity to be prepared for our global world when others have that opportunity?

Reflections on 227's Impact

I am often asked about the impact Proposition 227 had on me personally. I can really say that it changed my life. Being an advocate for English learners ever since the early 1970s, I learned about effective bilingual instruction as I worked on a Masters in Bilingual Education. It was in those early years of my career that I had found an educational program that might have changed the direction of my life—I would have loved school and would have gone into college right out of high school. I would have understood that while I was different I was a person of worth and that I could achieve academically. While my parents instilled the value of education, bilingualism, and love of my heritage, I felt that I did not fit in school. Thankfully, as a young adult—seven years after I graduated from high school and after a failed marriage, I found that I could meet with success—even complete a doctorate. After the passage of 227 I felt that it was even more important to continue my advocacy on behalf of English learners. As CABE president and later CABE CEO (2000–2012) I joined with others to carry on this rewarding work. The challenges and frustrations faced in the 227 campaign, however, run deep. In my travels and advocacy work I often encounter the number 227 and I get a surge of unpleasant memories—once again experiencing the events and outcomes. I steer clear of this number, for example, at a symposium I attended in Mexico City in a hotel being assigned to room 227 and asking them to change my room, or even more intense feelings just recently, after being hospitalized for a heart attack and taken to the intensive care unit and assigned to room 227—praying that I would not die in this room.

I know that the quest for equitable and socially just programs will be our greatest challenge. I continue to champion for English learner instructional programs that recognize the centrality of language and culture and the importance of bilingualism and biliteracy for the 21st century. For many language minority students, public schools play a key role in their education. Advocacy organizations such as CABE and coalitions such as Californians Together, of which CABE is a member, will remain vigilant to ensure policies, practices, resources, and instructional programs meet a standard for ensuring equity and access. With students of color being the majority of students in California's schools in 2015, it will be more and more difficult to look away and label them "those" children. Nativist sentiment cannot continue to be a factor in how we educate California's children. I hope I see the day when this proposition's intent is overturned, and we are currently working towards that goal with new legislation. If we don't acknowledge that English learners and other diverse students are our future and educate them to the highest levels, not only we will see a decline in our economy, but we will suffer the tremendous loss of human potential that can enrich and sustain this diverse State of California. Will we meet this challenge for equity? Only time will tell, but we won't stop trying.

Notes

1. In 1967 Governor Ronald Reagan signed SB 53, the legislation allowing the use of other languages of instruction in California public schools. This bill overturned the 1872 law requiring English-only instruction.
2. The U.S. English organization was heavily involved in all facets of the proposition beginning with a "survey" where on their website they asked for stories about experiences in bilingual education programs. With their "results" they used the stories during the campaign calling it a formal survey and "research."
3. There is no research that supports students becoming proficient in a second language in one year and being able to function academically.
4. Even though research in support of well-implemented bilingual education programs is indeed available, the goal of the campaign was to malign these programs that were reaching fewer than 20% of English learners. The overwhelming majority of English learners were in programs that were taught in English from pull-out English Language Development programs to "sink or swim" mainstream settings.
5. It is sad to say that Mr. Unz's attitude prevails in 2011. When asked by an *LA Times* reporter about his authoring Proposition 227 he told the reporter, "Well you know that there is no research to substantiate bilingual education" (personal conversation with reporter, December 2011).
6. This statement is a distortion of the research stating that there was little or no difference in outcome measures between programs. Advocates would respond to Mr. Unz by stating—if there is no difference why are you promoting one program over the other. Later research results of the CA legislatively mandated study of the impact of Proposition 227 programs found that while there was little difference, there seemed to be a greater advantage for students who learned in their primary language.
7. It is interesting to note that the very fields of science that Unz claimed gave him a sound bearing for his initiative are the very ones that now tell us that individuals with bilingual skills have an advantage—even delaying the onset of Alzheimer's.
8. Unz was 36 years old yet he continually stated that he had been interested in bilingual programs for over 10 years. Could it have been that he was frustrated and could not communicate with his Central American housekeeper?
9. Jay P. Green stated it best by writing, "During the debate over Proposition 227 in California that sought to eliminate the use of native language in the instruction of children with limited English proficiency (LEP), competing claims were made about what the research in the area concluded. Christine Rossell, for example, argued that the review of the literature she conducted with Keith Baker suggested that children learn English best when they are taught in English (Rossell & Baker, 1996). Kenji Hakuta, on the other hand, argued that the review of the literature he conducted as part of the

National Research Council report on bilingual education, suggested that native language approaches are indeed beneficial for children learning English (National Research Council, 1997). Bewildered by these conflicting claims, the media and electorate in California generally paid little attention to researchers and Proposition 227 was passed into law."

References

Bruni, F. (1998). "The California entrepreneur who beat bilingual teaching." *New York Times*. Published on June 14, 1998. Retrieved June 16, 2015 from: http://www.nytimes.com/1998/06/14/us/the-california-entrepreneur-who-beat-bilingual-teaching.html

Dolson, D. P., & Burnham-Massey, L. (2011). *Redesigning English-medium classrooms: Using research to enhance English learner achievement.* Covina, CA: California Association for Bilingual Education.

Gendzel, G. (2009). "It didn't start with Proposition 187: One hundred and fifty years of nativist legislation in California." *Journal of the West, 48*, 76–85.

Greene, J. P. (1998). *A meta-analysis of the effectiveness of bilingual education.* Claremont, CA: The Tomas Rivera Policy Institute.

Green, L. C. (1998). "Cruising the web with English language learners." *Annual editions: Teaching English as a second language.* I. A. Heath & C. J. Serrano (Eds.). Sluice Dock, Guilford, CT: Dushkin/McGraw-Hill.

Ingram, C. (1998). "Wilson backs ballot measure to ban bilingual education." *Los Angeles Times,* May 19, 1998.

Lau v. Nichols, 414 U.S. 563 (1974).

MacKaye, S.D.A. (1990). "California Proposition 63: Language attitudes reflected in the public debate." *The Annals of the American Academy of Political and Social Science, March 1990: Vol. 508,* 1135–146.

Mailman, S. (1995). "California's Proposition 187 and its lessons." *New York Law Journal,* January 3, 1995.

McLaughlin v. State Board of Education, 75 Cal.App. 4th 196 (1999) California Court of Appeal, First Appellate District, Division Two.

Olson, L. (2010). *Reparable harm: Fulfilling the unkept promise of educational opportunity for California's long term English learners.* California Tomorrow.

Parrish, B., Merickel, A., et al. (2006). *Effects of the implementation of Proposition 227 on the education of English learners, K–12: Findings from a five-year evaluation.* Final Report for AB 56 and AB 1116. American Institutes for Research and WestEd, January 24, 2006.

Peterson, J. (1998). "White House to announce opposition to Prop. 227." *Los Angeles Times,* April 27, 1998.

Quezada, M. S. (1991). District remedies to eliminate the shortage of qualified teachers of Limited English Proficient students in California. Doctoral dissertation, University of Southern California.

Quezada, M. S. (1999). "And the beat goes on . . . The debate over bilingual education continues: Proposition 227 one year later." In *The Multilingual Educator,* a publication of the California Association for Bilingual Education.

Ramirez, D. J. (1999). *Preliminary findings of the impact of Proposition 227 in school districts in California.* Center for Language Minority Education and Research (CLMER).

Ramirez, D. J., Pasta, D. J., Yuen, S. D., Billings, D. K., & Ramey, D. R. (1991). *Executive summary of the final report: Longitudinal study of structured English immersion strategy, early-exit and late-exit bilingual education programs for language-minority children,* as prepared for the United States Department of Education under Contract No. 300–87–0156. San Mateo, CA: Aguirre International, February.

Smith, D. & Groves, M. (1999). "Small gains on Stanford 9 scores cut across all levels of languageability." *Los Angeles Times*, August 4, 1999. Retrieved June 16, 2015 from: http://articles.latimes.com/1999/aug/04/news/mn-62523

Thomas, W. & Collier, V. (2002). "A national study of school effectiveness for language minority students' long-term academic achievement." UC Berkeley: Center for Research on Education, Diversity and Excellence. Retrieved June 16, 2015 from: http://escholarship.org/uc/item/65j213pt

Unz, R. (April 1998). Speech in New York where he was seeking donations for his campaign.

15

LATINOS AND SOCIAL CAPITALIZATION

Taking Back Our Schools

Magaly Lavadenz

This chapter proposes social capitalization as an approach for Latino/a parental involvement in schools to respond to policy decisions that significantly violate their educational rights in selecting the language of instruction for their children's education. A multi-year ethnography is used to document the development of social capital in two specific areas: 1) the acquisition of political, economic, and cultural resources to overturn a local school board with an anti-bilingual agenda; and 2) the sociopolitical process to elect parents who represent parent-choice. The entire process included a powerful alliance of parents and teachers who collaboratively employed networks of community support, resources, and grassroots organizing to eventually become a majority on the school board. Two election cycles ultimately reinstated school policies that supported parents' choices in program options for their children.

Latinos and Social Capitalization: Community Resistance to Restrictive Language Policies

The devastating effects of Proposition 227 have been further compounded by the standardized testing requirements of No Child Left Behind (NCLB) and of California's Academic Performance Index frenzy. Even in districts that have historically followed the legal options for parent waivers,[1] such as Liberty District, the political pressure of the label "low or underperforming" led the Liberty School Board to announce in October 2004 that there would be a radical reversal in honoring parents' requests for their elementary-school-aged children to participate in alternative bilingual programs offered in the district's five K–5 schools (Lavadenz, 2003). Amidst protests and distressed reactions from teachers present on a mid-October afternoon in 2004, district officials also announced that parents had not yet been informed of these changes. Many in the audience, bilingual teachers, themselves graduates of Liberty's bilingual programs who returned to teach in their community, burst into tears. Several of the teachers in the audience were my former students—graduates of our bilingual teaching credential program. Shortly after this board decision, two of my former students, along with several parents and veteran teachers, approached me to share their concerns about the decision and to ask for my support in brainstorming possible action steps.

For parents who had already been granted waivers, their initial response to the Liberty School Board decision to drastically reduce the number of local schools offering bilingual program options (from six schools to one school) varied. In essence, two bilingual teachers joined several parents and subsequently other bilingual teachers to form a powerful political network of allies in response to the violation of parents' rights. This social and political network of parents, bilingual teachers, and community organizers initiated a 14-month process of collaboration involving much dialogue and communication that culminated in the replacement of two of the five school board members on the Liberty School Board. Incrementally, this alliance of parents and teachers garnered support in the Liberty community, while simultaneously arming them with knowledge and social capital to protest, organize, and resist district English-only policies.

Six months after the Liberty Board announced the restriction of bilingual program options for children in that district, the Padres Unidos de Liberty group eventually identified and successfully elected two new school board members in the November 8, 2005 election. These newly elected officials became advocates of parents' rights to choose the educational programming for their children as well as to hold the district accountable for providing quality education for bilingual English Learners. However, the two new board members still did not constitute a majority in the five-member board. Soon after this election, one of the bilingual teachers who formed part of the social and political network resigned from her teaching position, moved into the Liberty School District community, and was elected to the Liberty School Board in the November 2007 election. Her candidacy, campaign, and subsequent election reflect yet another powerful acquisition and enactment of social capital. In 2010, she was successfully re-elected and chosen from among the board members to serve as board president.

Inspired in part by an article published in the 2005 conference edition of the *Multilingual Educator*, which outlines eight steps in engaging minority parent participation through communication, support, and organizing, the Padres Unidos de Liberty also:

- developed a voter registration campaign to register voters;
- consistently and continually were present and vocal at all school board meetings;
- provided citizenship classes for those seeking naturalization as U.S. citizens;
- analyzed community voter registration patterns;
- developed an election committee and campaign;

- contacted the media, especially the Spanish language media to publicize the oppression of parents' rights;[2]
- created a Political Action Committee to fundraise for the election;
- submitted written complaints to the Office of Civil Rights, to the Uniform Complaints branch of the California Department of Education;
- sought support and collaboration with Loyola Marymount University;
- invited and actively participated in parent and community leadership development provided by Mexican American Legal Defense Fund (MALDEF)[3] and California Association for Bilingual Education (CABE).[4]

This intensive, all-encompassing effort was based on solidarity, courage, and sacrifice by parents and teachers alike. The outcome, although an overwhelmingly successful effort, was a result of a highly committed, engaged, and outraged community that actualized the social, cultural, and political capital to resist and counter English hegemony. This school district had a history of valuing the linguistic and cultural "funds of knowledge" (Amanti et al., 1993) of this predominantly Latino immigrant community. Despite this history, district elected officials and administrators still succumbed to the false notion that more English is the answer to respond to policies such as NCLB. What they failed to realize when they made this decision was that, ultimately, public school educators must answer to the communities they represent.

The multi-year ethnography documents the development of social capital in the form of the acquisition of political, economic, and cultural resources to overturn local school board anti-bilingual members and elect community members who represent parent-choice (Délimon-Théramène, Monkman, & Ronald, 2005). The process included a powerful alliance of parents and teachers who collaboratively employed networks of community support, resources, and grassroots organizing to eventually become a majority on the school board.

The following research question guided the study:

- *How do Latino/a communities respond to exclusionary language and education policies as a result of Proposition 227 and state/federal accountability measures?*

Drawing upon three broad conceptual frameworks—social capital theory, social network theory, and sociocultural theory—social capitalization can be applied to explain and to facilitate the involvement of minority parents in complex, locally situated contexts that have historically excluded their participation in meaningful ways. I use the case of the K–8 Liberty School District, located within a 1.09 square mile unincorporated area of Los Angeles, near Los Angeles International Airport. From an overall student population of 7,562, 79% of the students enrolled in Liberty schools are classified as English Learners; 99.7% of English Learners have Spanish as their first language (California Department of Education, R-30, 2006–2007).

Data Sources

Data collection began in October 2004, when I was invited to attend a meeting of parents and bilingual teachers who were meeting to discuss the new Liberty School Board policy. Over the course of the three years, I collected field notes, observational records, as well as interviews of parents and teachers. I also collected district policy documents, memos, and correspondence. Additional data collected include relevant media reports (both written and televised) and photographic journals.

Methods

Content analysis with coding was used to analyze data (Hutchinson, 2001). Figure 15.1 represents a visual modeling of the three conceptual frameworks that inform the conceptualization of social capitalization. I provide examples of the consolidation of social capital theory, social networks theory, and sociocultural theory that were evident in the actions and activities of the parent and teacher networks. The networks that emerged were a response to Liberty School Board action in 2004 that severely restricted bilingual instruction in that district. In the next section I briefly summarize these theories in relation to parents' and teachers' collaborative resistance.

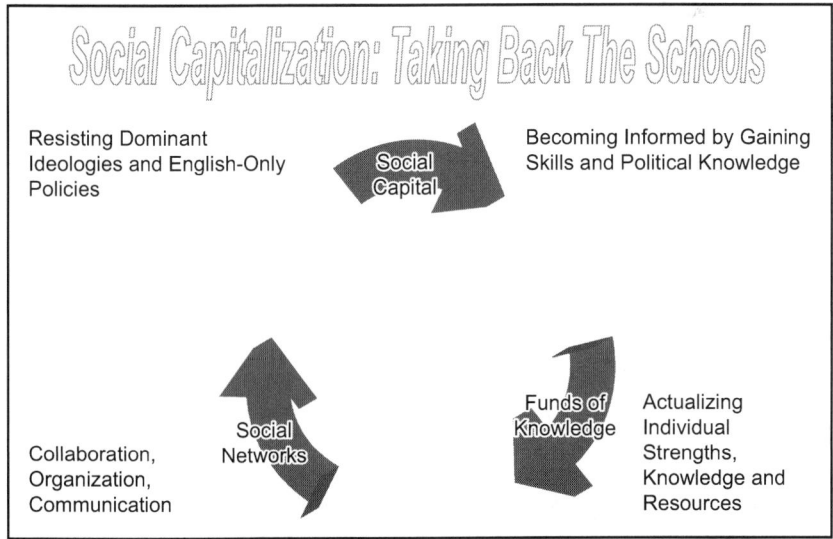

FIGURE 15.1 Social Capitalization: Taking Back The Schools

Findings: Social Capitalization: Liberty Community Resistance to Restrictive Language Policies

The conceptual framing of social capitalization presented in Figure 15.1 is represented by linking three theoretical frameworks: 1) social capital theory, 2) social networks theory, and 3) sociocultural theory. The data collected throughout the four-year trajectory of this narrative was complex and constantly evolving; nonetheless, the experiences of resistance from a collaborative community of teachers, parents, and community members are further elaborated in this chapter.

Social Capital Theory—Acquiring Political Strategic Knowledge and Skills

Bourdieu and Passeron (1977) and other scholars of social capital theory define it as the reproduction of social stratification as facilitated by the inherent possession and behaviors of middle class norms and values, thereby advantaging and privileging this class over others, especially in schools (i.e., dominance, hegemony). The theory contends that human beings have various types of capital. In U.S. society, varying types of resources and strategies are used to retain and hand down human and social capital. Individuals and groups from other societies who possess different human or social capital from those operationalized in schools and other institutions are at a disadvantage when the functions of those institutions are based on values, practices, and perspectives other than their own. As the coalition of parents and teachers of Liberty acquired U.S. political and social capital by learning about running campaigns, for example, they began to acquire the middle-class practices that enabled them to take action, create change, and begin to counter the hegemonic practices of the school board.

Social Networks Theory—Community Collaborative

Occurring within all classes, social networks consist of interpersonal ties and connections that cross institutions, ethnic groups, families, and cultures (Stanton-Salazar & Urso Spina, 2000; Lareau, McNamara-Horvat, & Weininger, 2003). Networks of support and community are important for the continuation of an infrastructure that keeps communities working. Parental engagement in formal spaces such as the Parent Teachers Association (PTA) is an example of a social network of support. For minority parents who rely on tools or resources within the school, participation is fostered by a shared language and cultural similarities to their children's teachers (Arriaza, 2003; Calabrese-Barton, Drake, & Pérez-Carreén, 2005; Daniel-White, 2002). Jasis and Ordoñes-Jasis (2004) address the development of social networks as parental *convivencia*, or an avenue of the empowerment of parents to exercise their rights through collective action. In the case of Liberty, the power of the social networks that included parents, teachers, and community organizers resulted in an expanded and sophisticated knowledge that extends far beyond the normal participation in a PTA meeting. One very telling example occurred during a heavily attended and heated school board meeting in February 2005. Liberty School Board members, realizing that consistent parent presence at school board meetings was to be the norm, called the local sheriff's office because of the perceived "threat" of parents. The hefty sheriff who came to the meeting stood guard at the door, intimidating some of the parents. One of the parents, however, called the local television media, who later televised the presence of the sheriff, along with a heated exchange between a board member and a parent (Olivos, 2004).

Sociocultural Theory—Enacting Community Funds of Knowledge

Amanti et al. (1993) use the term *funds of knowledge* to define the internal resources existing in all homes, but particularly in diverse communities that traditionally have been ignored in school curriculum, instruction, and practices. In applying sociocultural approaches, both theoretically and methodologically, this study has identified the centrality of the Latino/a family's role and their strength in resisting hegemonic district policies. A key vignette that depicts the use of individual and familial funds of knowledge in this study occurred during the campaigning for the election of 2005. The community organizer who served as political consultant for both campaigns stressed to the collaborative the importance of precinct walking, telephone banking, and fund raising (these as examples of social capital). In order to participate in the phone banking (calling registered voters to ensure the support for their candidates), the incorrect assumption was made that everyone participating had a phone. Once they discovered that several parents did not have phones at home, the collaborative quickly identified who did have phones, scheduled the phone banking sessions, and exchanged childcare duties and food preparation during the evenings and weekends of the phone banking sessions.

Conclusion

My role as a "sounding board," supporter, and encourager to this process was a privilege and honor—it symbolizes to me the importance of participatory action, responsibility, and solidarity that those of us in universities have to *respond* and not just document critical historic oppressive moments in our communities (Freire, 1994). This study's significance lies in framing social capitalization as an approach for increasing minority parental involvement in schools in response to decision-making policies that have historically violated parents' educational rights in the selection of the language of instruction in their children's education. This process provides a model of a resistive response towards seeking a more democratic education.

Notes

1. Proposition 227 passed in California with a 60:40 vote in 1998. Its aim was to sever bilingual education in California. The only alternative option parents have had for bilingual instruction in lieu of English Only is via a waiver process, which is subject to administrative approval.
2. An interesting incident was captured by UNIVISION, a major Spanish-language television station. Parents had called the media to ensure coverage; this excerpt was of the incident in which the police were called in to "stand guard" during the board meeting and while parents and their children picketed a board meeting. This action was a key example of some retaliation efforts by the district in response to the community's right to free speech.
3. Mexican American Legal Defense Fund is a lawyer group that defends civil rights cases.
4. California Association for Bilingual Education is an educator group that promotes bilingual education.

References

Amanti, C., Floyd-Tenery, M., González, N., Gonzalez, R., Moll, L. C., Rendón, P., & Rivera, A. (1993). *Teacher research on funds of knowledge: Learning from households.* Educational Practice Report: 6. National Center for Research on Cultural Diversity and Second Language Learning, 1–25.

Arriaza, G. (2003). Schools, social capital and children of color. *Race, Ethnicity and Education, 6*(1), 71–94.

Bourdieu, P., & Passeron, J. (1977). *Reproduction in education, culture and society.* London: Sage.

Calabrese-Barton, A., Drake, C., & Pérez-Carreón, G. (2005). The importance of presence: Immigrant parents' school engagement experiences. *American Educational Research Journal, 42*(3), 465–498.

Daniel-White, K. (2002). Reassessing parent involvement: Involving language minority parents in school work at home. *Educational Linguistics, 18*(1), 3–23.

Délimon-Théramène, F., Monkman, K., & Ronald, M. (2005). Social and cultural capital in an urban latino school community. *Urban Education, 40*(1), 4–33.

Freire, P. (1994). *Pedagogy of hope: Reliving pedagogy of the oppressed.* New York: Continuum Press.

Hutchinson, S. (2001). Education and grounded theory. In: R. Sherman & R. B. Webb. (Eds.), *Qualitative research in education: Focus and methods.* London: RoutledgeFalmer.

Jasis, P. & Ordoñes-Jasis, R. (2004). Convivencia to empowerment: Latino parent organizing at la familia. *The High School Journal, 88*(2), 32–42.

Lareau, A., McNamara-Horvat, E., & Weininger, E. B. (2003). From social ties to social capital: Class differences in the relations between schools and parent networks. *American Educational Research Journal, 40*(2), 319–351.

Lavadenz, M. (2003). La educación bilingüe y la teoría del caos: Implicaciones para la política educativa y lingüística en California. In: G. Persinotto. *Ensayos de lenguaje y pedaogogía.* Santa Barbara, CA: University of California Linguistic Minority Research Institute.

Olivos, E. M. (2004). Tensions, contradictions, and resistance: An activist's reflection of the struggles of latino parents in the public school system. *The High School Journal, 87*(4), 25–35.

Stanton-Salazar, R. D., & Urso Spina, S. (2000). The network orientations of highly resilient urban minority youth: A network-analytic account of minority socialization and its educational implications. *The Urban Review, 32*(2), 227–261.

16
LATINO PARENT ENGAGEMENT
Struggle, Hope, and Resistance

Pablo C. Ramírez

> *There is nothing more unequal than treating unequals as equals.*
> —*Lau v. Nichols, Supreme Court Decision, 1974*

Introduction

My parents are immigrants from Mexico. Throughout my K–12 educational experience, I was taught and encouraged to think that immigrants, especially undocumented immigrants, were a detriment to the United States. In elementary school, my parents were never taken into consideration. During this time (1980s) in Southern California, multiple immigration raids were undertaken. Fear of these raids, coupled with no authentic support from the public school system, kept my parents from actively engaging in my school. I recall that during my high school years in Southern California, teachers referred to Latino/a undocumented immigrant parents as criminals, gangsters, and non-American. The purpose of this chapter is to illustrate the process I have engaged in as a teacher, advocate, and researcher to support Latino immigrant parents in the educational system. First, I will share the personal story of my parents and its significance to my work. Second, I will describe key experiences with parents that transformed my perception of parent involvement. Third, I will review relevant literature concerning Latino parents in the educational system. Next, I will describe action research projects conducted with parents in California and Arizona. Lastly, I will pose possible recommendations for teachers, educators, schools, and communities in regard to Latino immigrant parents.

My Past

My life as a Mexican American living in San Diego, California changed dramatically in 1985 when I was 10 years old. During the summer of 1985 my parents were told by the United States government to leave the country. In other words, we were all being deported indefinitely. Although my brother and I were born in California, when my parents were deported, everyone left. My mom used words such as "summer vacation" and "visiting *abuelita*" as comfort words to avoid telling us the truth. The deportation was so traumatic that my mother did not reveal the truth about it until recently. She, like other immigrant parents, was told by American society that they have no cultural value through discriminatory practices (Olivos, 2006; Shannon, 1996; Valencia, 1997); one such practice is the deportation itself. Scholars Suárez-Orozco and Suárez-Orozco (2001) explain that Latino parents feel a sense of shame for being portrayed as criminals and leeches to the American economy. Both of my parents have been very quiet about our immigrant experiences. As parents, they have always shielded my brother and me about the discriminatory manner in which they were treated in the community and at work. In spite of their efforts to shield us, at the age of 10, I had already internalized the manner in which society negatively perceived my parents, our culture, and me.

In 1987 my parents decided to return to California from Mexico with my father leading the way. We followed. I do not know how my parents crossed the border. I did not care. From this pivotal moment in my life, *la migra, los coyotes, el racismo, el otro lado,* and *el sueño* have all been topics of dinner conversations, testimonies, and personal family narratives. A day does not go by that we do not talk or comment about the current issues impacting immigrant parents and our collective struggle for equality.

Parent Advocate

At the age of 23 I began teaching in a low-income Latino community in San Diego County. Almost 100% of the population was of Latino immigrant descent. History began to reproduce itself and trigger traumatic experiences from my past. The Latino parents that I served and worked for reflected all the struggles and fears my parents had felt 20 years before. Being a naive new teacher, I believed that the public school system had the great intention of understanding the injustice and oppression Latino immigrant parents faced in American society and schools. I willingly participated in the Parent Teacher Association, School Governance Committees, and English Language Advisory Committees. All governing bodies are supposed to, in theory, encourage parents and offer important information about their children's academic achievement and ultimately build parents' leadership skills. I believed that in this setting, parents would have what my parents never had: access to information and encouragement to voice their opinion.

It did not take long, however, to realize that the public school system in fact operationalized societal views towards Latino immigrant parents. I observed that the public school system reproduces discriminatory practices via parent involvement practices that stigmatize parents. One such practice is the exclusion of Latino parents in key school decisions involving the quality of education for Latino youth. My parents were told by the school what to do. Years later, I was told by the school administration what to tell parents to help their children. Was I going to relive and reproduce the same discriminatory practices my parents faced? For the next three years, I reflected on the role and value of Latino parents in the educational system. I understood that Latino immigrant engagement in the public school system is a political act (Gaitan-Delgado, 1990). As a result, advocating for Latino parents' rights in school communities has been a major part of my academic and research career. Latino parents' lack of agency in school communities is a significant societal issue that continues to impact schools across the United States (Olivos, Jimenez-Castellanos, & Ochoa, 2011).

Brief Literature Review

This section will review two landmark court cases that have chronicled the struggle for equality in education for Latinos in the past 80 years. Second, the section will examine the complexities of Latino parent engagement in the public school system. Lastly, a discussion on transformative resistance is presented as potentially having an impact on Latino parent agency in school communities.

Court Cases

Latinos have challenged the educational system in the courts. The two court cases briefly summarized here exemplify the struggle for equality for Latinos families.

Plyler v. Doe *(1982)*

The ruling of *Plyler v. Doe* (1982), which took place in the state of Texas, affirms that undocumented students shall be granted legal access to educational institutions from kindergarten to 12th grade. Further, it protects them from undue scrutiny and exclusion on the basis of perceived immigration status. This landmark decision is the first to suggest, theoretically, that immigrant youth have rights in the United States. This court case chronicles the struggle and resistance efforts by Latino parents and communities for educational equality. Although this case favored Latinos and culturally and linguistically diverse groups, the issues of segregation, racism, and deportation continue to plague Latinos in the United States.

Horne v. Flores *(1992)*

In the *Horne v. Flores* (1992) case, Latinos sued the Nogales Unified School District (NUSD) for failing to provide an adequate education to English Language Learners (ELLs). Further, the suit claimed that the NUSD did not provide prepared teachers, effective instructional materials, or programs provided by sufficient district funds. In 2009, the Supreme Court ruled that Arizona had sufficiently complied with the law. Thus, ELLs are still not receiving an adequate education per the Equal Educational Opportunity Act.

Latino Parent Engagement

Research literature on Latino parent engagement in public schools suggests that Latino parents continue to be excluded by the educational system (Olivos, 2006; Olivos, Jimenez-Castellanos, & Ochoa, 2011; Shannon, 1996). According to scholars Olivos, Jimenez-Castellanos, & Ochoa (2011), Latino parents are treated unequally and the evidence is in the underachievement results of Latino youth. Traditionally, public schools that involve parents have employed practices reflective of mainstream White middle-class values (Nuñez, 1995; Olivos, Jimenez-Castellanos, & Ochoa, 2011). These traditional paradigms have come under examination and critique because of established practices that have often disempowered and marginalized culturally and linguistically diverse parents and community members (Nuñez, 1995). To this end, Olivos (2006) posits that:

> Inequality is represented in the inertia found in the school system that binds educators into enforcing institutional beliefs that reinforce inequality by excluding bicultural parents from important input and decision-making authority. Inequitable treatment by educators leads to inequitable relationships with bicultural students and bicultural parents, and ultimately to inequitable educational results.
>
> *(p. 22)*

Further, the public school system is unwilling to critique its parent involvement practices and instead blatantly blames Latino parents. This assault is evident because Latino parents are characterized through a deficit perspective (Pearl, 2005). Transformative resistance in school communities has shown to be an essential piece leading to more equality for Latino parents and their children.

Resistance

Solórzano and Delgado Bernal (2001) identify transformational resistance as a form of resistance that is motivated by social justice and has a critique of social oppression. In this level of resistance parents are not merely avoiding school meetings, satisfied with participating in low-impact roles, or exclusively blaming themselves and their fellow parents for their children's low-academic achievement. Instead, parents are working to improve the condition of the entire school as well as working to name those elements of the schooling process that are detrimental to their children and not in the best interest of their community—in other words, challenging dominant ideologies such as school neutrality and seeking equal opportunities for students and parents from marginalized communities.

Using Solórzano and Delgado Bernal's (2001) framework, in this chapter, I examine Latino parent resistance in a specific public school setting in San Diego County (CA). In the following action research projects, resistance on the part of the Latino parents is seen taking on various forms, not all of which are easily discernable or predictable. The form of resistance these parents chose (either consciously or subconsciously) drew from the parents' agency, their political outlook, and their attempt to challenge dominant forms of power and ideology.

Action Research

Parent Training

In 2004 I conducted multiple meetings with parents through action research. The objective of action research is emancipation: to uncover and apply change in procedures that constrain justified claims for equity (Stringer, 1992).

I was frustrated by the way in which Latino parents in my school community were being marginalized. I understood from my first two years of working in the public school system as a teacher that authentic agency for Latino parents derived from community organizations (Nuñez, 1995). The parents and I had multiple discussions about the needs they wanted addressed. This process was enacted to understand underlying issues parents felt were important. Many of the issues emerged via parents' observations and reflections about our school. After three months of parent discussion and reflection, parents decided they wanted a program that supported leadership skills and wanted to learn how to navigate the educational system. Parents and I met with school administrators for three months. We encountered discouraging comments from, "Parents do not need leadership skills," to "It's a waste of time and money."

After multiple conversations and meetings with school administration, the school allowed a grassroots Latino organization, the Parent Institute for Quality Education (PIQE), to conduct, in collaboration with parents, a ten-week parent training. I collaborated with parents to coordinate PIQE in the school community. To this end, we were able to recruit over 100 Latino parents to participate in the training. Many parents were excited about the program, as it matched some of their needs. Although PIQE did not solve the issue of inequality towards Latino immigrant parents, it encouraged parents to be more critical about the way in which schools engage parents and disseminate information. PIQE provided parents with tools they could utilize in schools to access information.

From the school's perspective, the parent training with PIQE was seen as radical, and ultimately, unnecessary. After PIQE had left, our action research group followed up with the school. The parents from PIQE and I began a process of dialogue with the school administration about biliteracy and school finances, considered by the parents to be the most significant issues that they wanted to learn about. Parents began questioning school administration about these topics. We were met with negative attitudes and angered school administrators. Parents and I continued to push issues and concerns in other meetings such as School Site Council and English Language Advisory Council (ELAC), but our concerns were neglected in each of these committees.

Parents and I met regularly to reflect upon their efforts to become more active and informed and the reactions this caused. We began a process of problem-posing practices where we discussed how we could engage more parents and, consequently, disseminate information about the needs of parents. Parents began to understand the process of transformative resistance. They were able to decipher the method in which the education system built barriers impeding parents from truly and fully participating in the school. We challenged the school; however, the school's power exerted on the parents marginalized and isolated us in the school. We were characterized as troublemakers seeking a personal agenda. Further, we were labeled as too political and as a source of problems. As I worked with parents, I would reflect on the struggles my own parents faced 20 years ago. Lamentably, even when Latino parents are actively engaged in their school community and, consequently, seek information as to how to best to support the academic success of their children, they are portrayed as radicals, nosy/*chismosos*, and uneducated.

Biliteracy

In 2006, I was part of a parent resistance movement. It was a moment in my life where I witnessed the power of parents. In a Southern California school district, Latino parents were denied a bilingual program. Parents were upset and outraged and felt betrayed by the school. Parents were angry that their school district had taken away their biliteracy program even after the school had promised it would "support biliteracy in the classroom." The school board had strategically met behind closed doors to make a decision on the biliteracy program. Only a few pre-selected parents were invited to this meeting. Further, the educational system had dictated to Latino parents once again what was best for their children. Through action research approaches, I participated with community organizations and led parent meetings in the neighborhood to reflect on an action plan. Our discussions were focused on listening to what parents wanted to do to interrupt the exclusionary practices enforced by the school district. Most of the parents were Mexican immigrants and more than half were undocumented. The reason I note this is that during 2006 in San Diego County multiple immigration raids were being executed in the community. However, this did not deter parents from participating in community and parent discussions. Many parents showed no fear in defending their children's education and future. Again, I was reminded of my own parents during the 1980s and felt encouraged to see Latino parents collectively unafraid and seeking equality for their children. Together with a community organization, a handful of teachers met with parents for five months. Consequently, parents sent out flyers and enacted a process of going door to door informing other parents about the lack of a quality education their children were receiving. Parents led this resistance movement. They met with school board officials and school district figures. I would support parents by facilitating information and helping them organize their ideas, mostly in Spanish. During these meeting parents were very articulate and critical about the conditions placed on their school. Parents spoke eloquently in school board meetings and in multiple community forums about the need for a quality education for the community's children. After eight months of parent activism, the community was able to maintain their bilingual program. As a participant and observer, I was able to document a transformative resistance process enacted by parents and community figures that led to the interruption of status quo practices enforced by the public school system. In the presence of fear and marginalization, Latino parents and community members challenged the educational system and empowered the community.

Arizona and SB1070

I am currently working in Arizona. My mother asked why I was going to work for such an anti-immigrant state. Perhaps this comment was made because my family and I are still traumatized by our collective experience with *la migra* in California.

Senate Bill 1070 requires individuals (not born in the United States) over the age of 14 who remain in the United States for longer than 30 days to register with the U.S. government, and to have registration documents in their possession at all times; violation of this requirement is a federal misdemeanor crime. Issues of equality and democracy have been fought for a long period of time. In 2012 the state of Arizona argued about the language and provisions of SB1070. In the end all of the provisions under SB1070 were upheld. Thus, "show me your papers," continues to be a practice enforced in Arizona and other states. This practice has produced fear and trauma, greatly impacting the Latino parents of public school children.

After the passage of SB1070, the clock has turned back to the early 1980s. However, this time it is much worse. The fact is, we are living in a time in the United States where a person can be harassed and arrested by law enforcement by "looking" Latino through profiling. The xenophobia that exists at a national level reminds me of how my parents were negatively characterized by schools. So how do Latino parents in Arizona feel walking their children to school every morning? How do their children feel? As I engage in an action research project in Arizona, Latino parents are preparing and wanting change. One parent insightfully describes hope:

> No le tenemos miedo a la injusticia ni a la migra. Nuestros hijos son el gran futuro de nuestro país. Mucha gente cree que no tenemos el derecho de estar aquí, sin embargo, seguimos en nuestra lucha. Nos pagan mal y trabajamos duro y muchos padres de familia no se quejan. Queremos igualdad. Ya basta.

Latino parents in Arizona are working, living, and providing for their children in the presence of fear, in a down economy, during a period of high deportation rates and consequently, and ironically, there is hope.

Fear

The implications of the phrase "show me your papers" carry profound consequences for Latino populations. This practice creates fear and an unwelcoming environment by instilling fear tactics in undocumented populations. In my conversation with parents in Arizona, I have heard parents state that they will not leave their home for weeks, fearing deportation. For instance, one parent stated that a school administrator had called their home due to their child's absence and explained some of the ramifications, on voice mail, for not reporting the absence to the schools. Parents did not know or understand what the information was about since the information was in English and consequently, both parents stayed home and did not work for weeks for fear of being deported.

Economic Impact

Undocumented parents work for free. Under the context of SB1070, undocumented parents now face less opportunity to work and to eventually provide financial support for their families. Due in part to the cost of living and other economic conditions, undocumented individuals accept labor jobs that pay at or below the minimum wage in the United States. Conversely, no insurance or benefits are provided to parents leaving them extremely vulnerable. Show-me-your-papers provisions impact parents and families, thus, the conditions placed on parents put undue psychological stress. Maria, a single mother of three, has worked on a golf course for the past three years. She works from 4:00 a.m. to 3:00 p.m. six days a week. Maria has stated that she has to be strategic about work especially since "show me your papers" has been enforced. She states that she has to accept the working conditions that are presented to her for fear of been fired. Moreover, she has commented that there are no other alternatives, especially when you have three children and only one source of income.

Deportation

Families are being separated and deported at a national level within the context of anti-immigrant policies. According to the Pew Hispanic Center, more than 1.5 million unauthorized immigrants were deported from 2008–2011 (Passel, 2012). The implications of family separations are severe and profound. Separating a child from his/her mother is a scene that has been witnessed and is pervasive in many anti-immigrant states. Suárez-Orozco & Suárez-Orozco (2001) argues that separating a child creates high levels of psychological stress impacting the overall health of children. Parents that I have met and interviewed in Arizona have stressed that being deported and kept from being with their children is their biggest fear. Furthermore, many children born to undocumented parents have gone through this painful process. Children in this context are placed with other family members or placed in detainee centers for a period of time. The impact of this process on youth is cruel and inhumane.

Dreamers

In times of great tension and adversity, Latino families are collective and strong. In 2012, a deferment provision, President Obama's Deferred Action for Childhood Arrivals program, protects some undocumented youth from deportation. In addition, it authorizes them to live and work in the United States for two years. In the context of "show me your papers," undocumented parents are seeking rights for their children and are politically astute. Consequently, from August 2012 to December 2012, a high average of deferments was submitted at a national level (Passel, 2012). In Arizona, the data show that undocumented families are applying for the Deferred Action for Childhood Arrival program. These data reveal that although many sociopolitical, and language barriers result in unwelcoming environments, parents are politically astute in seeking due process for unauthorized youth even if means that they may be deported. Manuel, a parent I have talked with on several occasions, affirms that, "si no nos pueden dar la mica/green card a nosotros, que se las den a nuestros hijos que han estado aquí y son más americanos que nada."

Recommendations

Based on the current conditions of Latino immigrant parents in many school communities, changes need to be implemented in schools to disrupt the manner in which parents are being mistreated. Schools, at a national level, need to continue to reach out and provide parents information regarding their rights and due process. Furthermore, schools must begin to equip themselves with more resources and counselors that can support and guide Latino undocumented parents in terms of coping with stress or issues related to immigration and education.

It is imperative that teachers continue to support Latino parents during these critical anti-immigrant periods. Teacher advocacy at a national level is required to encourage parents in schools. Moreover, teacher advocates should challenge districts to create authentic lines of communication so that parents can voice their ideas, questions, and concerns in regard to their children's future. More training is needed to support teachers working with immigrant parents and children. This training must focus on practices teachers can use in and outside the school to support parents and to collaborate with parents across the school year. This important relationship must be nourished so it can have a significant impact on the academic trajectory of Latino youth in the educational system.

A stronger bond must develop between schools and Latino immigrant communities. By creating a powerful alliance with schools, parents can seek support in terms of human rights, education, and information about immigration and possible questions about employment. The school should be guided by the needs of the community. Hence, community members must be major stakeholders giving key ideas concerning parents, education, and immigrant rights. This strong relationship provides political power needed to combat anti-immigrant practices at a national level.

A major shift in immigration policy at a national level must be operationalized in order for parents to be able to provide for their families. The psychological stress and constraining environment placed onto parents should be disrupted in favor of a process that would allow immigrants a clear path to citizenship. This process will benefit many families with regard to educational opportunities and financial stability. Moreover, it will have a positive impact on the U.S. economy.

Conclusion

In this chapter, I illustrated the effect that my early childhood experiences had on my beliefs about Latino parents in the educational system. It revealed how my experiences as a teacher and parent advocate have helped me face early on in my career the injustice and oppression perpetuated in the public school system on Latino parents. The review of the literature confirmed that Latinos have always fought for equality in education, yet are still facing the same chronic issues as in the past. Further, the literature review affirmed that Latino parent engagement is critical and needed for the success of youth in education. I asserted that transformative resistance is a construct that shows promise in the struggle for Latino parent agency in school communities. Lastly, I tried to show how the action research chronicled in California and Arizona highlights and expounds on the multiple systematic barriers that Latino immigrant parents face on a daily basis. In the case of Arizona, it is clear that we are fighting an uphill and dangerous battle. Nonetheless, this chapter illustrates that Latino immigrant parents are resilient and have the collective power to transform our current educational system.

References

Gaitan-Delgado, C. (1990). *Literacy for empowerment: The role of parents in children's education*. New York, NY: The Falmer Press.

Horne v. Flores (231 US434) (1992).

Lau v. Nichols (414 US 563) (1974).

Nuñez, R. (1995). *The bicultural home and traditional explanations for low academic achievement: A case of embedded racism*. Unpublished dissertation, San Diego State University & Claremont Graduate University Doctoral Program.

Olivos, E. M. (2006). *The power of parents: A critical perspective of bicultural parent involvement in the public schools*. New York, NY: Peter Lang Publishers, Inc.

Olivos, E. M., Jimenez-Castellanos, O. & Ochoa, A. M. (2011). *Bicultural parent engagement: Advocacy and empowerment*. New York, NY: Teachers College Press.

Passel, J. (2012). *Unauthorized immigrant population: National and state trends, 2011*. Washington, D.C.: Pew Hispanic Center.

Pearl, A. (2005). *Democratic practices in education: Implications for teacher education*. Lanham, MD: Rowman & Littlefield Education.

Plyler v. Doe 457 U.S. 202 (1982).

Shannon, S. M. (1996). Minority parental involvement: A Mexican mother's experience and a teacher's interpretation. *Education and Urban Society, 29*(1), 71–84.

Solórzano, D. G. & Delgado Bernal, D. (2001). Examining transformational resistance through a critical race and LatCrit theory framework: Chicana and Chicano students in an urban context. *Urban Education, 36*(3), 308–342.

Stringer, E. T. (1992). *Action research*. Thousand Oaks, CA: Sage Publications.

Suárez-Orozco, C. & Suárez-Orozco, M. M. (2001). *Children of immigration*. Cambridge, MA: Harvard University Press.

Valencia, R. (1997). *The evolution of deficit thinking: Educational thought and practice*. New York, NY: Teacher College Press.

17

A CONCISE HISTORY OF THE NATIONAL LATINO/A EDUCATION RESEARCH AND POLICY PROJECT

Origins, Identity, Accomplishments, and Initiatives

Angela Valenzuela and Patricia D. López

Background

Before the National Latino/a Education Research Agenda Project, the "NLERAP Council" as we know it today, existed, an agglomeration of education researchers formed a working group as part of the Inter-University Program for Latino Research (IUPLR). Within a time span of two to three years, by 2000 this working group became NLERAP. Our group was primarily comprised of university faculty involved in both teacher preparation and research on the education of Latina and Latino youth in the public school system. NLERAP was founded by Professor Pedro Pedraza within the Centro de Estudios Puertorriqueños at the City University of New York at Hunter College.

The purpose of NLERAP at that time was to engage in a consensus-building dialogue concerning the educational crisis confronting, in particular, the Puerto Rican and Mexican-origin communities across this nation and to develop an actionable research agenda that would address this reality. This agenda was always coupled with the Council's desire to exert influence at local, state, and national levels in the policy and practice of certain areas of educational reform. Because of the makeup of the Council, secondary education and English language learners were also constants of our focus. While we retain a focus as a collective on issues pertaining to teacher preparation, Council membership has evolved over time to include leaders from community-based organizations in those sites where we are located, nationally, as outlined further in this chapter.

The First Decade

In 2000, Pedro Pedraza and his assistant, Melissa Rivera, embarked on a two-year effort that involved diverse stakeholder meetings comprised of educators, community activists, university scholars, and other educational constituencies with Latino communities in eight regions throughout the country and Puerto Rico. This effort crystallized into a national and regional board structure, with Council members serving as liaisons and members of their respective regional boards. Valenzuela herself became a NLERAP Council member in 2001.

The top four, most widely voiced concerns in the stakeholder meetings were high-stakes testing, teacher quality, equity, and the need for a greater focus on arts in the curriculum. A need for quality bilingual education was also expressed; however, because it was ranked fifth as a concern and because it is an area that is addressed fully by other organizations, NLERAP decided not to make this a specific focus. The community also "talked back" to hegemony in research approach and indicated that the kind of research conducted by academics for the kinds of changes sought by their communities was untenable. Not only were academic researchers typically non-collaborative, but neither were they community oriented. Moreover, the timeline from research conceptualization, design, implementation, and policymaking was not responsive to the urgent needs of community. To remedy this situation, the community called for a multi-methods research orientation predicated on participatory and collaborative research.

Pedro Pedraza and Melissa Rivera developed a research agenda booklet that summarized the outcomes of their two-year investigation (Pedraza, Rivera, & Nuñez, 2003) and subsequently produced an anthology with contributions by Council members (Pedraza & Rivera, 2005) that became useful in conversations with other scholars, community groups, and potential funders wanting to know the concerns of the Latino community at large (Pedraza et al., 2003; Pedraza & Rivera, 2005). These documents also helped lay the foundation for NLERAP's community-based research approach that not only legitimated the participatory research that some members were already conducting, but also presaged the more policy-oriented, if not a more direct advocacy, role as NLERAP members at the regional, grassroots level.

This emerging identity took form in 2007 when the group decided that NLERAP should move to the University of Texas at Austin under the leadership of Angela Valenzuela, who by then directed the Texas Center for Education Policy (TCEP). The original equity concerns laid out by Latino community stakeholders years earlier further crystallized at the January 31, 2009 meeting of the NLERAP Council meeting in New York City when the group seized Dr. Sonia Nieto's idea for the group to create and cultivate a "grow-your-own" Latina/o teacher education pipeline in each region. A grant in 2009 from the Ford Foundation helped to begin laying the foundation for the Grow-Your-Own Teacher Education Institutes (GYO-TEI) to coincide with NLERAP's move to its new home at the University of Texas at Austin. Council membership also expanded during this time period to include younger research faculty and seasoned leaders associated with partnering community-based organizations in participating sites as discussed more fully later in this chapter. But first, a look at TCEP, NLERAP's policy arm.

TCEP and Engaged Policy

Throughout NLERAP's first decade that included the advent and unfolding of the No Child Left Behind Act of 2001, together with testing and accountability mandates that paralleled policy making in many states, the need for the organization to accord more attention to policy at multiple levels encouraged members to consider TCEP as an appropriate home for NLERAP. The group appreciated TCEP's approach to policy, namely, "engaged policy," because of the way that it aligns with the actionable, community-centered research approach that stakeholders identified as necessary.

TCEP is a non-partisan source of credible, policy-relevant, research-based information in various areas, including standardized testing, accountability, English language learners, and college readiness. TCEP cultivates a deep level of understanding about policies and policy production by creating opportunities for researchers and education communities statewide to engage the multiple aspects of policy, while staying tuned in to issues of power and conflict that exist in these shared contexts. We also connect policy makers and legislators with associated faculty and researchers whose research has direct bearing on the production of educational policy in local, state, national, and international contexts.

TCEP's conceptualization of policy goes beyond a limited focus on the actions and intentions of government or end goals and outcomes to include sociocultural and political processes of policy production (see Ball, 1990; Levinson & Sutton, 2001; López, 2011). This can mean tracking policy discourses, individual and organizational actors and their (shifting) identities and interests, and the histories and trajectories of specific policies themselves. In the case of the co-authors, this also means we play a role in educating individual legislators and their staff about the implications of the policies that they are either considering or actually pursuing in terms of the existing research base (see López, Valenzuela & Garcia, 2011).

Our engaged policy approach is in great part responsible for the elimination of high-stakes testing on standardized state exams for third graders in the state of Texas, positively affecting over 300,000 children. Children will now be holistically assessed based on factors such as grades, attendance, classroom performance, teacher assessment, parent input, and test performance. TCEP continues its critical work in this area of policy in support of the complete elimination of the misuses of standardized testing in our state and beyond.

As NLERAP's policy arm, our goal within TCEP is to help build similar capacity in the area of policy in every site in a way that honors and builds on NLERAP's commitment to community-based research and collaboration. This goal is integral to the GYO-TEI initiative to which we now turn.

NLERAP's Grow-Your-Own, Teacher Education Institutes initiative

The primary goals of the Ford-funded GYO-TEI were twofold: build and implement a national and regional structure to support the NLERAP mission of creating a collective, national voice for improving the quality of life among Latinos in the United States through education; and second, to create a critical mass of culturally competent educators in our states and nation. Sites for the GYO-TEI initiative were purposefully located in large cities where Council members are located and where Latino/as are highly represented.

The regional board at each site consists of at least one well-established, community-based organization and a higher education university partner, each with a local district strategy for channeling future graduates back into their communities as culturally and politically aware, community-conscious teachers:

- Brooklyn College, New York, partnering with El Puente, involving students from the El Puente High School Project for Peace and Justice and other high schools serving the Williamsburg and Bushwick communities of Brooklyn.
- University of Illinois in Chicago, partnering with the Puerto Rican Community Center, involving students from Roberto Clemente High School.
- California State Sacramento University, partnering with Families in Schools in Los Angeles, involving students from the Sacramento area.
- University of Wisconsin, Milwaukee, partnering with La Casa de Esperanza, Inc., involving students from Pulaski, Riverside, Rufus King, and South Division high schools, as well as Milwaukee-area high schools located in Kenosha and Racine.
- University of North Texas, Dallas, partnering with the League of United Latin American Citizens (LULAC), LULAC National Educational Service Centers, Inc. (LNESC), Hispanic Institute for Progress, Inc. (HIPI), and involving Sunset High School in Dallas, Texas.

Related to our first goal, we also now have, in addition to the Council, a national 501(c)3 nonprofit called NLERAP, Inc. that provides the infrastructure and capacity to lead and sustain a national-level education effort. NLERAP, Inc.'s capacity includes a communications strategy, accounting services, and a legal board structure together with a fundraising strategy that primarily targets a select segment of the corporate sector at each locale, as well as nationally.

Regarding our second goal of creating a mass of culturally competent scholars, we outlined our values and principles, research, and evaluation approach for our

GYO-TEI initiative. This further involves the development of an action plan that draws from an extensive literature review authored by multiple NLERAP Council members and sponsored by the Spencer Foundation titled, "Charting a New Course" (Nieto, Rivera, & Quiñones, 2011). This work, coupled with two additional documents based on the work of our two national subcommittees—that is, the Community Action Research in Education (CARE) and the Curriculum and Pedagogy (C & P) Committees—provides an orientation and guidelines for the theoretical and curricular dimensions of a GYO initiative.

An accomplishment to date is NLERAP's efforts through the GYO-TEI initiative to influence curricular reform in our partnering colleges of education teacher preparation programs. The university adoption of two signature courses where pre-service teachers are expected to acquire sociocultural and sociopolitical awareness, respectively, and gain access to NLERAP's community action research approach through either value-added, or substitute, courses is significant. Finally, conversations about how the pre-service GYO-TEI teachers might receive these signature courses in a community-based setting, rather than at the university, are also taking place. Our expectation of the GYO-TEI initiative's goals is that, in addition to sociocultural and sociopolitical awareness, pre-service and current teachers will develop critical literacies in the areas of reading, writing, numeracy, science, and personal finance.

New Directions

With a second major investment from the W.K. Kellogg Foundation that builds on efforts under the Ford Foundation grant, we work to solidify our partnerships at the grassroots level, develop our national visibility, advance our teacher preparation curriculum together with an action research approach, strengthen our focus on policy, and be a powerful voice in inserting research-based solutions to educational and social problems. Together, these efforts will trigger a new era for teacher preparation among GYO-TEI's partnering universities, in particular, as well as community-centered reform efforts, in general.

References

Ball, S. J. (1990). *Politics and policy making in education: Explorations in policy sociology.* New York: Routledge.

Levinson, B. A. & Sutton, M. (2001). Introduction: Policy as/in practice—A sociocultural approach to the study of educational policy. In B. A. Levinson & M. Sutton (Eds.), *Policy as practice: Toward a comparative sociocultural analysis of educational policy.* Westport, CT: Greenwood Publishing Group, Inc.

López, P. D. (2011). Deconstructing the interdisciplinary in policy: Critical education policy analysis, social justice, and the politics of urgency. (Unpublished specialization paper). University of Texas at Austin, Austin, Texas.

López, P. D., Valenzuela, A. & Garcia, E. (2011). The critical ethnography for public policy. In B. Levinson & M. Pollock (Eds.), *Companion to the anthropology of education*. Malden, MA: Wiley-Blackwell Press.

Nieto, S. (S.Ed.), Rivera, M. & Quiñones, S. (Eds.), Cammarota, J., Cannella, C., Garcia, E., González, M., Irizarry, J., Moll, L., Nieto, S., Perez, B., Romo, H. and Valenzuela, A. (2011). *Charting a new course: Understanding the sociocultural, political, economic and historical context of Latino/a education in the United States*. NY and TX: NLERAP for Spencer Foundation.

Pedraza, P. & Rivera, M. (2005). Origins of the national Latino/a education research and policy project. In P. Pedraza and M. Rivera, (Eds.), *Latino education: An agenda for community action research* (National Latino/a Education Research and Policy Project) (pp. 3–10). Philadelphia, PA: Lawrence Erlbaum Associates.

Pedraza, P., Rivera, M. & Nuñez, V. (2003). National education research agenda project: Educational research framework and agenda. Centro de Estudios Puertorriqueños and the Research Foundation, City University of New York.

AFTERWORD

Peter McLaren and Suzanne SooHoo

It is by now a commonplace assumption that history runs inexorably forward. But this forward motion—call it the Big Bang or a storm from paradise caught in the wings of the Angel of History—does not necessarily lead to progress. It can lead to a standstill of all kinds—moral, epistemological, political and social. Sometimes that standstill can be stretched enough so that it breaks away from the encrustations of the old and bounds into the realm of the new. Yet sometimes the standstill can send progress catapulting backwards into the nihilistic darkness out of which humanity has so dauntingly and fitfully emerged, crawling and clawing its way towards modernity and more recently, towards what Enrique Dussel calls "transmodernity."

Our voyage through history is often dizzying and never less than bewildering and we cannot but imagine with trepidation what future we are making as we make our paths by walking.[1] Jouncing along the highways and byways, the throughways and thoroughfares, the causeways and cobblestoned alleys, we stop to stretch our legs in the restless rest stops along our journey—what some of us call 'research'—where we can pause to take stock of where we are headed.

Educators, it seems, are the most tireless and restless of travelers. Once respected and revered, we have now become the scapegoats of our failing schools, and by extension, of the continuing collapse of the U.S. financial empire. The era of de-industrialization has done little to add to the public perception of the professional virtues of being a teacher. Since the 1970s and onwards it seems as though we have been headed towards an impending educational crisis or frantically attempting to make a fast exit out of one. Whether these are true educational crises or fabricated by the stewards of post-industrial progress, we always seem to be destined towards oblivion. Given the contingencies that surround these crises—social, historical, cultural, economic—and the indeterminacies that characterize each of them, none of the crises is easily understood or predicted.² This is because the systems of intelligibility and explanatory vocabularies for understanding earlier crises cannot fully illuminate the hydra-headed characteristics and dimensions of the most recent, and so on. Again, this is because educational crises are inextricably intertwined with the economic, social and cultural logics of the times, not to mention the socioeconomic forms of society in which such crises are spawned, nurtured, resisted and played out on the battlefields of teaching, learning, and of reproducing and/or transforming the world. No educational crisis, however familiar, is what it appears to be since the lenses that we use to gauge their meaning are always misting up (take Fox News as one wretched belligerent but there are many more), and the meanings that we try to glean from such crises are often furiously obstinate, if not downright crotchety. No crisis exists in a vacuum, each crisis is welded to the everyday conditions that give rise to it and upon the way in which we define each crisis, and this situation necessarily forecloses as many questions as it raises. Furthermore, we find it difficult to grasp the entire significance of the unending crises in education because it is difficult to step outside of the phenomena and interrelated layers of antagonistic relations that we believe constitute such a crisis in order to discern their significance and eventually overcome them. We are, it seems, increasingly unable to free our intellects from a narrow grasp of what it means to be educated in the 21st century.

The problem with the term crisis is that it seems as though there will be a time when the crisis is over and resolved, perhaps even to our liking and subsequent rejoicing. But the crisis of education has now become like the war on terror, and likely will be unending. Unless, of course, teachers, students, administrators, and community workers take a definitive stand against the war being waged upon them and work towards not only educational change, but changes that will ultimately affect the nature of our social and economic relations throughout the planet. For we believe that the crisis of education is always already present within the contradictions of the capitalist system of accumulation in which women and ethnic minorities suffer disproportionately to the white male majority.

There are many factors which must be taken into consideration when we talk about the current corporate takeover of education—which school boards euphemistically refer to as 'makeovers'—and many of them have to do with the consolidation of the transnational capitalist economy after the current crisis of 2007–2008 featuring the subprime mortgage collapse. Outside of the United States, the death rattle of public education follows in the wake of the austerity measures imposed on various countries by the International Monetary Fund. Here educational funding has been gutted like a fish in your local fish and chips restaurant. While some refer to this crisis as a global financial crisis or a structural or cyclical crisis, it is clear that however you wish to describe it, it has serious underpinnings that economic analysts on the left have identified as involving, among other conditions, underconsumption, overproduction, Marx's tendential fall of the rate of profit, the increased dominance of finance capital throughout our social universe, neoliberalism or a combination of all of these factors. There have been student uprisings across the globe contesting the effects of the near-complete privatization of the education system—most notably the Chilean student uprising of 2010—and it is hard to forget the trials and tribulations associated with the Arab Spring, which began in Tunisia and Algeria and impacted Egypt and other countries of the Middle East. Students are very clear about the impact the crisis of capitalism has had on education. Education now is mainly about professional training for corporate and commercial interest replacing the social interest of democratic life, about creating consumer citizens instead of critically informed democratic citizens. It is now quite common to talk about students as customers, teachers as paid laborers, and institutions of 'higher' learning that we call universities as public or private service providers who are interested now mainly in knowledge-driven capital (innovation, organization, distribution techniques, procedures and programs affecting the stability and expansion of corporations, the marketability of academic products, the economic return on property-rights-protected knowledge, etc.) in what is now considered a knowledge-driven economy. Rarely is knowledge discussed today in terms of how to meet the needs of the working-class, immigrant groups, the unemployed and underemployed or those otherwise considered redundant because they have little to produce or little to consume. Rarely is knowledge discussed with an eye to saving the planet from imploding due to the ecological crisis wrought by capitalist growth.

In today's public square, much of the debate in the United States surrounding the demise of education by means of the 'businessification' of schooling practices has to do with the disappearance of 'education for the sake of education,' that is, for the sake of the joy of learning itself, for the sake of creativity and learning how to learn as a means of navigating today's increasingly complex society undergoing revolution after revolution in technology. But the entry point of our defense of education does not begin with defending education for its own sake, because we do not believe that education is ever for its own sake since education is always for the sake of someone, some group, some social class and some ruling regime.[3] Public education has always been Janus-faced, camouflaging the interests of one class, one ethnic group, one gender under some concrete universal that is supposedly in the interests of the social whole. While we emphasize the importance of transdisciplinary intellectuality and encourage our students to self-reflexively grasp their interior selves in the search for their own agency, we do not believe such agency is forged in a political vacuum; it requires moral and political choices related to how the world is understood and the global reach of suffering of our brothers and sisters. For us, the arc of education must always point toward the practice of social justice. Social justice is not simply an option but an obligation. We are, after all, critical educators seeking not only our own ontological clarity but political clarity in an era of gangster capitalism that has brought about wage stagnation, mass unemployment, the casualization and informalization of the labor force, deepening wealth and income inequalities where the value relationship is denominated in market prices, foreclosures, increasing debt peonage and a perilous and cowardly retreat from civil rights.

The exploitative relations that exist between the workers and capitalists are now being transferred to the classrooms of our nation where students are taking on debt levels that nearly match those of home ownership. We also decry the growing tendency of mainstream multicultural approaches in education to sever race from its historical origins in the accumulation of capital through colonialism and imperialism, reducing domination by race and ethnicity to personal attitudes and behaviors. Race, after all, helps to structure the social order of neoliberal capitalism leading to the school-to-prison pipeline and mass incarceration, where a disproportionate number of African-Americans and Latina/os—considered only as surplus labor that the dominant class is unwilling to support materially—are forced out of the school system through neglect, the so-called war on drugs and zero tolerance policies and garrisoned inside prisons where they are treated as waste matter in a system that views them as already dead. The increasing flow of immigrants from America Latina looking for work are now commodified as raw material for globalized circuits of capitalist accumulation and exported to wherever they are needed at the moment; yet at the same time their dignity is deformed and their character is defamed, and they remain expendable and are denied access to social labor such as food stamps, medical insurance and welfare benefits. Those who remain in the classrooms across the United States are offered a curriculum defanged and depotentiated, one that is dominated by acquiring standardized skills over knowledge-seeking. We recognize the problems with understanding 'difference' and 'otherness' in privileged spaces in universities in the States with their antiseptic presentation of other cultures, ethnicities and histories. Here, as Davis (2014)[4] notes, engaging with otherness takes place at a safe distance, within students' own comfort zones and thus neutralizes and turns into pleasantries issues like poverty, women's struggles, and resistance to capitalist exploitation, projecting the student's own privilege into otherness and violently turning the other into the same.

Fortunately there exist—however small and besieged they might be—spaces of protagonistic agency, spaces of hope and possibility that have been carved out over generations in the atavistic arena of educational struggle. Many of the most important spaces of liberation that exist in our schools of education, high schools, middle schools and elementary schools, as well as meeting places within our communities (such as churches, mosques, synagogues, community centers, human rights centers and institutions designed to assist immigrants, homeless populations and people with disabilities) have been created by educators and cultural workers of color. Intrepidly carrying the light of critical pedagogy into the dark corners of our unmercifully 'capitalized' communities, including both urban and rural constituencies, have been Latina/o educators. Our particular praxis of struggle that has been forged in the crucible of Freirean education and the tradition of community-based popular education owes a great deal of debt to Latina/o philosophers, educators and activists. Here we take a principled position against what we call the 3-cides: genocide, ecocide (the destruction of the biosphere) and epistemicide (the elimination of ways of knowing of indigenous cultures), all of which are implicated in the transnational accumulation of capital. We struggle against the new normal of high-stakes standardized tests scores that are privileged over the production of critical knowledges and educational imperatives that serve technology, science, mathematics and engineering over the arts and humanities, thus confirming our charge that economic growth is more important than social equality.

While some critics decry Freirean education as a North American 'industry' that gives academic cache to those who operate mainly in academic settings, we have been spending time working with marginalized groups in the surrounding communities of Orange County as well as in international geopolitical arenas in Venezuela, Mexico, Colombia, Brazil, Argentina, China, New Zealand and elsewhere. We have struggled as allies with our Latina/o comrades—which include professors, schoolteachers, parents, students and community activists—in the theoretical fields of critical race theory, decolonizing pedagogy and Freirean-inspired critical pedagogy, but most importantly in our daily lives as colleagues and friends, on the picket lines and in neighborhood gatherings and in classrooms. We understand that the struggle for equity and social justice must be one of solidarity and *comunalidad* and cannot exist without a transnational united front comprised of all marginalized communities—including poor white communities—currently facing the juggernaut of capital. This will mean we cannot advance purely educational solutions to the current crises of education without at the same time being concurrently involved in larger labor struggles, community struggles and political struggles. Part of the struggle means sharing pain that for many is unshareable, the pain of bodies humiliated, starved, naked, tortured and brutalized by a system of unremitting violence, a violence that is becoming increasingly institutionalized within the state. All of this is occurring at a time in which our humanity is no longer self-evident but can only be discovered retrospectively, in the rag-and-bone shop of distant memory. While current systems of domination—the surveillance state, the militarization of local and regional police forces and the rapidly expanding power complexes of the arms industry and high tech corporations—thrive in the milieu of social amnesia they have so carefully cultivated, we refuse to allow our memories to be policed, to be commodified or otherwise devalued.

As we write this afterword, the words of Nita Freire from her recent visit to Chapman University (October 25, 2014) inspire our consciousness as she described Paulo's concept of untested feasibility: "It is a word that brings in itself the germ of possible transformations geared toward a more human and ethical future. It carries within itself, the beliefs, values, dreams, desires, aspirations, fears, anxieties, the yearning ability to learn and the fragility and greatness of human beings." Untested feasibility is part faith, part hope, part dream of transformation anchored by glaring realities of dehumanization, injustice and suffering. It is a notion that we can 'be more' than we are, we can overcome oppression and subjugation, and with moral and spiritual centerdness, we can transform our world and the roles we play in it. Untested feasibility, fueled by the belief we can be more, unites despair and struggle with action for justice with our newfound abilities to reason and love. Paulo believed there is no thinking or being without love. Love encourages us to be generous and tolerant of other human beings while recognizing and accepting both our and their human condition of unfinishedness.

In this book, you found untested feasibility as the resounding mantra in each chapter. The authors demonstrated personal and public courage powered by hope and conviction to contest and address unjust conditions in their communities and institutions. In intimate detail, their narratives describe the courage it takes to face one's self in the oppressor's world—to question, how did I become disconnected from my own culture, language and beliefs. Who am I now and could I be more? They showed us the critical consciousness that allowed them to claim rightful space in the world—to know where one comes from, to use one's own language, to bring forth one's spirituality, to boldly awaken one's own and another's consciousness, to engage with others in authentic ways and to transform the world with moral clarity. These developments are all necessary so the person and "the world does not lose its memory" (Freire, 2007, p.22).[5] These authors recognized their public mission to overcome historical errors by turning historical losses into fertile ground for struggle (Souza de Freitas, 2007).[6] What emerges is Latino solidarity in being active builders of their history. While addressing racism, sexism, linguicism and class exploitation, they dedicated their public lives to humanizing the world with dreams of untested feasibility. The unsuredness and undeniable vulnerability of challenging unjust practices is moored with a base collective consciousness and faith.

The authors of this book, who are activists and scholars, offer first-hand accounts of their work and struggle for educational equity, bilingual education and pro-Latino policies. Using their own lived histories as text, they challenge what they call 'distilled Latino history from non-Latino perspectives.' Their aim was to assert their voices in order to provide a more balanced view of history to classrooms and libraries, to show how Latinos have been involved in the civil rights in education in our nation. It is their hope coupled with untested feasibility that this book described where Latinos have been and will help define where they will want to go as they continue to struggle for civil rights and human dignity. We applaud their unyielding activism and stand by their work to fight against historical amnesia.

We believe that if we work diligently and avoid diffidence, unknown friends and critical allies will come to us. Not every culmination of events, such as our struggle against various causes of suffering and oppression, becomes a new beginning and not every arrival at a new place of understanding becomes a point of departure where there exists no reiteration of pain and suffering, where the world suddenly appears a better place. The truth is that it is very likely that the suffering of the world will worsen in the years to come, despite our efforts. Understanding that our suffering and those of our fellow humans will continue, perhaps unabated, in our own lifetimes does not compel us to advocate renouncing the world for the sake of divine love or a feeling of equanimity in this world or for the sake of entering a state of unqualified reverence for the phantasmagoria of everyday life. We work instead to develop a critical consciousness commensurate to the demands made by the historical present, that is, commensurate to the demands that the current historical conjuncture imposes upon us as political and moral agents. We do not seek balance, rather, we seek a fierce and loving engagement with the world, a critical engagement, amplified in every aspect of our lives when the spirit of imperishable absoluteness ruptures our everyday, mundane existence and we fight tooth and nail for a better world. A critical engagement with no guarantees of success. We search outwardly and inwardly in the place of intellection and action, that is, in the place of praxis, a praxis of being and becoming that while at times might seem urgent and perhaps even imperious is designed to transform the world along the arc of social justice. For there is no love without justice. And there is no justice without love. And there is no greater path than this. We speak of love not as something fungible, not as something you are given or can acquire or that takes this form or that; love is not a thing, but that which brings forth and illuminates the other. We can only know such love through our loving engagement with the other, in other words, though our purposeful and resolute action with others in this world of unmet needs and shattered dreams.

Notes

1. As used in the book *We Make the Road by Walking: Conversations on Education and Social Change* by Myles Horton and Paulo Freire, edited by Brenda Bell, John Gaventa and John Peters, 1990, Temple University Press. The book title was inspired by a popular Spanish verse, "*Caminante, no hay camino, se hace el camino al andar . . .*" in the original poem by Antonio Machado, "Proverbios y cantares XXIX" [*Proverbs and Songs 29*], *Campos de Castilla* (1912); trans. Betty Jean Craige in *Selected Poems of Antonio Machado* (Louisiana State University Press, 1979).
2. For an excellent discussion of the crises in education, see Glenn Rikowski, *Crises in Education, Crises of Education*. A paper prepared for the Philosophy of Education Seminars at the University of London Institute of Education 2014–15 Programme, 22nd October 2014, online at Academia: https://www.academia.edu/8953489/Crises_in_Education_Crises_of_Education
3. See Rikowski, G., *Crises in Education, Crises of Education*.
4. Davis, Creston. (2014). *Six Lessons Learned from Starting GCAS*. Retrieved May 7, 2014 from https://crestondavis.wordpress.com/author/crestondavis/
5 Freire, P. (2007). *Daring to Dream: Toward a Pedagogy of the Unfinished*. D. Macedo & N. Araujo Freire, Eds. Boulder, Co: Paradigm.
6. Souza de Freitas, A. (2007). Foreword. In Freire, P., *Daring to Dream: Toward a Pedagogy of the Unfinished*. D. Macedo & N. Araujo Freire, Eds. Boulder, Co: Paradigm.

APPENDIX

A Chronology of Educational Experiences of Latinos in Latin America and the United States 1500s–2012

Date	People/Subject	Events	Impact	Source
The Colonial Era 1500s–1821				
1523	Spanish Royal Crown, Spanish missionaries	Doctrina Schools and Evangelization of indigenous people of Tlaxcala	Acculturate and teach superiority of Spanish culture.	MacDonald, Victoria-María (Ed.). (2004). *Latino Education in the United States*. New York, NY: Palgrave Macmillan.
1538	Spanish Royal Crown, Spanish settlers	Formal elementary schools in Texcoco	Teach reading, writing, singing, and music among indigenous elites.	Ibid.
1551	Spanish Royal Crown, Spanish settlers	Spanish founded University in Santo Domingo, Hispaniola.	Children of families of means were educated beyond the settler schools.	Ibid.
1551	Spanish Royal Crown, Spanish settlers	Spanish founded university in Lima, Peru.	Children of families of means were educated beyond the settler schools.	Ibid.
1580	Spanish Royal Crown, Spanish settlers	Spanish founded university in Mexico City.	Children of families of means were educated beyond the settler schools.	Ibid.

(Continued)

Date	People/Subject	Events	Impact	Source
1606	Franciscans	Spanish founded University in Bogotá, Colombia. A classical school and preparatory seminary opens in St. Augustine.	Children of families of means were educated beyond the settler schools. Children of Spanish settlers attend school.	MacDonald, Victoria-María (Ed.). (2004). *Latino Education in the United States.* New York, NY: Palgrave Macmillan.
1634	Spanish Royal Crown	Another school opens in St. Augustine.	Children of Spanish settlers attend school.	Ibid.
1680	Native Americans, Spaniards	Native Americans stage the Pueblo Revolt of 1680.	Deadliest insurrection against Europeans in North American history; included destruction of churches and schools.	Ibid., p. 11.
1717 and 1720	Residents of Santa Fé, New Mexico	Residents of Santa Fé discuss the creation of schools.	No concrete results recorded.	Ibid.
1794–1800	Governor Diego de Borica	Governor Borica spreads and enforces settlers' schools in Alta California.	Several schools open in San José, Monterrey, Santa Barbara, San Diego, and San Francisco.	Ibid.
1802	San Antonio's governor, Juan Bautista Elguézabal	San Antonio governor issues an 1802 proclamation requiring all parents to place their children in school or face "severe penalties."	San Antonio residents must find appropriate schools per the 1802 proclamation.	Ibid., p. 11.
1805	Colonial Government of Spain	Colonial Government sends two teachers from Mexico City to Santa Fé.	Trade school to teach weaving opens.	Ibid.
1805–1821	Colonial Government of Spain	Several schools open in Santa Fé, Albuquerque, Taos, Belen, San Miguel, and Santa Cruz.	Children of soldiers and officers attend schools; neighboring "vecino" children also attend.	Ibid., p. 11.
1812		San Antonio residents donate funds to create a schoolhouse.		Ibid.
1819		San Antonio school is finished and teacher is requested to teach religion.	Low teacher salary, irregular curriculum, and poor teacher preparation becomes characteristic of all rural, 19th-century schools.	Ibid., p. 13.

Date	People/Subject	Events	Impact	Source
Education During the Mexican Era 1821–1848				
1800–1821	Spanish Crown	Royal orders requiring public primary schools increase.	In practice, government resources favored universities for the upper classes and missions for Native Americans.	MacDonald, Victoria-María (Ed.). (2004). *Latino Education in the United States.* New York, NY: Palgrave Macmillan.
1827	Governor José María Echeandía	Governor José María Echeandía orders the establishment of public schools in the missions.	By 1829, Echeandía reported that seven of the southern missions had established schools.	Ibid.
Americanization and Resistance 1848–1912				
1848	Schools established in Southwest	Catholic, Protestant, and private schools established throughout Southwest	Shift from additive to subtractive Americanization.	MacDonald, Victoria-María (Ed.). (2004). *Latino Education in the United States.* New York, NY: Palgrave Macmillan.
1848–1900	Schools established in Texas	Catholic schools for children established in Texas	Students came from Texas and Mexico to learn traditional subjects in addition to music, painting, sewing, and embroidery.	Ibid.
1851–1876	Latino students in higher education	Santa Clara College, Notre Dame College, other Catholic Colleges, and other Jesuit colleges actively recruit Latinos.	Higher education, a rare commodity for most, was pursued among Latinos when finances permitted.	Ibid.
1858	Anglo parents withdraw children from bilingual schools	Anglo parents win the battle for English-only instruction. Mexicans enroll their children in Catholic schools permitting Spanish.	Approximately 500 school-age children (majority Mexicans and Californios) were then schooled in English. Antonio Jimeno del Recio offered to teach Spanish-speaking children at public expense.	Ibid.
1871	Radical Rule under Reconstruction	Texan public school system was created with more flexible approach to languages.	Teachers are permitted to teach the German, French, and Spanish languages "provided the time so occupied should not exceed two hours each day."	San Miguel, Jr., G. (1987). *"Let All of Them Take Heed": Mexican Americans and the Campaign for Educational Equality in Texas.* Austin: University of Texas Press.

(Continued)

Date	People/Subject	Events	Impact	Source
1898–1900s	Puerto Rican students and teachers	English was imposed as language of instruction in Puerto Rican island schools.	From the moment of the American occupation in 1898, the Commissioner of Education imposed English as the language of instruction causing great turmoil.	Negrón de Montilla, Aida. (1971). *Americanization in Puerto Rico and the Public School System 1900–1930*. Río Piedras: Editorial Edil.
1900	Puerto Rican students	Children of the wealthy criollos sent to Indian Americanization schools to learn English and assert American allegiance.	Changing loyalties from Puerto Rico to United States; disconnecting with culture and families. Attempting to provide an education that would prepare the students to an American lifestyle and commit them to American ideals.	Navarro-Rivera, Pablo. (n.d.). *Acculturation Under Duress: The Puerto Rican Experience at the Carlisle Indian Industrial School 1898–1918*. http://home.epix.net/~landis/navarro.html Osuna, Juan José. (1932). "An Indian in Spite of Myself." *Summer School Review*, X(5).
1900–1940s	Puerto Rican students and teachers	Periodic boycotts and walkouts	Periodic boycotts and walkouts by teachers, and students and teachers resulted in the reinstallation of Spanish as a means of instruction. English became a subject taught from elementary school that increased up the grades and into higher education.	Ibid.

Segregation and New Arrivals Begin to Take Action 1898–1960

Date	People/Subject	Events	Impact	Source
1898–1930s	Anglo residents of the American Southwest, Mexican-American families and children	Newly implemented linguistic and cultural policies increasingly segregated Mexican-American children and deprived them of equal educational opportunities.	Anglo fear, residential segregation, racism, political economy, and influx of Mexican-Americans in Southwest create segregation of Latino children.	MacDonald, Victoria-María (Ed.). (2004). *Latino Education in the United States*. New York, NY: Palgrave Macmillan, p. 118.

Date	People/Subject	Events	Impact	Source
1920s–1950s	More Latinos enter college and were pioneers	Philanthropy, increasing numbers of middle-class Latinos, and the G.I. Bill were major contributors to this shift.	Often the only Latinos in their classes, they provided leadership and talent to the formation of the first Chicano/Puerto Rican civil rights movement of the 1960s and 1970s.	MacDonald, Victoria-María (Ed.). (2004). *Latino Education in the United States*. New York, NY: Palgrave Macmillan.
1930s	League of United Latin American Citizens (LULAC), parents in Del Rio Independent School District of Texas, Plaintiff: Jesus Salvatierra	Parents in Del Rio Independent School District of Texas sued, citing that they had been denied use of facilities used by "other white races."	Plaintiff Jesus Salvatierra lost because the court found that Mexican children were separated as a result of "special language needs."	Ibid., p. 119.
1930s and 1940s	Puerto Rican organization challenges public schools	Puerto Rican families begin arriving to the United States in increasing numbers.	In the 1930s in New York, Puerto Rican organization Madres y Padres Pro Niños Hispanos questioned the school officials' use of intelligence testing, which channeled Puerto Rican children into classrooms for "backward" children rather than recognizing the inherent language bias in such testing.	Ibid.
Cuban Arrivals 1959–1980				
1960–1972	Dade Country Public School, Cuban immigrant children	Dade County public schools received more than $130 million for bilingual education programs. Puerto Ricans in New York had encountered barriers to receiving bilingual schooling, but such programs in Florida were opened without controversy and received adequate staffing and funding.	According to James and Judith Olson, "the field of bilingual education was born in those Dade Country Schools when it became clear that when Cuban-American children were able to become literate in their mother tongue as well as learn English, their success rates in school were dramatic."	Ibid., p. 186.

(Continued)

Date	People/Subject	Events	Impact	Source
1961	HEW's Office of Education, Cuban immigrant students, south Florida	HEW's Office of Education created a college loan program for Cuban students. 5,500 Cuban immigrants benefited. $34 million was distributed to Cuban American college students between 1962 and 1976 through the Cuban Refugee Program.	The combination of direct and indirect assistance to Cuban pupils and teachers during the 1960s and 1970s translated into positive educational and economic outcomes, creating a successful Latino enclave in south Florida.	MacDonald, Victoria-María (Ed.). (2004). *Latino Education in the United States*. New York, NY: Palgrave Macmillan, p. 188.

Chicanos Search for Educational Opportunities and Access 1960s and 1970s

Date	People/Subject	Events	Impact	Source
1968	Latino students at Wilson High School in Los Angeles, California	On March 1st, 1968, 300 students at Wilson High School walked out when the principal cancelled the student production of *Barefoot in the Park*. Other schools walked out as well, as students staged massive walkouts during the spring of 1968.	The cancellation of the play symbolized the failure of teachers, administrators, and school board members to address student demands. Students at Wilson, Garfield, Roosevelt, and Lincoln (the 4 East L.A. high schools with majority Chicano populations) demanded improved school conditions. The demands were often ignored or marginalized.	Ibid.
1968	Supporters of Walkouts—United Mexican-American Students (UMAS), Brown Berets	College students who were members of the newly formed L.A. chapters of United Mexican-American Students (UMAS), the Brown Berets, and local activists provided support and ideas.	Sal Castro, one of the few Mexican-origin teachers at Lincoln, actively supported the student strikes. The Educational Issues Coordinating Committee (EICC) in California met with school board members to follow up on student demands.	Ibid., p. 218.

Date	People/Subject	Events	Impact	Source
1968	Pete Tijerina, Ford Foundation, Mexican-American Legal Defense and Education Fund (MALDEF), National Association for the Advancement of Colored People (NAACP) in the Southwest	Ford Foundation awarded $2.2 million to be spent over 5 years on civil rights legal work for Mexican-Americans; $250,000 of the grant was to go for scholarships to Chicano legal students.	Pete Tijerina is credited with founding MALDEF, along with the influence of the NAACP and the Ford Foundation grant. With the necessary financial resources, MALDEF began to combat discrimination against Mexicans in the Southwest through litigation.	MacDonald, Victoria-María (Ed.). (2004). *Latino Education in the United States*. New York, NY: Palgrave Macmillan, p. 219.

Puerto Rican Organizations Seek Social Justice and Change 1950–1970s

Date	People/Subject	Events	Impact	Source
1940s and 1950s	Puerto Ricans	Migration to New York and Chicago, in search of jobs	The city's Board of Education commissioned the Puerto Rican Study. A conclusion was that extensive bilingual preparation for teachers and support staff was needed immediately.	Ibid.
1949–1968	Puerto Rican numbers increased from 29,000 to 300,000	The city's Board of Education commissioned the Puerto Rican Study (1953–1957).		
			Another was to hire Puerto Rican women and former teachers as Substitute Auxiliary Teachers (SATs).	
1952	Government	Commonwealth status was granted.	As people moved from rural to urban areas, and later NYC, few resources were available for Puerto Rican youth.	Ibid.

(*Continued*)

Date	People/Subject	Events	Impact	Source
1957	Puerto Rican Community in New York and Chicago	Puerto Rican families and the Puerto Rican and Latino community at large	Puerto Rican-Hispanic Leadership Fund	MacDonald, Victoria-María (Ed.). (2004). *Latino Education in the United States.* New York, NY: Palgrave Macmillan.
1961	New York	ASPIRA founded by Antonia Pantoja.	Antonia Pantoja created ASPIRA (aspire) to prevent high school dropouts and promote the schooling of Puerto Rican children in New York City.	Ibid.
1964	New York	Puerto Rican Community Development Project	Community and advocacy groups not willing to quietly assimilate to American culture and language.	Ibid.
1965	Bronx, NYC	United Bronx Parents, Inc. (UBP, 1965) founded by Dr. Evelina Antonetty to access better schooling for the children.	Founded to forge legal battles of the Puerto Rican community regarding civil rights issues including education.	Ibid.
			Youth and young adult organization that was formed to challenge the pervasive inequities in the Puerto Rican Community in major cities such as New York and Chicago.	
1967	The fall of 1967 witnessed the birth of several Mexican-American student organizations	Mexican-American Youth Organization (MAYO), several chapters of United Mexican-American Students (UMAS), Mexican-American Student Association (MASA), and Political Association of Spanish-Speaking Organization (PASO) were formed.	The Chicano movement received inspiration and training from African-American organizations, particularly the Black Panther Party and the Student Non-Violent Coordinating Committee (SNCC).	Ibid., 224–225.
1969	UC Santa Barbara conference of 1969	The Santa Barbara conference of 1969 holds the most significance for Latino higher educational history.	Detailed articulation of the demands of Latino college youth and focused specifically on higher education.	Ibid.

Date	People/Subject	Events	Impact	Source
1969–1970s	Higher Education College campuses New Latino scholars and college students	Push for Open Admissions and Ethnic Studies; greater diversity on campuses Increased enrollment, scholarship and activism	Chicano and Puerto Rican studies and research centers on college campuses. Increase in Mexican, Puerto Rican, and other Spanish-descent faculty and students. Ethnic Studies at San Francisco State University was one of first in higher education history. The number of Latinos entering college was meager, increasing in the 1970s, with students pouring into community colleges, state universities, and Ivy League campuses. Latino scholars entered the academy teaching ethnic studies, history classes and writing culturally relevant books.	MacDonald, Victoria-María (Ed.). (2004). *Latino Education in the United States.* New York, NY: Palgrave Macmillan.
1969–1976	Chicago and New York and other cities with significant Puerto Rican populations	Young Lords Organization and Young Lords Party	The Young Lords connects with the Black Panthers and evolves from a turf gang starting in Chicago to a political organization. It spreads to New York and other major cities and makes an impact on the lives of poor Puerto Ricans and other Latinos by radically challenging the establishment in education, health and politics.	Abramson, Michael. (1971). *Palante: Young Lords Party.* New York: McGraw-Hill. Melendez, Miguel "Mickey." (2003). *We Took the Streets: Fighting for Latino Rights with the Young Lords.* New York: St. Martin's Press. Ogbar, J.O.G. (2006). "Puerto Rico in My Heart: The Young Lords, Black Power and Puerto Rican Nationalism in the US, 1966–1972." *Centro Journal, 18*(1), 148–169.
1972	Chicago and New York	Lawyer's group established to take on legal battles affecting Puerto Ricans	Puerto Rican Legal Defense and Education Fund was established (1972).	MacDonald, Victoria-María (Ed.). (2004). *Latino Education in the United States.* New York, NY: Palgrave Macmillan.

(Continued)

Date	People/Subject	Events	Impact	Source
Latinos and Schooling 1980s and 1990s				
1981–1990	States	15 states voted to make English the official language.	U.S. Senator S. I. Hayakawa urged passage of an amendment to the U.S. constitution declaring English the official language of the nation. Legislation for this amendment eventually failed.	MacDonald, Victoria-María (Ed.). (2004). *Latino Education in the United States.* New York, NY: Palgrave Macmillan.
1986	Hispanic Association of Colleges and Universities (HACU)	HACU brought together Hispanic leaders in business and two- and four-year colleges and universities with large numbers of Latinos.	The mission to improve the access and quality of college education for Hispanics, is carried out through offices in San Antonio, Texas, and Washington D.C. HACU's most successful victory was the establishment of Hispanic Serving Institutions (HIS), securing eligibility for federal funds.	Ibid., p. 283–284.
1994	Passage of Proposition 187	The "Illegal Aliens, Ineligibility for Public Services Verification, and Reporting Initiatives Statute." Prop 187 would have rendered public services such as schooling at all levels (K–20), health care, and other social services unavailable to undocumented immigrants. It required local and state officials to report to the INS.	MALDEF and LULAC sued the state. Due to its conflict with *Plyler v. Doe*, which forbids such immigration, Prop 187 was declared unconstitutional in September 1999 without being implemented.	Ibid., p. 280.
1994	H.R. 5240, The Higher Education Act Amendments of 1984, Paul Simon	Paul Simon introduces H.R. 5240, which recommended several reforms to aid Hispanic access and retention.	Modification of Title III to provide direct aid to institutions with high concentrations of Hispanic students.	Ibid.

Date	People/Subject	Events	Impact	Source
1994	Executive Order 12900, "Educational Excellence for Hispanic Americans" Gary Orfield Harvard Project on School Desegregation	President William Clinton signed Executive Order 12900 that created a special taskforce "to advance the development of human potential, to strengthen the nation's capacity to provide high-quality education, and to increase opportunities for Hispanic Americans to participate in and benefit from federal education programs."	One result of the order was the 1996 publication of *Our Nation on the Fault Line: Hispanic American Education*. The findings were alarming and critical of the nation's attention to Latinos and schooling. *Our Nation* reported that Latinos and African-Americans were disproportionately clustered in large urban schools with few white pupils.	MacDonald, Victoria-María (Ed.). (2004). *Latino Education in the United States.* New York, NY: Palgrave Macmillan.
1995		Number of states making English the official language increased to 23.	The English-only movement began in 1980 and spread throughout the country, particularly in areas of rapid immigrant or refugee arrival.	Ibid.
1998	Passage of Proposition 227: The Unz Initiative	Most divisive and potentially harmful measure in influencing Latino educational equity in the 1980s and 1990s	Essentially eliminated most forms of bilingual education in California schools, despite the fact that one out of every eight children in California's schools in 1990 were considered of limited English proficiency (LEP).	Ibid.

(*Continued*)

Date	People/Subject	Events	Impact	Source
2002– Ongoing	Development, Relief, and Education for Alien Minors Act (DREAM Act)	The complicated legal status of undocumented immigrant students was brought to attention by the proposal of the DREAM Act.	If passed, the bill would grant legal residency to undocumented students with no criminal records who have been U.S. residents for at least five years and graduated from an American high school or received a GED. Due to inaction by Congress, the Deferred Action for Childhood Arrivals (DACA) Program was initiated by President Obama on June 15, 2012.	MacDonald, Victoria-María (Ed.). (2004). *Latino Education in the United States.* New York, NY: Palgrave Macmillan.
2003	Grutter v. Bollinger	The U.S. Supreme Court affirmed the use of race as a legitimate tool in law school admissions and that "diversity is essential to its [University of Michigan Law School] educational mission."	Decision held that "the law school's narrowly tailored use of race in admissions decision to further a compelling interest in obtaining the educational benefits that flow from a diverse student body is not prohibited by the Equal Protection Clause."	Ibid., p. 284.
2010– Ongoing	HB 2281, signed by Governor Jan Brewer	HB 2281 bans teaching classes that are designed for students of a particular group, promote resentment, or advocate ethnic solidarity over treating pupils as individuals.	A bill to ban ethnic studies in Arizona schools was signed into law by Gov. Jan Brewer. It was challenged and upheld, but is still being contested at the time of publication.	Santa Cruz, Nicole. (2010, May 12). Arizona bill targeting ethnic studies signed into law. *Los Angeles Times.*

Date	People/Subject	Events	Impact	Source
2012	High School Graduates/ Executive Action: Deferred Action for Childhood Arrivals (DACA)	Under the auspices of the US Secretary of Homeland Security provides undocumented graduates of US high schools or with a GED with work authorization.	"Deferred action is a use of prosecutorial discretion to defer removal action against an individual for a certain period of time." Lawful status is not assured.	http://www.uscis.gov/humanitarian/consideration-deferred-action-childhood-arrivals-daca

ABOUT THE AUTHORS

Evangelina "Gigi" Brignoni was Professor of Education for University of Nebraska, Omaha. She initiated the first bilingual credential program for the University. Brignoni began as a bilingual teacher and was an activist for the language rights of children throughout her academic career. She succumbed to cancer in 2012 after a long trajectory as a dedicated bilingual educator.

Anaida Colón-Muñiz is Associate Professor of Education for Chapman University's College of Educational Studies. She currently directs Community Education Programs for Libreria Martinez de Chapman University, a community-based bookstore and education center based in downtown Santa Ana, California. Colon-Muñiz has spent her career concerned with equity and Latino civil rights issues; she is a proponent of bilingual education, and an advocate for Latino children and their families.

Luis Fuentes was Professor Emeritus, University of Massachusetts (UMASS), Amherst. Fuentes was the first Puerto Rican principal in New York City for Ocean Hill-Brownsville District during the early years of community control and bilingual education, and later superintendent of District 1 in Manhattan. He spent his career seeking educational opportunities for his students and advocated avidly for them and their parents. For years, he directed the Bilingual Professions in Education doctoral program at UMASS, Amherst, greatly expanding the number of Latino leaders in the field of education. In his 80s, he succumbed to illness in Puerto Rico in 2014.

Magaly Lavadenz is Professor of Education at Loyola Marymount University. Lavadenz currently directs several funded bilingual teacher education projects and coordinates graduate level programs in bilingual education. She is an avid advocate and leader in the State of California on equity matters related to the schooling of English learners, helps to prepare related policy protections for bilingual students, and presents at international conferences on her research and development.

Patricia D. López was a doctoral candidate, with a portfolio in Mexican American Studies, in Education Policy and Planning at the University of Texas at Austin, where she was also a Research Associate for the Texas Center for Education Policy. She is now an assistant professor at San José State University.

Donaldo Macedo is Distinguished Professor of Liberal Arts and Education at the University of Massachusetts, Boston. He has been a central figure in the field of critical pedagogy for more than 20 years. His work with Paulo Freire broke new theoretical ground, as it helped to develop a critical understanding of the ways in which language, power, and culture contribute to the positioning and formation of human experience and learning. Macedo was Freire's chief translator and English language interpreter. He has published more than one hundred articles, books, and book chapters in the areas of linguistics, critical literacy, and multicultural education, which have been translated to several languages. This book on the civil rights of Latinos is a contribution to his Series in Critical Narrative.

Mike Madrid was Education Director for Chapman University's College of Educational Studies. Madrid has been in public education for over 35 years and has advocated for better educational opportunities for Latinos, especially English learners. He became fascinated with the history of U.S. Latino struggles, researching past cases such as Lemon Grove and continues to present on these little known histories.

Peter McLaren is Distinguished Professor in Critical Studies for the College of Educational Studies at Chapman University. He also serves as Co-Director and International Ambassador for Global Ethics and Social Justice for the Paulo Freire Democratic Project and Co-Editor of the *Radical Imagine-Nation* journal. He defines himself as a transdisciplinary scholar who works in the area of critical pedagogy, critical social theory, Marxist humanist philosophy, and ethnographic research. His activist work involves engaging educational workers worldwide, and developing a philosophy of praxis directed at creating a post-capitalist, socialist future.

Theresa Montaño is Professor of Chicano Studies and Education at California State University, Northridge. An active unionist, Montaño was also on the staff of United Teachers Los Angeles, where she worked in professional development and as an area representative for nine years, and continues to work for greater collaboration between the union and the Latino/a-Chicana/o community in areas of mutual concern. Montaño's research interests include Teacher Activism, Chicana/a-Latino/a Educational Equity, Critical Multicultural Education, and Bilingual/ELL education.

Sonia Nieto is Professor Emerita, University of Massachusetts, Amherst. She is a renowned multicultural educator, scholar, author and noted speaker. Nieto has dedicated her life to equity and social justice issues for students from diverse backgrounds and their teachers. She has an impressive record of preparing future scholars in the areas of critical multicultural education and bilingual education. She is a prolific writer, who continues to influence the field of education with publications and presentations in the United States and abroad.

Alberto M. Ochoa is Professor Emeritus for San Diego State University, San Diego's Policy Studies. Ochoa has been a longtime advocate of Latino civil rights in education and has a deep understanding of the policies and legal trajectory of Latinos in education. He continues to advocate strongly for parent rights.

Pedro Pedraza is a scholar who served as Research Director of El Centro de Estudios Puertorriqueños (the Center for Puerto Rican Studies) in Hunter College, City University of New York for over 38 years. During that time he helped to found the national initiative for Latino research known as the National Latino/a Research Education and Policy Project. He continues to support Latino educational rights initiatives.

María S. Quezada is past Executive Director of the California Association for Bilingual Education (CABE). She has dedicated her life to the education of English learners. Quezada was CABE state president the year that Prop 227 passed, engaging in a long battle with Mr. Unz and his English Only proponents. Quezada is currently the director of Project Inspire, a parent advocacy and development program, which she helped to found while at CABE. She is still active politically in Latino issues.

Pablo C. Ramírez is Assistant Professor at Arizona State University in the Mary Lou Fulton Teachers College. Ramirez's research and teaching interests focus on critical Latino parent engagement, secondary English learners, immigrant students, and teacher ideology in the education system. His life's work is greatly influenced by civil rights issues, and he continues to advocate on behalf of students and community.

Sandra Robbie is the producer of the Emmy Award-winning KOCE documentary on the 1946 Mendez v. Westminster case "For all the Children/Para todos los niños." She has been instrumental in the founding of an archive at Chapman

University as well as promoting awareness of the case on statewide and national levels, helping it to become part of the curriculum content for history/social science.

Marta E. Sanchez is Professor of Education at Loyola Marymount University in Los Angeles. Her areas of expertise are in teacher education, language acquisition and learning, and cultural diversity. Sanchez is a longtime advocate of better access to higher education for Latinos and continues to serve these efforts.

Herman Sillas, Esq. is an attorney with the Law office of Herman Sillas. He was one of the attorneys who defended Sal Castro after the Walkouts in Los Angeles and served as legal counsel for the California Association for Bilingual Education for many years. He understood this struggle from his own experiences in school as well as from the evidence in the case. He continues to write regularly.

Suzanne SooHoo is Professor of Education for the College of Educational Studies at Chapman University. She is currently the Jack and Paula Hassinger Chair in Education, Co-Director of the Paulo Freire Democratic Project, and Co-Editor of the *Radical Imagine-Nation* journal. She teaches courses in multicultural education, critical pedagogy, teacher research, and culturally responsive research methods at both the doctoral and master's levels. A former elementary school principal, Suzanne enjoys working in the community with partners in democratic civic engagement.

Angela Valenzuela, from 2007 to 2012, served as Associate Vice-President for School Partnerships located within the Division of Diversity and Community Engagement at the University of Texas at Austin. She continues to direct TCEP and NLERAP.

NATIONAL LATINO/A EDUCATION RESEARCH AND POLICY PROJECT

National Advisory Board Members

René Anthop González
    University of Wisconsin, Milwaukee
Julio Cammarota
    University of Arizona, Tucson
Miguel Carranza
    University of Nebraska
Ursula Casanova
    Arizona State University, Phoenix
Maria Casillas
    Families in Schools, Los Angeles
José Cintrón
    California State University, Sacramento
Oscar Cruz
    Families in Schools Los Angeles
Richard Durán
    University of California, Santa Barbara
Barbara Flores
    California State University, San Bernardino
Hector M. Flores
    Director, Intergovernmental Affairs at Dallas ISD and Past National LULAC President
Nilda Flores González
    University of Illinois, Chicago
Marvin Garcia
    Alternative Schools Network of Chicago
Ofelia Garcia
    The Graduate Center, City University of New York

John Guerra
    Aztec Worldwide, Inc., Dallas, Texas
Kris Gutierrez
    University of Colorado, Boulder
Jason Irizarry
    University of Connecticut, Storrs
José López
    Puerto Rican Cultural Center, Chicago, Illinois
Frances Lucerna
    El Puente, New York
Victoria Maria MacDonald
    University of Maryland, College Park
Carmen Mercado
    Hunter College, City University of New York
Luis Moll
    University of Arizona, Tucson
Sonia Nieto
    University of Massachusetts, Amherst
Pedro Noguera
    New York University, New York
Pedro Pedraza
    Center for Puerto Rican Studies, Hunter College, CUNY
Pedro Portes
    University of Georgia, Athens
Maria del Refugio Robledo
    Intercultural Development Research Association San Antonio, Texas
Pedro Reyes
    University of Texas, Austin
Melissa Rivera
    Center for Puerto Rican Studies, Hunter College, CUNY
Harriett Romo
    University of Texas, San Antonio
Richard Ruiz
    University of Arizona, Tucson
Nora Sabelli
    SRI International
Dean Sheryl Santos-Hatchett
    College of Education, University of North Texas, Dallas
Maria Elena Torre
    City University of New York
Angela Valenzuela
    University of Texas, Austin
Ana Maria Villegas
    Montclair State University

INDEX

AB 540 40; *see also Martinez v. Regents of the University of California*
Abrahamsen, Samuel 84
ACLU *see* American Civil Liberties Union
Acosta, Oscar 105, 106; *Brown Buffalo* 108n4; *Revolt of the Cockroach People* 108n4
Acuna, Rudy 136
activism 10, 21, 22, 70, 72, 76, 82, 83, 86, 105, 111, 115, 122–3, 154
advocacy 8, 10, 103, 112, 113, 154, 166, 186, 189
Aguirre, Frederick P. 62
All Handicapped Children Act 39
Alvarez, Roberto, Jr. 53; *see also Roberto Alvarez v. the Board of Trustees of the Lemon Grove School District*
Alvarez v. Lemon Grove see Lemon Grove Incident; *Roberto Alvarez v. the Board of Trustees of the Lemon Grove School District*
AMAE *see* Association of Mexican-American Educators
Amanti, C. 176
American Civil Liberties Union (ACLU) 105
Anderson Bill 48, 62
Anglada, Mario 95
Anzaldua, Gloria 151; *Haciendo Caras / Making Face, Making Soul* 112
Arab Spring 196
Ardila-Rey, A. 152

Arizona 163; action research projects 177; Deferred Action for Childhood Arrival 185; deportation 185; English language learners 165, 180; farm worker rights 111; internment camp 60; Latino immigrant parents 186; No Child Left Behind 40; *see also Flores v. Arizona; Horne v. Flores;* Nogales Unified School District; Proposition 203; SB 1070
ASPIRA 8, 69, 76, 94, 95, 149, 155n2
Aspira v. Board of Education of New York City 33
assimilation theory xviii
Association of Mexican-American Educators (AMAE) 102, 127, 141

barriofication xiv, xv
BC 44 9, 21, 72, 83, 85, 86; ethnic studies and transformative education 72–87
BCC *see* Bilingual Certificate of Competence
Beaumont High School: walkouts 133
"Becoming Me in the World" 147–57; false to critical consciousness 150–1; hope through critical multicultural/bilingual education 153–4; introduction 148; recalling dangerous memories 148–50; reflecting on dangerous memories and hegemonic forces 151–3; role today 154–5
bias, biases 150
bigotry, 150

Index

Bilingual Certificate of Competence (BCC) 124, 125
bilingual certification 124, 125, 128
Bilingual Education Act 32, 43, 123, 124
bilingual education policy 95, 126, 127, 182–3
biliteracy 25, 166, 182–3
Birkenhead, Bruce 80
Black Berets 9, 103
Black Panther Party 103
Bliss, George 51
Bliss Bill 48, 51, 56
Bonilla, Frank 89
Bourdieu, P. 174
Bowman, K. 48, 49, 50, 56
boycott 53, 85, 109, 110, 111
Brignoni, Evangelina "Gigi" viii; death 21, 146n1; "I Don't Speak My Mother's Tongue" 10, 143–6
Brinkley, A. C. 52, 53
Brown Berets 9, 103, 104
Brown v. Board of Education of Topeka, Kansas 29, 30, 33, 39, 43, 49, 58, 59, 62–3, 108n5
Brown/White paradigm 50, 56
Burnham-Massey, L. *Redesigning English-Medium Classrooms* 164
Bush, George H. 36
Bush, George W. 42
Bushwick 191

Cadiero-Kaplan, Karen 124
California 25, 114; Bilingual Certificate of Competence (BCC) 124; bilingual education policy 126, 127, 182–3; Black Panther Party 103; college students 135; "debilingualization" of public education 127; demographics 136; desegregation 7 (*see also* Lemon Grove Incident); "dismissive period" 124; equal access to instructional materials 40 (*see also Williams v. State of California*); farm workers 110, 119n4; grape industry 111; high school xiv; immigration raids 177; *la migra* 183; Mexican schools 50; school segregation 8, 27, 29, 50, 51, 56, 62; teacher certification 125, 130; *see also* AB 540; Anderson Bill; Bliss Bill; *Covarrubias v. San Diego Unified School District*; *Crawford et al. v. Board of Education of the City of Los Angeles*; *Diana v. California Board of Education*; Latino parent engagement; *Lopez v. Seccombe*; *Mendez et al. v. Westminster*; Los Angeles School System; Operation Chicano/a Teacher Program; *Pasadena City Board of Education v. Spangler*; *Perez v. Lippold*; *Piper v. Big Pine School District*; Proposition 63; Proposition 187; Proposition 209; Proposition 227; *Roberto Alvarez v. the Board of Trustees of the Lemon Grove School District*; Student California Teachers Association; United Teachers Los Angeles; *University of California Regents v. Bakke*; *Ward v. Flood*; *Williams v. State of California*
California Academic Performance Index 170
California Agricultural Labor Relations Act 110, 111
California Association for Bilingual Education 129, 139, 141, 158, 160, 172, 176n4
California Association of Teachers of English as a Second Language (CATESOL) 141
California Civil Rights Initiative 41; *see also* Proposition 209
California Council on Teacher Credentialing (CCTC) 128
California Delegation Against Hate Violence 41
California Department of Education 40, 164, 172; *The Status of Hispanics in California Public Education* 135–6
California Education Code 51, 105
California Federation of Teachers (CFT) 122, 23
Californians Together 129, 163, 166; *Reparable Harm* 165
California State Sacramento University 191
California State Seal of Biliteracy 166
California State University Commission on Hispanic Underrepresentation 136
California State University System (CSU) 136
California Superior Court 53
California Supreme Court 40
California Teachers Association 141
Carter, Robert L. 62
Carter, T. P. 135
Castañeda v. Pikard 38, 124
Castillo, Jose Mariano 105
Castro, Sal 18, 20–1, 103, 104, 105, 107, 108n6
Castro v. Superior Court 9, 106

Center for Puerto Rican Studies 9
Chacón-Moscone Bilingual-Bicultural Education Act 124
Chambers, Claude 54, 55, 56
Chapman University 47, 198
Chávez, César xiv, xx, 1, 12n1, 110, 113, 119, 119nn3–4; water fast 111
Chicano Movement 24, 25, 26
Chicanos Por La Causa 12
Cintron, Elis et al. v. Brentwood Union Free School District et al. 34, 35
City University of New York (CUNY) 8, 75, 88, 188; *see also* El Centro de Estudios Puertorriqueños
Civil Rights Act xiii, xiv, xvi, xviii, xix, xx, 30, 32
civil rights activist 18, 127; *see also* Huerta, Dolores
civil rights movement xiii, 6, 7, 15, 18, 30–6, 133; Black 48–9; impact in higher education 88–99; Latina(o) xx, xxi, 86, 109; Mexican-Americans/Chicanos 24
Civil War 25, 26–7
Cofer, J. O. 151
Colón-Muñiz, Anaida: "Becoming Me in the World" 147–57; critical multicultural education 153–4; dangerous memories 147, 148–50, 151–3, 154; hegemony 151–3; "Introduction" 1–14; "La Lucha Sigue" 109–20; "Latino Educational Civil Rights" 15–23; *see also* Fuentes, Luis
Coloradans for Language Freedom 122
Colorado: Amendment 31 42; Civil Rights Initiative 42; English Only Initiative 122; *see also Otero v. Mesa County Valley School District*
concientización 16, 20
Coral Way Elementary School 32
Covarrubias v. San Diego Unified School District 35, 36
Crawford et al. v. Board of Education of the City of Los Angeles 39
critical consciousness 17, 22, 148, 150, 154–5, 199, 200
critical discourse analysis 20
critical pedagogy 147, 152; critical bilingual multicultural education 154, 155; critical pedagogical approach 154
critical sociohistorical narrative 16–18; concientización 17; hope and love 18; naming and denunciating 17; problem-posing 17; reflection and action = praxis 18

Cubans, Cuban Americans 4, 30
Cuban Revolution 30
cultural displacement, 150
culturally relevant pedagogy 152
culturally responsive pedagogy 152
CUNY *see* City University of New York

Dangerous memories 147, 148, 150, 151, 154
Darder, A. 151
Davis, Creston 197
"debilingualization" of public education 127
decategorization 37
decentralization 36, 94
Deferred Action for Childhood Arrivals 185
Delano Grape Strike 111, 119n3
Deleon, Marcus 102
Delgado Bernal, D. 181
Delgado et al. v. Bastrop Independent School District of Bastrop County et al. 29
deregulation 36, 38
desegregation vii, 7, 33, 38, 39; *see also Crawford et al. v. Board of Education of the City of Los Angeles*; *Keyes*; Lemon Grove Incident; *Mendez et al. v. Westminster*; *Roberto Alvarez v. the Board of Trustees of the Lemon Grove School District*
Deukmejian, George 127
Dewey, John 153
dialogic(al) process 21, 22
Diana v. California Board of Education 35, 36
Dinos, Carmen 75
disabilities discrimination 35, 39; *see also* All Handicapped Children Act; Individuals with Disabilities Education Act
Dolores Huerta Foundation 1, 2, 112
Dolores Huerta Foundation of Community Organizing 115, 118
Dolson, D.: *Redesigning English-Medium Classrooms* 164Douglas, Frederick 82–3
Dream Act 40

East Louisiana Railway 27
egocentric speech 96, 99n2
El Barrio 65, 70n1, 88, 94, 96, 97
El Centro de Estudios Puertorriqueños (The Center for Puerto Rican Studies) 9, 88–99; beginning 89–90; Centro Staff Fund 92; challenges of structure 92–3; community engagement 97; community

research 95–7; growth in various areas 97–9; introduction 88–9; Language Policy Task Force 93; language rights 93–5; Marxist framework 90–1; scholarship production 91–2
Elementary and Secondary Education Act (ESEA) 42, 114, 160
English language learners 11, 15, 115, 123, 124–6, 128, 129–30, 158–68, 165, 171, 172, 180; *see also* Proposition 227
English only 42, 49, 116, 123, 124–6, 127, 128, 129, 130, 148, 153, 160, 164, 171
Equal Educational Opportunity Act of 1974 32, 38, 180
Erasmus Hall High School 73
Escobar, Dolores 138, 139
ethnic studies, ethnic studies movement 8, 21, 76, 77, 79, 83, 86, 113, 149, 150

farm worker rights 111
Ferreira, Enrique 52
Ferrin, R. L. 135
Fifth Circuit Court of appeals 38
Filipino farm workers 110, 112
Flores v. Arizona 39
Florida 30–1; *see also* Coral Way Elementary School
Ford Foundation 66, 89, 136, 137–8, 189, 192
Free Academy 88
Freire, Nita 198
Freire, Paulo xx, 43, 75, 115, 122, 151, 152–4, 197–8; critical consciousness 17, 22; critical sociohistorical approach 19–20; dispensers of false generosity 152; emancipatory education 7, 16–17, 22; hope and love 18; naming 17; *Pedagogy of the Oppressed* 153; problem-posing 17; reflection and action 18
Fuentes, Carlos xv
Fuentes, Luis vii, 6, 21–2; "My Recollection of a Failed Attempt to Return the Schools to the Public" 8, 65–71; *see also* Erasmus Hall High School; Ocean Hill–Brownsville Demonstration District

Garcia, Jorge 137
Gates, Louis xviii
Gay, G. 152
Gee, J. 20
Gendzel, G. 159, 160
ghetto 73, 74, 149
Giroux, Henry xxi

Gómez v. Illinois State Board of Education 38
Gonzales, N. 151
Govea, Jose 127
Graf, Luis de 85
grape industry 109–10, 111
Green, Jay P. 167n9
Green, Jerome T. 52, 54, 55
Groves, M. 169
Grow-Your-Own-Teacher Education Initiative 189, 191–2
Guadalupe Organization, Inc. v. Tempe Elementary School District 35, 36

Harrington, Ron 83, 85
heritage language 148
Hernandez v. Texas 30
HEW *see* U.S. Department of Health, Education, and Welfare
hidden curriculum 148
Hiller, Richard 95
hope and love 18, 22
Horne v. Flores 40, 42, 180
Huerta, Dolores vii, xx–xxi, 1–2, 6, 9, 18, 109–20; from the classroom to the fields and beyond 110–12; conversation with 112; denouncing school conditions for (im)migrant children 114–16; improve schools' understanding and respect for parents 116–18; schools as sites in the quest for social justice 113–14; "sí se puede" xv, xx–xxi, 1, 112, 119; woman warrior 112–13
Hughes, Marie 61
Hunter College *see* El Centro de Estudios Puertorriqueños
Huntington Park High School: walkouts 121
Hyman, Lawrence 84

Idaho Migrant Council v. Board of Education 38
"I Don't Speak My Mother's Tongue" 143–6
Immigration and Nationality Act 30
Independent School District v. Salvatierra 29
Individuals with Disabilities Education Act 39
inquiry approach 18–19; call to contribute 18–19; process 19
International Monetary Fund 195
internment camp 59–60, 62
interracial marriage 29
I.S. 55
Itliong, Larry 110, 112, 119n3

Jackson, Jesse 126
Jim Crow 27
Johnson, Lyndon 76, 135
Johnson, Paul xv
Johnson, Wayne 125, 127
Jose Peter v. Ambach 35, 36

Kansas *see Brown v. Board of Education of Topeka, Kansas*
Keyes v. Denver School District 38
Kneller, John 81, 83–4
Korean War 29
Kraus, P. 106

Landy v. Daley 108n6
Language Policy Task Force (LPTF) 91, 93, 94, 95, 96, 97
language submersion 150
LASA *see* Latin American Students Association
Latin American Students Association (LASA) 89, 90
Latino immigrant parents 177, 178, 179, 181–2, 185, 186
Latino parent engagement 177–87; action research 181–5; Arizona and SB1070 183–4; biliteracy 182–3; court cases 179–81; deportation 185; dreamers 185; economic impact 184; fear 184; history 178; *Horne v. Flores* 180; introduction 177; Latino parent engagement 180; Latino parent resistance 180–1; literature review 179–91; parent advocate 178–9; parent training 181–2; *Plyer v. Doe* 179; recommendations 185–6
Latinos: population 3; U.S. Census Bureau 4, 49
Latinos and social capitalization 170–6; community collaboration 174–5; community funds of knowledge 175; community resistance to restrictive language policies 170–2, 174; data sources 173; findings 174; methods 173; political strategic knowledge and skills 174; social capital theory 174; social networks theory 174–5; sociocultural theory 175
Lau Remedies 33
Lau v. Nicols xiii, 32–3, 34, 38, 95, 124, 145, 158, 177
Lavadenz, Magaly xiii, xvii, xix; "Introduction" 1–14; "La Lucha Sigue" 109–20; "Latino Educational Civil Rights" 15–23; "Latinos and Social Capitalization" 170–6; *see also* Fuentes, Luis
Lavin, David 89
LEAD *see* Learning English Advocates Drive
Learning English Advocates Drive (LEAD) 125–7, 128, 129
Lemon Grove Grammar School 54, 55
Lemon Grove Incident 7–8, 47–57; Brown/White paradigm 49–50; different racial paradigm 48–9; education of children of Mexican descent in 1930s 50–2; history and trial 52–3; introduction 47–8; lawsuit 53; Mexican school desegregation 48–9; significance of decision 55–6; trial and decision 54–5; *see also Roberto Alvarez v. the Board of Trustees of the Lemon Grove School District*
Lemon Grove Neighbors Committee 52, 53
LEP *see* limited English language proficient
Levins-Morales, A. 151
liberation 18; liberation theology 148
Liberty School District 170–5
limited English language proficient (LEP) 30, 33, 167n9
long-term English Learners 164–5
Lopez, Margarita 94
López, Patricia D.: "A Concise History of the National Latino/a Education Research and Policy Project" 11–12, 188–93
Lopez v. Seccombe 29, 48
Los Angeles Chicano Walkout in 1968 9, 18, 20–1, 24, 100–8, 136; aftermath 107; background 100–2; court battle and victory 106; indictment of the ELA 13 104–5; legal defense team 105; Mexican-American educators and students 102–3
Los Angeles County Human Relations Commission 101
Los Angeles School System xiv
Los Angeles Unified School District 24, 39, 102, 128, 141
LPTF *see* Language Policy Task Force
Lugo, Elba 78, 80–1, 83, 85

MacDonald, V. M. 6–7, 12
Macedo, Donaldo vii, 115, 152; "Foreword" xiii–xxii

MacKaye, S. D. A. 159
Madrid, Mike: "The Lemon Grove Desegregation Case" 7–8, 47–57
Malcolm X xxi
Mancilla, G. 53, 54, 55
Manhattan, Intermediate School (I.S.) 201 66
Manifest Destiny 26
Marcus, David 61
Marquez, Roberto 87
Marshall, Thurgood 41, 49, 62
Martinez v. Regents of the University of California 40
Marx, Karl 195–6
Marxist framework 90–1, 98
Massachusetts: Question 2 Initiative 42, 163, 165
Matthews, Chris xvi
McCormick, Paul J. 61–2
McLaren, Peter: "Afterword" vii, 194–200
McLaughlin v. State Board of Education 165
Méndez, Estrada, Guzmán, Palomino, and Ramírez families 61
Méndez, Felicitas 58
Méndez, Gonzalo vii, 8, 58, 60
Méndez, Jerome 60
Méndez, Sylvia xii, 58, 60
Mendez et al. v. Westminster vii, 2, 8, 21, 29, 47–8, 49, 51, 58–64; connecting *Brown* and *Mendez* 62–3; story 59–62
Mexican Americans 8, 9, 24, 26, 29, 30, 34, 36, 38, 47, 48, 49, 51, 56, 62, 63, 101, 102–3, 104, 105, 106, 107, 110, 121, 124, 127, 136, 138, 141
Mexican-American War of 1846–1848 26
Mexican Revolution 27, 28
Meza–Overstreet, Mark 127
Michigan Civil Rights Initiative 42
migra, la 178, 183
Montaño, Theresa: "I Am a Chicana, I Am Union, I Am an Activist" 10, 121–32
More Effective Schools 66
mother tongue 145, 146
Mueso Del Barrio 70n1

NAACP 62
Nadal, Tony 81, 84, 85, 86, 87
naming 16, 17, 20–1
National Defense Education Act 30
National Latino/a Education Research and Policy Project 11–12, 98, 188–93; background 188; first decade 189–90; Grow-Your-Own-Teacher Education Initiative 191–2; new directions 192; Texas Center for Education Policy 189, 190–1
native tongue 145
Nava, Julian 104
NCLB *see* No Child Left Behind
Nebraska: bilingual education 145; Civil Rights Initiative 42; *see also* University of Omaha
Negrón de Montilla, Aida 96–7
New Mexico *see Serna v. Portales Municipal Schools, U.S. Court of Appeals, Tenth Circuit*
New York 21; English-only schools 148; Puerto Ricans 79; Puerto Rican teachers 77; School Wars 94; *see also* 9/11; *Aspira v. Board of Education of New York City*; BC 44; City University of New York; El Centro de Estudios Puertorriqueños; National Latino/a Education Research and Policy Project; Nuyorican; *Rios v. Read*
New York City Board of Education 66, 77
Nieto, Sonia vii, 21, 22, 151, 152, 189; "The BC 44, Ethnic Studies, and Transformative Education" 8–9, 72–87
Nieves, Josephine 76, 77, 78, 86
9/11 xviii, 41
Ninth Circuit Court of Appeals 29, 35, 40, 42, 58, 61–2
No Child Left Behind (NCLB) 40, 42–43, 170, 172, 190
Nogales Unified School District 180
Noon, Fred C. 52, 53, 54
Northwest Arctic School District et al. v. Joseph A. Califano et al. 38
Nuyorican 76, 144, 150, 155n3

Obama, Barack xiv, xv, xvi, xviii, xx, xxi, 1; Deferred Action for Childhood Arrivals 185
Ocean Hill–Brownsville Demonstration District 65–71, 74
Ochoa, Alberto M. 6, 20; "Recognizing Inequality and the Pursuit of Equity" 7, 24–46
O'Connell, Jack 164
Office for Civil Rights 30, 38, 172
Okrand, Fred 105
Operation Chicano/a Teacher Program 10, 133–42; background 134–5; history of Chicano/a students 135–6; introduction 133–4; Operation

Chicano Teacher 136–8; role 138–9; uniqueness 139–41
oppression 148, 150, 172, 178, 180, 186, 199
Orange County 58–9, 61, 62, 198; *see also Mendez et al. v. Westminster*
Orange County Department of Education 60
Orfield, Gary xiv
Otero v. Mesa County Valley School District 34

Pantoja, Antonia 69, 155n2
Parent Institute for Quality Education (PIQE) 181–2
Pasadena City Board of Education v. Spangler 33
Passeron, J. 174
Pedraza, Pedro 188, 189; "Memoirs of El Centro" 9, 21, 88–99
Perenchio, A. Jerrold 129
Perez, Richie 82
Perez v. Lippold 29
Petersen, Sally 125
Piper v. Big Pine School District 48
PIQE *see* Parent Institute for Quality Education
Pledge of Allegiance xiii–xv
Plessy, Homer 27
Plessy v. Ferguson 27, 20
Plyer v. Doe 179
Portales Municipal Schools *see Serna v. Portales Municipal Schools, U.S. Court of Appeals, Tenth Circuit*
Pousada, Alicia 96
praxis 16, 18, 22, 86, 93, 197, 200
primary language 36, 122, 124, 125, 126, 128
PRLDEF *see* Puerto Rican Legal Defense and Education Fund
problem posing 16, 17, 20, 21, 182
Project Seek 69
Proposition 63 39, 159
Proposition 203 42
Proposition 187 41, 159
Proposition 209 41–2, 159
Proposition 226 129
Proposition 227 11, 42, 115, 128–9, 167nn5–6, 167n9, 170, 172, 176n1; approval 129; distorted facts 160–3; equity 163–6; and the loss of educational rights 158–69; reflections on impact 166–7
protest 5, 21, 41, 79, 83, 149, 150, 170, 171

PRSU *see* Puerto Rican Students Union
P.S. 25 74, 75, 82
P.S. 155 67, 69
Public School (P.S.) 155 67, 69
Puerto Rico 3, 68, 69, 72, 78, 80, 82, 88, 90, 98, 110, 146, 148, 189; Puerto Rican 8, 9, 21, 65–71, 143–55; Puerto Rican culture 148; *see also* BC 44; El Centro de Estudios Puertorriqueños; Nuyorican
Puerto Rican Legal Defense and Education Fund (PRLDEF) 94, 95
Puerto Rican Students Union (PRSU) 89–90

Quezada, Lupe 127
Quezada, María S. 22; "Proposition 227 and the Loss of Educational Rights" 11, 158–69
Quiñones, Gloria 97

racism 25, 28, 43, 56, 79; institutional xiii, xvi–xvii, 21
Rafael Hernandez Bilingual Mini-school 94
Ramírez, David 160, 164
Ramírez, Pablo C.: "Latino Parent Engagement" 11, 177–87
Ramirez, Rafael 95
Ramos, Evelyn 143
Ravitch, Dianne 43
Reagan, Ronald xiv, 36, 38, 167n1
rebellion 22, 148, 149
recognizing inequality and the pursuit of equity 24–46; introduction 24–5; period of civil rights movement and equal access 30–6; period of pre and post civil war and reconstruction 26–7; period of separate but equal and segregation 28–9; period on the movement to undo civil rights gains 36–43; sociopolitical educational framework 25
reflection and action 16, 18, 20, 21, 22, 154
resistance 9, 11, 21, 27, 33, 170–2, 174, 180–1, 182, 183, 186, 197
returning schools to the public 65–71; parent action and consequences 67–70
Rios v. Read 34, 35
Rivera, Gerardo 85
Rivera, Henry 21, 61
Rivera, Melissa 189
Rivera, Sylvia 95

Robbie, Sandra 21; "The Meaning of Méndez" 8, 58–64
Roberto Alvarez v. the Board of Trustees of the Lemon Grove School District 29, 47–57; *see also* Lemon Grove Incident
Roberts, Kenneth L. 50
Rodriguez, Richard 150, 153
Rosales, R. 49
Rubinstein, Annette: *Schools Against Children* 68
Ruiz, Raul 138
Ruiz, Vicki 3, 51

Salazar, Ruben 107
Sanchez, David 103
Sanchez, Leonel 53, 55
Sánchez, María Engracia 77, 78, 80, 81, 83, 85, 86
Sanchez, Marta E.: "Operation Chicano/a Teacher Program" 10, 133–42
Sánchez-Korrol, Virginia 85
Santana, O. 151
Santa Rita Hall 1, 12n1
Santiago, E. 151
SB 1070 41, 183–84
SCTA *see* Student California Teachers Association
self-identity 148; self image 148
separate but equal 25, 26, 27, 28–9, 30, 48, 63
Serna v. Portales Municipal Schools, U.S. Court of Appeals, Tenth Circuit 34
Shanker, Albert 68, 122–3
Sillas, Herman 18, 21, 22; "The 1968 Los Angeles Chicano Walkout" 9, 100–8
Smith, D. 163
social justice 2, 5, 6, 7, 10, 21, 25, 43, 56, 87, 89, 92, 98, 109, 113–14, 116
sociohistorical narrative analysis 7, 15–23; analyzing narratives 19–20; critical discourse analysis 20; finding 20–2; Freire's critical sociohistorical approach 19–20; inquiry approach 18–19; schooling context for Latinos in the United States 15–16; significance of findings 22; theoretical framework 16–18
Solórzano, D. 17, 180, 181
SooHoo, Suzanne 155n1; "Afterword" vii, 194–200
Spanish Harlem 65, 70n1

Springer, Joanne xiv–xv
Spritzler, David xiv
Student California Teachers Association (SCTA) 141
Suárez-Orozco, C. 185
Suárez-Orozco, M. M. 185
subtractive schooling 15
Sunset High School 191
Swann v. Charlotte-Mecklenburg Board of Education 33

Teitelbaum, Herbert 95
Texas 190; walkouts 24; *see also Castañeda v. Pikard*; *Delgado et al. v. Bastrop Independent School District of Bastrop County et al.*; *Hernandez v. Texas*; *Independent School District v. Salvatierra*; *Plyer v. Doe*; Sunset High School; *United States of America v. State of Texas, et al.*; University of North Texas, Dallas; University of Texas at Austin
Texas Center for Education Policy 189, 190–1
Texas War of Independence 26
Title III 43
Title VI 30, 38
Title VII 70, 93, 94, 139, 160
Title IX 35
Treaty of Guadalupe 26, 110
transformative resistance 179, 180, 182, 183, 186
Tuchman, Gloria Matta 129

UFW *see* United Farm Workers
union 121–32; activism 122–3; certification 129–31; community or union 122–3; "debilingualization" of teacher quality 127–8; English only and UTLA 124–6; politics of language 123–4; Proposition 227 128–9; teacher's strike and the battle against LEAD 127; union before Chicana 121–2; union policy 126
United Farm Workers (UFW) 1, 18, 111, 112, 119nn3–4
United Farm Workers Organizing Committee (UFWOC) 111
United Federation of Teachers 65, 66, 74
United States of America v. State of Texas, et al. 33, 38
United Teachers Los Angeles (UTLA) 121, 123, 124–6, 127, 128, 129
University of California Regents v. Bakke 41

University of North Texas, Dallas 191
University of Omaha 10
University of Texas at Austin 189, 190
Unz, Ron 42, 129, 161, 162, 163, 164, 167nn5–8
U.S. Department of Health, Education, and Welfare (HEW): Lau Remedies 33; *Memorandum, May 25, 1970* 32
U.S. Immigration and Customs Enforcement (ICE) 41
U.S. State Department of Education 33; Section 504 35; Title VI 38
UTLA *see* United Teachers Los Angeles

Valdivia, Alberto 127
Valenzuela, Angela: "A Concise History of the National Latino/a Education Research and Policy Project" 11–12, 151, 188–93
Vargas, Herminio 75, 84–5
Vasquez, Eliana 107

Vera Cruz, Philip 110, 119n3
Vietnam War 24, 25, 74, 79, 107, 149
Vygotsky, Lev 19, 96, 99

walkouts 9, 18, 20–1, 24, 100–8, 121, 124, 133, 136
Ward v. Flood 27, 48
Warren, Earl 29, 49, 59, 62
Watts Riots 9, 101
White ideology xvi–xvii
White supremacy xv, xvi, xvii, xviii
Williams, Jack 111
Williams v. State of California 40
Wirin, A. L. 105
Wong, Rachel 137
World War I 28
World War II 29, 73
Wysinger v. Crookshank 27

Yosso, T. 17
Young Lords 82, 89